# Infertility in the Modern World: Present and Future Prospects

As we enter the twenty-first century, a number of medical, environmental and social changes have profoundly affected human reproduction. This book discusses some of the more dramatic changes in an accessible way that will be useful to graduate students, as well as the more general reader interested in such issues. Topics include medical technologies that equip us with potential cures for many causes of infertility: diseases such as AIDS that have a devastating impact on the reproductive and social lives of humans, particularly in areas with limited access to medical care. Also discussed are increasing industrialization and the development of fabricated materials that pollute our environment in unforeseen ways with possibly devastating effects on human health and fertility, and social revolutions that profoundly alter human relationships, such as nonmarital unions between heterosexual couples, same-sex relationships, adoption and surrogacy which are becoming increasingly common.

GILLIAN BENTLEY is a Royal Society Research Fellow in the Department of Biological Anthropology, University of Cambridge, where her work focuses on reproductive ecology. She is currently involved in collaborative projects examining the relationship between interpopulational variation in reproductive hormone levels and fecundity among women in industrialized and nonindustrialized areas.

C. G. NICHOLAS MASCIE-TAYLOR is Professor of Human Population Biology and Health, and Head of the Department of Biological Anthropology, University of Cambridge. His main fields of research are biosocial studies, quantitative human genetics and disease, and reproductive ecology.

THE BIOSOCIAL SOCIETY SYMPOSIUM SERIES
Series editor: Professor G. A. Harrison, University of Oxford

The aim of the Biosocial Society is to examine topics and issues of biological and social importance and to promote studies of biosocial matters. By examining various contemporary issues and phenomena, which clearly have dimensions in both the social and biological sciences, the society hopes to foster the integration and inter-relationships of these dimensions.

**Previously published volumes**
1. Famine *edited by G. A. Harrison*
2. Biosocial Aspects of Social Class *edited by C. G. N. Mascie-Taylor*
3. Mating and Marriage *edited by V. Reynolds and J. Kellet*
4. Social & Biological Aspects of Ethnicity *edited by M. Chapman*
5. The Anthropology of Disease *edited by C. G. N. Mascie-Taylor*
6. Human Adaptation *edited by G. A. Harrison*
7. Health Interactions in Less-developed Countries *edited by S. J. Ulijaszek*
8. Health Outcomes: Biological, Social & Economic Perspectives *edited by H. Macbeth*
9. The Anthropology of War *edited by M. Parker*
10. Biosocial Perspectives on Children *edited by C. Panter-Brick*
11. Sex, Gender and Health *edited by T. M. Pollard and S. B. Hyatt*

*Volumes 1–9 are available from Oxford University Press*

# Infertility in the Modern World: Present and Future Prospects

Edited by

GILLIAN R. BENTLEY
and
C. G. NICHOLAS MASCIE-TAYLOR
*University of Cambridge*

CAMBRIDGE
UNIVERSITY PRESS

PUBLISHED BY THE PRESS SYNDICATE OF THE UNIVERSITY OF CAMBRIDGE
The Pitt Building, Trumpington Street, Cambridge, United Kingdom

CAMBRIDGE UNIVERSITY PRESS
The Edinburgh Building, Cambridge CB2 2RU, UK
40 West 20th Street, New York, NY 10011–4211, USA
10 Stamford Road, Oakleigh, VIC 3166, Australia
Ruiz de Alarcón 13, 28014 Madrid, Spain
Dock House, The Waterfront, Cape Town 8001, South Africa

http://www.cambridge.org

First published 2000

Printed in the United Kingdom at the University Press, Cambridge

*Typeface* Monotype Baskerville 11/5/14pt    *System* 3b2    [CE]

*A catalogue record for this book is available from the British Library*

*Library of Congress Cataloguing in Publication data*
Infertility in the modern world : present and future prospects /
edited by Gillian R. Bentley, C. G. Nicholas Mascie-Taylor.
    p. cm. – (The Biosocial Society symposium series: 12)
Includes bibliographical references and index.
ISBN 0 521 64364 3 hardback – ISBN 0 521 64387 2 paperback
1. Infertility.    2. Infertility – Social aspects.    3. Fertility, Human – Social aspects.
I. Bentley, Gillian R., 1957–  .    II. Mascie-Taylor, C. G. N.    III. Series.
RC889.I5635    2000
616.6′92–dc21

ISBN 0 521 64364 3 hardback
ISBN 0 521 64387 2 paperback

# Contents

# Contributors

GILLIAN R. BENTLEY

Dept. of Biological Anthropology, University of Cambridge, Downing Street, Cambridge CB2 3DZ, England, U.K.

ALAN H. BITTLES

Centre for Human Genetics, Edith Cowan University, Perth, Western Australia.

JOHN C. CALDWELL

Health Transition Centre, National Centre for Epidemiology and Population Health, The Australian National University, Canberra, ACT 0200, Australia.

PATRICIA CALDWELL

Health Transition Centre, National Centre for Epidemiology and Population Health, The Australian National University, Canberra, ACT 0200, Australia.

LYNDA CLARKE

Family Policy Studies Centre, 9 Tavistock Place, London WC1H 9SN, England, U.K.

and

London School of Hygiene and Tropical Medicine, Centre for Population Studies, 49–51 Bedford Square, London WC1B 3DP, England, U.K.

KENNETH DOWELL

Centres for Assisted Reproduction, CARE at the Park,
The Park Hospital, Sherwood Lodge Drive,
Burnstump Country Park, Arnold, Nottingham NG5 8RX,
England, U.K.

LISA V. FRIEL

21 N. Stafford Avenue, #6, Richmond, VA 23220, U.S.A.

SIMON FISHEL

Centres for Assisted Reproduction, CARE at the Park,
The Park Hospital, Sherwood Lodge Drive,
Burnstump Country Park, Arnold, Nottingham NG5 8RX,
England, U.K.

FIONA MCALLISTER

19 Stavordale Road, London N5 1NE, U.K.

C. G. NICHOLAS MASCIE-TAYLOR

Dept. of Biological Anthropology, University of Cambridge,
Downing Street, Cambridge CB2 3DZ, England, U.K.

PHILLIP L. MATSON

Hollywood Fertility Centre, Hollywood Private Hospital,
Monash Avenue, Nedlands, Western Australia 6009.

CHARLOTTE J. PATTERSON

Department of Psychology, Gilmer Hall, P.O. Box 400400,
University of Virginia, Charlottesville VA 22904, U.S.A.

SIMON THORNTON

Centres for Assisted Reproduction, CARE at the Park,
The Park Hospital, Sherwood Lodge Drive,
Burnstump Country Park, Arnold, Nottingham NG5 8RX,
England, U.K.

# 1

## *Introduction*

G. R. BENTLEY AND C. G. N. MASCIE-TAYLOR

This book illustrates the ways in which human biology and culture can affect fertility and outlines some of the modern technologies that, at least in the Western world, can alleviate the physiological problems associated with infertility. It results from a Biosocial Society Symposium held in Cambridge, U.K. in May 1998. It is organized into three sections, each containing two chapters. The first section (with chapters by co-authors S. Fishel, K. Dowell and S. Thornton as well as A. H. Bittles and P. L. Matson) covers the more technical and clinical aspects of infertility that are primarily relevant to industrialized nations with access to modern technologies and the research capabilities to address (and often ameliorate) specific issues of infertility. The second section (with chapters by G. R. Bentley, and J. C. and P. Caldwell) deals with environmental aspects of infertility, including the consequences of industrial pollution for human fertility, and the effects of sexually transmitted diseases (STDs) in the area of sub-Saharan Africa. Finally, the third section (with chapters by F. McAllister and L. Clarke, as well as C. J. Patterson and L. V. Friel) addresses the social aspects of infertility and the importance of behaviour in determining infertility.

It is impossible to compute the incidence of human infertility as a raw statistic or to reduce it to a simple figure. Infertility varies from country to country and from cohort to cohort, depending on the sample, the population surveyed, whether males are included together with females, and whether these figures include 'social infertility' (such as childlessness by choice) as opposed to physiological infertility. Mirroring such variance are the different figures offered in the chapters here. For example, J. C. and P. Caldwell, using

1

data from noncontracepting, healthy populations with couples who married when young, estimate that sterility from physiological causes other than STDs may be as low as 2%, a figure that is matched in other demographic studies from similar populations (e.g. Early and Peters, 1990; Wood, 1994). In contrast, S. Fishel, K. Dowell and S. Thornton estimate the rate of infertility to be 14% among Western populations, although this figure probably includes women who delay conception until they are older, when subfecundity is likely to be high. In addition, 32% of this rate can be attributed to male-factor infertility. A. H. Bittles and P. L. Matson again give rather different figures for Western countries, namely 5–8% for primary infertility, presumably related to physiological causes.

These figures should be contrasted with rates for primary infertility of 30% in areas of sub-Saharan Africa covered by J. C. and P. Caldwell's chapter, where STDs are an important factor determining this figure. G. R. Bentley informs us that many studies indicate a regional decline in sperm quantity that is reported to be as high as 50%, although how this translates into fecundity and fertility remains unclear. Dealing with the issue of 'social infertility', F. McAllister and L. Clarke cite data indicating that approximately 20% of women born in 1975 in the United Kingdom (U.K.) will remain childless by the end of their reproductive lives, compared with only 11% of women born in 1942. C. J Patterson and L. V. Friel present new data suggesting that up to 86% of gays and 70% of lesbians in the U.S.A. (using the most conservative definition of 'gay' and 'lesbian') will not have their own biological offspring.

As the previous paragraphs suggest, the causes of infertility are manifold and complex. Infertility is highly variable from region to region depending on a number of biosocial factors, none of which is amenable to a single solution. For example, the infertility of older women in developed countries who have delayed childbirth for a variety of social and economic reasons can be reduced through the use of assisted conception technology. For men and women in same-sex relationships, having biological children may also require the use of techniques adapted from assisted conception technologies, as will individuals afflicted with particular kinds of genetically inherited diseases that affect the reproductive tract. For younger women with STDs in sub-Saharan Africa, infertility can only be solved by access to (often unavailable) medicines, or in cases of human immunodeficiency virus/acquired immune deficiency syndrome (HIV/AIDS) will probably remain unsolved and end with the premature death of affected individuals. The situation in this part of the world should be compared with that of HIV-infected individuals in industrialized Western countries, where access to new drug-cocktails to counteract the effects of HIV/AIDS have led to considerably extended life-spans and to a greatly improved quality of life. If increasing infertility becomes evident from our polluted world, cleaner and greener policies will have to be implemented to reduce the dangers to human and other populations. For policy-makers concerned with increasing numbers of individuals who remain childless by choice, the institution of specific policies designed to increase the attractiveness and ease of parenting in the modern world may be required. Each of the chapters in this volume offers solutions for the unique problems of infertility.

The two chapters in the first section counterbalance one another. Chapter 2 outlines the kinds of new technologies that can, in many cases, permit infertile individuals to conceive, while Chapter 3 concentrates on genetic causes of infertility that may require reproductive technologies for conception to occur. Chapter 2 thus provides a comprehensive overview of assisted conception technologies currently available to infertile couples. It covers topics such as ovarian stimulation, *in vitro* fertilization (IVF) and intracytoplasmic sperm injection (ICSI), now used routinely for males with exceptionally low sperm counts. The chapter also outlines some of the key areas of future development that are a focus of attention for fertility treatment specialists. One such area is the use of spermatids instead of fully mature spermatozoa for *in vitro* conception. Similarly, another area is to achieve successful *in vitro* maturation of primary (immature) oocytes rather than a fully developed follicle. Such a development would then obviate the need for artificially stimulating ovarian cycles, a procedure that can cause both short- and long-term health risks for the women involved. Instead, a single biopsy sample of ovarian tissue could be taken, which could then provide innumerable oocytes for potential conception. Furthermore, if the development of viable embryos *in vitro* could be extended beyond the current limits, it would provide the opportunity for implanting fewer embryos and reduce the risk of multiple conceptions. It would also increase the possibility of genetic analysis from multi-celled embryos to assess potential conditions of risk. Such preimplantation diagnoses offer couples who may produce offspring with inherited diseases the possibility of aborting *in vitro* as opposed to *in utero* at a much later stage of embryonic development.

Other areas of increasing research include further development of cryopreservation technologies, particularly for oocytes as opposed to embryos, and the preservation of testicular and ovarian tissue from patients treated for diseases in childhood (such as cancer) that would otherwise render them sterile. Future technologies may also focus on the donation not just of oocytes but of cytoplasm, which may improve oocyte quality in women, thus preserving the genetic identity of their offspring. Transplantation of the egg nucleus is also theoretically possible and has been used in bovines, albeit with poor results. This new technology may prove beneficial for women who have defective mitochondrial deoxyribonucleic acid (DNA), which affects conception rates.

Chapter 3 concentrates on genetic factors that contribute to human infertility, ranging from conditions that relate to structural defects of the reproductive tract to conditions that result in increased risk of spontaneous abortion including maternal-fetal red cell incompatibility, and maternal-fetal human leukocyte A system (HLA) incompatibility. A. H. Bittles and P. L. Matson specifically clarify how early fetal loss (EFL) among humans (who experience among the highest rates compared to other mammalian species) is related to specific chromosomal problems. Indeed, more than one study suggests that around 78% of all conceptions end in EFL. The rate of genetic abnormality in conceptuses that abort prior to the eighth week of gestation is approximately 66%, with autosomal trisomies accounting for most of these anomalies. In other words, the human system attempts to eliminate potential genetic abnormalities early in the developmental process. The incidence of EFL is also higher among older women, because of the ageing of their oocytes. Those embryos that remain viable and continue to mature in humans account for a relatively small proportion of conceptions.

Genetic causes of primary infertility range from chromosome numerical disorders such as Turner Syndrome and Klinefelter Syndrome, to structural disorders such as balanced reciprocal X-autosome translocation, or Y chromosome microdeletions. Other genetic disorders can lead to subfertility. These include autosomal dominant disorders such as Noonan Syndrome, and autosomal recessive disorders such as cystic fibrosis – probably one of the most prevalent of genetic problems in modern human populations that can lead to infertility. More rare autosomal recessive conditions include 5-α reductase deficiency documented consistently in only a few human isolates. There are also a number of genetic disorders with incompletely understood modes of inheritance, such as Stein–Leventhal Syndrome. Finally, A. H. Bittles and P. L. Matson briefly discuss the possibility that mutations in the mitochondrial DNA may lead to conditions of male infertility.

A. H. Bittles and P. L. Matson specifically include sections that complement the chapter by S. Fishel, K. Dowell and S. Thornton by focusing on the potential clinical treatments of genetically infertile individuals, and the genetic outcome of progeny conceived using such technologies. Individuals with such genetic abnormalities are, however, a minority of cases of those seeking assisted conception technologies. Similarly, both chapters are complementary in the way in which they deal with the ethical issues surrounding reproductive technologies. S. Fishel, K. Dowell and S. Thornton are understandably greater advocates for forging ahead with new developments, whereas A. H. Bittles and P. L. Matson urge for more caution in adopting reproductive technologies that may have unforeseen consequences. For example, it is not yet resolved whether offspring resulting from some of the newest technologies (including ICSI) might suffer any health effects. Doubts about the health of artificially conceived progeny have also resulted in a current ban on the use of spermatids for conception. Both chapters caution about the need to evaluate causes of azoospermia and oligospermia which, if resulting from genetic abnormalities, might result in offspring who inherit the same condition. S. Fishel,

K. Dowell and S. Thornton cover some of the ethical areas that surround egg donation and surrogacy, while A. H. Bittles and P. L Matson have a small section dealing with the potential for inbreeding caused by the possibility of mating by related offspring conceived using sperm from the same anonymous donor. This latter issue also relates to Chapter 7, by C. J. Patterson and L. V. Friel since lesbian women might opt for artificial insemination as a preferable route for conception.

In Chapter 3, A. H. Bittles and P. L. Matson also discuss the significant emotional and physical costs to individuals suffering from conditions such as Klinefelter Syndrome who elect assisted conception. These may include multiple testicular biopsies, pre-implantation diagnoses and so forth. They advocate the need for comprehensive counselling, which should accompany treatments for such individuals. Similarly, women with cystic fibrosis need particular counselling about the risks associated with pregnancy and gestation, as well as the provision of clear information about the usually shortened life expectancies for afflicted individuals. This would necessarily mean arranging for suitable guardians for the offspring of these individuals in the event of their early death.

In the second section, Chapters 4 and 5 deal with environmental aspects of infertility, but differ substantially in the topics under review. Chapter 4 addresses the issue of whether increasing amounts of environmental pollutants are affecting human fertility in subtle ways, whereas Chapter 5 concerns the evident effect of STDs on human fertility in sub-Saharan Africa. Both represent problems that are relatively intractable for different reasons. In the first case, reducing the kinds of environmental pollutants that are implicated as problematic for fertility would require socioeconomic and political adjustments on a scale that would meet with massive public resistance despite increasing public concern about the issues at stake. Solving the second situation in sub-Saharan Africa remains problematic because burgeoning socioeconomic and political problems in this region continue to prevent the distribution of adequate medical care. In addition, the kinds of behavioural adjustments that are needed to reduce transmission rates of HIV/ AIDS are understandably difficult to implement.

During the past eight years increasing attention has been focused on the potential problem of specific environmental pollutants (called xenoestrogens) that mimic the effects of reproductive hormones. It has already been hypothesized that increasing amounts of such substances have contributed to a decline in human sperm quantity and quality, with frightening forecasts for future male fertility. In Chapter 4, G. R. Bentley describes many of the substances that act as xenoestrogens, and covers their effects on different species in the wild and in the laboratory. She also reviews the evidence for the alarmist claims about human sperm counts. Most of the publicity surrounding the purported decline in human sperm quality can be traced to a paper published by Danish researchers in 1992 in the prestigious *British Medical Journal* (Carlsen *et al.*, 1992). The large numbers of criticisms and reanalyses of the data from this paper have not received the same attention. However, G. R. Bentley reviews and collates these many criticisms. This chapter also deals with the possible effects on female reproductive development, a topic that has not been fully addressed in the literature about environmental pollutants. While admitting that xenoestrogens have the potential to affect fertility in many species, she concludes that the current data are misleading. Further studies on these issues are urgently needed.

In Chapter 5, J. C. and P. Caldwell concentrate on infertility in sub-Saharan Africa, which has the highest reported levels of infertility primarily associated with STDs. This includes HIV/AIDS, although historically the most important STDs to affect women in this region are gonorrhoea and chlamydia. Data from as far back as the 1930s onwards have consistently demonstrated a high proportion of infertility in this region of Africa. The depth of the problem is illustrated by recent data from Gabon where a third of the population in one area are childless. The cause of female infertility in 83% of cases here was tubal occlusion, with chlamydia and gonorrhoea probably primarily to blame.

The authors skilfully combine the sociocultural, historical and behavioural aspects of their data to show how circumstances in sub-Saharan Africa have led to the ready transmission and rapid spread of STDs. Systems of marriage, lineage, inheritance, land-rights and postpartum sex prohibitions, as well as the relative freedom of women in comparison with those in Eurasia have created a unique system that J. C. and P. Caldwell refer to as the 'sub-Saharan African sexual system'. The advent of colonialism, the increasing migration that occurred for work opportunities, as well as forced labour exacerbated these social conditions. They also point out that the social premium on fertility in sub-Saharan Africa encourages women to seek alternative partners with whom to conceive if they fail to do so with their husbands.

A separate section in Chapter 5 deals with the specific problem of AIDS and infertility in sub-Saharan Africa. It reminds us that two-thirds of all world cases are concentrated in this region, inhabited by only 3% of human populations. Here, as many as 30% of urban groups are affected. Two other factors are critical in determining these high rates. First, unlike in other areas, transmission of HIV/AIDS is primarily heterosexual; second, high rates of other untreated STDs facilitate infection.

The final section of the book focuses on social aspects of infertility. Chapter 6 deals with the issue of childlessness by choice among women and men in the U.K., while the second evaluates the incidence of infertility amongst gays and lesbians mostly from the U.S.A.

F. McAllister and L. Clarke cite data indicating that approximately 20% of women in the U.K. born in 1975 will remain childless by the end of their reproductive lives, compared to only 11% of women born in 1942. They also point out that, although the data are less reliable for men, figures for childlessness may be even higher for this sex. Although these figures seem alarmingly high, F. McAllister and L. Clarke provide us with a historical perspective from which to view them, pointing out that a similar proportion of women remained unmarried and childless in the early 1920s. This trend was sharply reversed in the years following the Second World War. In earlier times, from the sixteenth century onwards, a high proportion of women and men also remained childless, although due to causes somewhat different than those that characterize the patterns seen today. These include a high proportion of individuals who never married and a number of individuals who married late. This contributed towards a pattern referred to as the 'Western European marriage pattern'.

What, then, are the characteristics of individuals who choose to remain childless in the U.K. today? F. McAllister and L. Clarke point to the many social factors that can contribute to a woman or a man never having children. This includes choice of careers and length of education, delays in marriage, the availability of reliable contraceptives and postponement of first births. Sometimes couples find themselves unwittingly the victims of age-related infecundity, where successful conception becomes increasingly difficult, and where they may be unwilling or unable to avail themselves of emotionally and financially costly assisted reproduction technologies. One of the problems in assessing such data is the paucity of reliable information for men. In addition, both men and women in later life may rationalize their lack of children in terms of desire, whereas a definite decision specifically to remain childless may not have been made.

What is particularly valuable about Chapter 6 is the unique contribution of both quantitative and qualitative data. In the qualitative section of the paper, interviews were conducted with 34 women aged between 33 and 49. These were grouped into categories depending on how firm their 'choice' had been to remain childless. These categories include 'certain,' those who were 'certain now', those who 'accepted' the fact that they were childless, those who were 'ambivalent', and those who felt the decision had been 'forced' on them. Between a third and one-quarter of respondents fitted into the 'certain' category, many of whom had made this decision relatively early in life as a teenager. These respondents tended to focus on the negative aspects of having children, including the loss of freedom and the heavy responsibilities that accompany parenting.

Those who fitted into the second category of respondents who were 'certain now' tended to have their opinion reinforced by their partners, but who otherwise might have been more uncertain. Many of these individuals were in second marriages or relationships. Those who accepted the fact that they were childless had often been forced into that situation by circumstance; many of these were women who had never married while young and who were now in their 40s. Many of these had wished for children when they were younger but not in relationships. In contrast, individuals who fell into the 'ambivalent' category either had a problem with infertility or had postponed having children until they felt they were too old to embark on parenthood. Many of these expressed the wish that they had children. Finally, there was a small group who felt the decision had been taken out of their hands. This group included women for whom there was a fertility problem for which a solution was never sought.

It is clear from these data that, in most cases, having a partner and the views of one's partner are crucial aspects in the decision of whether to have children. Childless women were obviously influenced by the perception in their own relationship that the division of labour would be unequal if they had children. Contrary to expectations, few of the childless interviewees listed their career as a major factor in the decision not to have children, thus challenging the stereotype that childless people are wholly career-minded. In fact, some of the older women who formed partnerships later in life took this transition as the moment at which to reduce their hours at work. Many childless individuals also looked forward to an early retirement.

In conclusion, F. McAllister and L. Clarke suggest that couples who are childless by choice do not represent a uniform and anomalous group of rejectionists, but rather nonconformists who accept the dominant paradigm of parenting and for that reason have often chosen to reject the attendant responsibilities. They close their chapter by covering some policy implications. They suggest that if the burden of parenting (particularly for working mothers) was reduced, many individuals and couples might find parenting a more attractive option. In addition, they advocate that health counselling about age-related declines in fertility should become as important as counselling on the problems of teenage pregnancies. They caution, however, that where government policies have been directed towards encouraging fertility in other European countries, such policies have often had little impact on long-term fertility rates.

In the final chapter in the book, C. J. Patterson and L. V. Friel discuss infertility among gays and lesbians in the U.S.A. In view of this homosexual lifestyle, many would expect gays and lesbians generally not to be biological parents, but the desire for parenthood is not limited to heterosexuals, and certainly lesbians are biologically able to achieve motherhood nowadays with comparative ease given the availability of reproductive technologies.

There have, however, been very few data collected on infertility among gays and lesbians, and what data exist may be unreliable. Figures for homosexual parents in the U.S.A. range from one to five million. In one study in the 1970s undertaken in San Francisco, 21% of lesbian women and 10% of gay men reported having children. These data were then compared to a heterosexual group matched for age, education and gender. Of these, 51% of women and 47% of the men reported having children. The problem with this study is its reliability and representativeness of the general population. A more recent study, which also has its limitations, found hardly any difference (5%) between lesbian and heterosexual women who defined themselves as having children at home (whether biological or not), but a much larger differential (30%) between gay and heterosexual men.

C. J. Patterson and L. V. Friel use data from the National Health and Social Life Survey (which assessed sexual orientation as well as issues of fertility) to try and provide better estimates of biological parenthood among gays and lesbians in the U. S. A. This survey interviewed over 3000 subjects ranging from 18 to 59 years old. Of these, 1.4% of women and 2.8% of men openly identified themselves as gay, lesbian or bisexual. A less conservative estimate of who might be considered gay or lesbian attempted to ascertain whether individuals had engaged in same-sex behaviour during adulthood. Using this criterion, 3.5% of women and 5.3% of men could be classified as lesbian or gay.

Of those women who identified themselves as lesbians, 30% were biological mothers, while 49% of those who were classified as lesbian by their behaviour were mothers. This should be compared to a figure of 73% of heterosexual women from the sample who were biological mothers. For the men, 14% of those who identified themselves as being gay were biological fathers, and 32% who had homosexual experiences were fathers. This could be compared with 59% of heterosexual men who reported being fathers. There are, of course, several limitations to this dataset which C. J. Patterson and L. V. Friel outline, but it does give some understanding of how gays and lesbians compare with the heterosexual population in terms of fertility. Approximately half the number of gays and lesbians achieve parenthood in comparison to heterosexual men and women.

Given that the overall number of gays and lesbians appears small from the surveys undertaken, and the number of infertile individuals among this population is lower than one might expect, the social implications of infertility among this group is unlikely to warrant much attention by policy-makers, particularly in comparison to the rather large number of individuals in the West who appear to remain childless by choice regardless of their sexual identity. The most pressing issue among gays and lesbians will probably remain how to achieve biological and social parenthood in a society that remains prejudiced against such a goal for this minority group.

Taken together, the chapters in this volume outline a major contradiction in the modern world: that technological advances can exist in one part of the world allowing infertile men and women to bear children even with conditions that, until a few years ago, would have been considered insurmountable. In contrast, vast numbers of infertile men and women exist in other parts of the world where simple and timely access to antibiotics could, in many cases, alleviate their reproductive health problems. Without wishing to diminish the personal psychological anguish that can accompany infertility, this condition often has social and economic consequences in developing nations that far outweigh the consequences for infertile couples in most industrialized nations. In addition, the social luxury of choosing to remain childless is simply not an option for many women and men where having children provides security for old age, social rank, and a source of labour for household activities and subsistence. Above all who can quantify the indescribable source of emotion, pleasurable and otherwise, that most children engender in their biological and social parents. It is perhaps this, above all else, that drives individuals to take extreme measures to achieve (or avoid) parenting in the modern world.

## References

Carlsen, E., Giwercman, A., Keiding, N., Skakkebaek, N. (1992) Evidence for decreasing quality of semen during past 50 years. *British Medical Journal* **305**:609–13.

Early, J. D., Peters, J. F. (1990) *The population dynamics of the Mucajai Yanomama.* New York: Academic Press.

Wood, J. (1994) *Dynamics of human reproduction.* Chicago: Aldine.

# PART I

# Biomedical perspectives on fertility

## 2

# *Reproductive possibilities for infertile couples: present and future*

S. FISHEL, K. DOWELL AND S. THORNTON

## Abstract

Infertility affects at least 14% of the reproductive population world-wide. Modern technology can provide genetically related offspring to 80% of couples seeking treatment, and pregnancy to a further 10–15% using donated gametes. However, that only a small proportion is able to acquire suitable treatment, even in the West, highlights the social, economic and political difficulties surrounding available resources for assisted conception technology.

Before 1992 approximately 95% of severe male-factor infertility cases were offered sperm donation – unacceptable in many cultures. Since the development of intracytoplasmic sperm injection (ICSI), 90–95% of male-factor cases can now be offered the chance of their own genetic offspring. The use of egg donation and of surrogacy further expands opportunities for infertile couples to have children. In the former the recipient gestates and delivers her child, albeit genetically unrelated to herself, whilst in the latter the commissioning couple can have their genetic offspring via host surrogacy. These technologies remain ethically challenging.

Developments in embryology technology have helped couples whose problem is one of implantation rather than conception, and this includes assisted hatching and zygote/embryo repair. The alliance of such technologies to the development of molecular genetics permits the biopsy of an eight- to ten-cell embryo for chromosome/genetics analysis on the extracted cells. This procedure has both social and economic advantages and makes it possible for couples to refrain from embarking on a pregnancy should the embryo carry a feared hereditary disorder.

More recently, techniques to preserve germ cells, both mature and immature, and the potential in prepubertal male cancer sufferers for ipsigeneic germ cell repopulation offer considerable opportunity to preserve the fertility of these boys. The technique of oocyte grafting after cryopreservation provides similar opportunities for females of all ages. The inherited disease of mitochondrial deoxyribonucleic acid (DNA) cytopathies, passed on through the maternal line via the egg cytoplasm, poses serious health risks to offspring, including epilepsy, deafness, blindness and muscular atrophy. Potential developments in embryo/zygote micromanipulation could provide the opportunity to preserve the genetic complement of the parents, while protecting the future offspring from diseased cytoplasmic mitochondria. Similar technology might help those couples who are infertile as a result of habitual miscarriage, rather than any problem with conception and implantation *per se*.

Hence, in the future, *in vitro* fertilization (IVF) and embryology technology will not only provide children for the subfertile, but will encroach on health and disease issues unrelated to infertility.

## Introduction

Evaluation of the incidence of infertility is difficult, not least because the reviewing of censuses cannot take into account voluntary infertility. The most reliable information comes from studies published during the last ten years, from which some of the summarized material in this paper is obtained.

Approximately one in seven individuals has a problem with infertility. At face value, an incidence of 14% of the reproductive population puts those who are infertile into one of the largest groups requiring medical attention. Although the figure of 14% is based on data derived from studying Western society, it is believed that a similar incidence exists in most cultures of the world, with rates rising to as high as 25% of the reproductive population depending upon the definition of the duration of infertility.

Table 2.1. *Causes of infertility / childlessness*

| Male | Female |
|---|---|
| Low count | Ovulation dysfunction |
| Poor motility | Endocrine dysfunction |
| Abnormal morphology | Tubal disease/absence |
| – | Endometriosis |
| – | Ovarian failure |
| Biochemical dysfunction | Uterine anatomical anomalies |
| Anti-sperm autoantibodies | Sperm antibodies |
| Endocrine dysfunction | Antizona pellucida antibodies |
| Chromosome dysfunction | Oocyte quality |
| Obstructive azoospermia | Chromosome dysfunction |
| Spermatogenic failure | Recurrent implantation failure |
| | 'Other' (e.g. cardiopathy) |

Despite claims that there appears to be an increase in the rate of infertility in Western Europe, studies over the last 20 years point to a fairly stable and consistent prevalence (Thonneau and Spira, 1990). Although there are varying views in the literature, a number of authors believe that nearly twice as many women born 45 years ago presented with problems of infertility compared to women born 60 years ago. This referral uptake of medical help varies considerably from country to country. Similarly, it has been reported that approximately 9% of women born in 1950 were voluntarily childless, compared to 1.9% of women born in 1935 (Johnson *et al.*, 1987).

In recent years the impact of male infertility has become more refined, and a current view predicts that at least half of the causes of infertility amongst couples are male-factor related. Table 2.1 provides an overview of the general causes of infertility presenting at specialized centres, and Table 2.2 the breakdown of some of these causes. Requirement for assisted conception technology continues to increase, as evidenced by the figures reported in the Annual Reviews of the Human Fertilisation and Embryology Authority. In their 1997 report there were a total of 36,994 IVF cycles from 26,967 patients during the period of 1 January 1995 to 31 March 1996.

Table 2.2. *Incidence of causes of infertility**

| Cause of infertility | Incidence (%) |
| --- | --- |
| Male factor | 32 |
| Hormonal anomalies | 28 |
| Tubal factors | 22 |
| Uterine abnormalities | 11 |
| Unknown causes | 4 |
| Cervical | 3 |

*Data from 'Infertility' Postgraduate Update Series 1995 edn. (Reed Healthcare Publication).

This chapter will concern itself predominantly with infertility management through assisted conception technology, rather than routine gynaecological and urological management.

## Ovarian stimulation

There are a considerable number of pharmaceutical agents available for stimulating and controlling follicular development (Table 2.3). Follicular stimulants may be administered either in synchrony with the menstrual cycle (normal or irregular), or after pituitary desensitization with gonadotrophin releasing hormone (GnRH) agonists or antagonists.

There are two distinct groups of women for whom exogenous follicular stimulants are prescribed: (1) those requiring treatment for menstrual and/or anovulatory disorders; and (2) normo-ovulatory women undergoing assisted conception. The distinction is relevant when considering the type of drug and dosage. For example, pituitary desensitization with GnRH agonists or antagonists provides a number of benefits both to patients and clinics. Once the pituitary is desensitized, the patient enters an acyclical phase without significant ovarian activity. Follicular stimulants can be superimposed, even after long-term pituitary desensitization. This permits clinics and patients to undertake programmed treatment cycles and further confers the advantage of stimulating a cohort of

Table 2.3. *Follicular stimulants*

| |
|---|
| Antioestrogens |
| Gonadotrophins |
|    Crude extracts – human menopausal gonadotrophin |
|    Recombinants – pure follicle-stimulating hormone and luteinizing hormone |
|    Gonadotrophin-releasing hormone agonists and antagonists |

follicles simultaneously. This regime circumvents the natural process whereby a dominant follicle suppresses the development of supernumerary follicles, and ovulation occurs in response to maturation of the dominant follicle. The natural process ensures that women avoid multiple ovulation and the consequences of multiple pregnancy. By superimposing follicular stimulants on a pituitary-desensitized programme, endogenous ovulation does not occur and ovulation is triggered by exogenous administration of human chorionic gonadotrophin (hCG). The cohort of follicles is programmed to ovulate synchronously with multiple oocytes entering the maturation phase. Hence, pituitary desensitization (often called 'down regulation') is also a means to achieve large numbers of mature oocytes which, once fertilized and cleaved, can be cryopreserved for future cycles. Having multiple embryos for transfer (up to three, as limited by law in the U.K.) maximizes the opportunity for pregnancy while minimizing the chances of multiple pregnancy. However, careful management of the patients with regard to the numbers of embryos transferred is a crucial issue practised very carefully by experienced doctors managing assisted conception cycles.

The use of programme cycles, often called the suppression of endogenous hormone production, followed by controlled ovarian hyperstimulation (COH) is now the first-line therapy for patients undergoing assisted conception. In a sense, this was the first ethical decision with which we were confronted early in the 1980s – the administration of potent follicular stimulants to normo-ovulatory women. The benefits have been considerable, with relatively inexperienced clinics achieving a high degree of efficiency in ovulation induction, fertilization and pregnancy because the negative effects of a patient's endogenous ovulation is negated. Previously, the rate of cancelled cycles for various endocrine anomalies during midcycle was around 30–40%, depending upon the clinic; today this has been reduced to around 5%.

Biotechnology made it possible to produce a genetic recombinant preparation of human follicle-stimulating hormone (FSH) *in vitro*. Genetically engineered Chinese hamster ovary cells, whose genome includes the genes coding for the human alpha and beta subunits, are utilized to produce biologically active (glycosylated) recombinant FSH (Chappel *et al.*, 1992). Until recently the pharmaceutical preparations of gonadotrophins contained a mixture of FSH and luteinizing hormone (LH) which was generically known as human menopausal gonadotrophin (hMG). The protein contents of these preparations are more than 95% nonspecific copurified urinary proteins. The new recombinant preparation (FSH) has no LH activity, is of very high purity, provides batch-to-batch consistency and can be administered subcutaneously. The literature is full of debate as to whether it confers a distinct advantage to the patient given that the cost, currently, can be up to four times that of the hMG preparations; furthermore, there is little evidence to demonstrate conferred outcome advantage.

Importantly, in parallel with the development of GnRH agonists and recombinant gonadotrophins, consideration is now being given to the 'old fashioned' simple (oral) preparation and inexpensive forms of follicular stimulation using anti-oestrogens (such as clomiphene citrate). For use before midcycle, and any impending ovulatory LH surge, new compounds, GnRH antagonists, have been developed to inhibit ovulation thus permitting more than a single follicle to enter the ovulatory phase. However, the GnRH antagonists' molecular structure is more complex than that of GnRH agonists, the latter having modifications at positions six and ten of the GnRH decapeptide, while the former has additional modifications in positions one, two, three and eight. The first generation of GnRH antagonists produced allergic side-effects due to histamine release and thus hampered clinical development. Modern GnRH antagonists [Ganirelix, Organon, or Cetrorelix (Cetrotide), ASTA-Medica] have overcome these difficulties. Our own preliminary data with Cetrotide have generated excellent results. Thus, future follicular stimulation regimes may see the reintroduction of the more simple oral antioestrogenic preparations combined with GnRH antagonist administration before midcycle, followed by ovulation induction with hCG when the follicles have matured. This will produce fewer follicles, and therefore fewer embryos to permit cryopreservation or prolonged culture to the blastocyst stage. However, early studies suggest that high pregnancy rates can still be achieved with the financial costs of the drugs reduced by 40- or 50-fold per cycle initiated with pituitary desensitization and administration of recombinant gonadotrophins. It is every practitioner's hope that in the very near future patients will receive an alternative for cheaper, safe and efficient ovarian stimulation.

## *In vitro* fertilization (IVF)/intracytoplasmic sperm injection (ICSI)

To assist a subfertile couple achieve a pregnancy, conception can be brought about either *in vivo* or *in vitro*, depending upon the indication. Specialists have differing views on when to use more invasive technologies but, in the main, ovulation induction with timed intercourse or intrauterine insemination is the 'simplest' procedure. A more invasive option is gamete intrafallopian transfer (GIFT) in which the oocytes are recovered from a mature follicle, mixed with washed and prepared sperm from the partner and the gametes returned to the ampullary region of the fallopian tube by either laparoscopy (the preferred route) or transcervical catheterization (currently, the least successful option). Clearly, any form of conception *in vivo* requires patent and functional fallopian tubes and an assumption that fertilization can occur.

Various conditions necessitate conception *in vitro*. For the females these include problems with oocyte pick up by the ampullary region of the fallopian tube; this can be caused by endometriosis, ovulatory dysfunction, tubal disease or bilateral absence of the tubes. Fertilization can also fail as a result of poor quality sperm (Table 2.1) or oocytes. The latter is extremely difficult to diagnose without a patient undergoing two or more cycles of IVF, including ICSI. Because of the inability to observe conception *in vivo* GIFT is becoming less popular as a main-line treatment therapy. It has largely been replaced by IVF, except in those cases where the ability of the patient's gametes to procure fertilization has been established.

Today, IVF is routine. Appropriate clinical management will determine whether patients should undertake *in vitro* insemination by the conventional IVF procedure or utilize the ICSI approach. Clinical judgement will often depend upon the sperm morphology, given that count and motility are sufficient. Approximately 20% of patients with unexplained infertility will have a problem at the level of the gamete. By definition the aetiology will be submicroscopic and subsequent cycles will require the use of ICSI.

ICSI was first demonstrated as a potential treatment for severe male-factor infertility in 1992 (Palermo *et al.*, 1992). It was not until elucidation of the appropriate technical procedure (Fishel *et al.*, 1995*a*) that ICSI became a revolution in achieving a consistently high incidence of pregnancies in many Units worldwide. Given that defective sperm function has been described as the single, largest defined cause of human infertility (Hull *et al.*, 1985) it is hardly surprising that ICSI has been heralded as a revolution. However, many causes of sperm dysfunction are unknown and therefore most likely related to a genetic anomaly. Conception in such cases will undoubtedly ensure that ICSI shall beget ICSI! The genetic implications of this are described elsewhere (see Chapter 3).

Prior to the introduction of ICSI, approximately 95% of cases of severe male-factor infertility were offered donor sperm as the only form of conception. Today approximately 95% of men with severe male-factor infertility can have their own genetic offspring. Sperm can now be taken from all reaches of the reproductive tract, including the seminiferous tubules. Successful fertilization and conception can occur in cases of severe azoospermia caused either by an obstruction or spermatogenic dysfunction. Sperm portraying 100% morphological abnormality, immobility and a range of other defects can procure conception *via* ICSI with the birth of healthy offspring. However, clear discriminative data on the success of each particular sperm condition have yet to be published from a large enough series of data. There are various conditions which undoubtedly produce a lower incidence of implantation and pregnancy, although the conception and birth of apparently healthy offspring is still attainable. By utilizing ICSI there appears to be no obvious distinction between ejaculated, epididymal or testicular spermatozoa in outcome data, provided they are morphologically normal and motile. There is some debate as to whether the latter produce a lower incidence of live offspring per case, but there are too few data to make a judgement at this time.

In cases of nonobstructive azoospermia, a biopsy of seminiferous tubules can be taken and then cryopreserved for later use. However, particularly in cases of nonobstructive azoospermia, a karyotype and detailed counselling of potential genetic dysfunction is mandatory. This needs to cover chromosome anomalies, genetic deletions such as Yq deletions and cystic fibrosis status. Oligospermic males have a higher risk of sex and autosomal chromosome anomalies, estimated from a number of studies to be approximately 4.6% (i.e. 1:25) men. However, with azoospermic males this figure is estimated at 2.8% exclusive of Klinefelter, and 13.6% including Klinefelter Syndrome.

There has been much discussion on the prevalence of Yq deletions (Reijo *et al.*, 1995; Vogt *et al.*, 1992), but it is imperative to evaluate scientifically the relevance of these particular deletions. There are probably 200–300 genes relevant to spermatogenesis on the autosomal chromosomes. Deletions in the Y have yet to be fully analysed, and the appearance of microdeletions in Yq in normal fertile males indicates that a deeper understanding of them is required before we can understand their relevance.

## Immature sperm conception

The generation of the mature male gamete during spermatogenesis takes approximately 70 days in the human. The process begins at puberty, with the stem cell, spermatogonium, actively dividing to give rise eventually to primary spermatocytes. It is these cells that activate the programme of meiotic division, duplicating their chromosomes and undergoing the long meiotic prophase during which new assortments of genes are generated. During this first meiotic division, two distinct daughter cells, the secondary spermatocytes, are produced. These cells rapidly undergo a second meiotic division producing two haploid spermatid cells. Although these round spermatids have a DNA protamine–histone incomplete transition, many researchers believe the cells are genetically indistinct from the fully formed spermatozoon. Evidence for this comes from the birth of normal, healthy and fertile animal offspring after spermatid injection. However, these studies have been performed using spermatids from healthy animals, which is distinct from the abnormal profile presenting in men requiring spermatid microinjection.

The round spermatids need to undergo dramatic changes in their structure and function to produce the highly specialized spermatozoon. Many authors believe that these modifications provide the male gamete with the ability to negotiate the female reproductive tract, the cells (cumulus oophorerous) surrounding the oocyte and the oocyte investments preceding fusion and fertilization. Indeed, the initial results with round spermatid injection in animals seem to have confirmed this hypothesis (Kimura and Yanagimachi, 1995; Ogura *et al.*, 1994). This was further confirmed by preliminary human clinical trials leading to pregnancies and birth with round spermatids (Tesarik *et al.*, 1995, 1996) and elongated spermatids (Fishel *et al.*, 1995*b*, 1996).

The data available from the literature (Table 2.4) demonstrate a highly variable and unpredictable outcome of human spermatid conception, especially using round spermatids. It appears that the implantation rate per embryo, significantly reduced from the 15–18% one would expect with mature spermatozoa, is similar between round and elongated spermatids. However, there is a significant difference in the incidence of fertilization and many authors believe this is due to both a technical and an identification problem. Once this is resolved, the opportunities for round spermatids to procure conception might improve to the level of that achieved with elongated spermatids (Aslam *et al.*, 1998). However,

Table 2.4. *ROSI and ELSI published data outcome for complete cycle histories*

| Type of cells injected | ROSI | ELSI |
|---|---|---|
| No. of cycles | 80 | 55 |
| No. of oocytes injected | 648 | 426 |
| No. of oocytes fertilized (2PN) | 203 (31.3%) | 245 (57.5%) |
| No. of embryo transfers | 75 (93.7%) | 55 (100%) |
| No. of transferred embryos | 155 (76.3%) | 198 (80.8%) |
| No. of clinical pregnancies | 10 | 12 |
| % of pregnancies/cycle | 12.5% | 21.8% |
| % of pregnancies/ET | 13.3% | 21.8% |
| % of transferred embryos | 6.5% | 6.1% |
| No. of live births | 9 | 11 |
| % of births/cycle | 11.3% | 20.0% |
| % of births/ET | 12.0% | 20.0% |
| % of transferred embryos delivered | 5.8% | 5.6% |

ELSI, elongating spermatid microinjection; ET, embryo transfer; 2PN, 2-pronuclei stage; ROSI, round spermatid microinjection.

despite the completion of meiosis in round spermatids, it is feasible that further epigenetic (nuclear and cytoplasmic) modifications occur during remodelling and maturation to the fully formed spermatozoon. Many authors remain concerned about possible health hazards for offspring resulting from spermatid conception. Currently there is much debate as to which patients would benefit from the opportunity of spermatid conception. The experience of a number of authors is that occasional fully formed spermatozoa are obtained from testicular biopsy samples from men ejaculating only spermatids; indeed, some authors believe it is inconsistent for spermatids to be produced without the presence of spermatozoa (Silber *et al.*, 1997). Conversely, in about 50% of patients who have had a previous biopsy and been informed of spermatogenic dysfunction without the presence of spermatozoa (e.g. Klinefelter Syndrome, partial Sertoli-cell-only syndrome, post-mumps orchitis, post-testicular atrophy chemotherapy, post-cryptorchidism, idiopathic maturation arrest), spermatozoa have been recovered following biopsy for an attempt at assisted conception. These spermatozoa have been successfully used to achieve pregnancies and the birth of healthy children.

Despite the clinical successes with spermatid injection, there are clear difficulties in achieving a high incidence of fertilization and implantation with round spermatids. Further research and arguably clinical trials (Aslam *et al.*, 1998) are required to fully evaluate the introduction of spermatid conception for reproduction. In the U.K., at the time of writing, there is a moratorium on the use of spermatid conception, and discussions are taking place amongst scientists and the Human Fertilisation and Embryology Authority as to the appropriateness of introducing a programme of clinical trials. More recent studies by ourselves and others cast doubt on the viability of embryos conceived after ROSI.

## Egg donation and surrogacy

Conditions for egg donation and surrogacy are listed in Table 2.5. Egg donation has been offered since 1984 (Lutjen *et al.*, 1984) and, with surrogacy, has become the most successful assisted conception programme – pregnancy rates are consistently around 50% in the most successful clinics. The egg donor is prepared in a similar manner to the conventional IVF management. Resulting embryos can be transferred to the recipient either fresh or after cryopreservation. For fresh embryo transfers the recipient is synchronized with the donor using GnRH analogues to desensitize the pituitary and generate a cyclical state. Endometrial preparation is by sequential oral administration of oestrogen, followed by progesterone. After cryopreservation, successfully thawed embryos are transferred to recipients during either their natural menstrual cycle or after desensitization and endometrial preparation.

## Oocyte maturation

One of the major difficulties for any successful oocyte donation programme is the supply of oocytes. Apart from a recent publication

Table 2.5. *Genetic/chromosomal conditions licensed by Human Fertilisation and Embryology Authority for preimplantation genetic diagnosis*

| | |
|---|---|
| X-Linked diseases | Sickle-cell anaemia |
| Translocations and gonadal mosaics | Tay–Sach's disease |
| Cystic fibrosis | Lesch–Nyhan Syndrome |
| Fragile X | Alpha-1 antitrypsin |
| Dominant cancer (polyposis coli) | Retinitis pigmentosa |
| β-Thalassaemia | |

(Wu *et al.*, 1998) demonstrating the presence of primordial follicles in routine aspirates from a mature follicle, the opportunity for a large, regular supply of mature oocytes depends upon women willing to undergo follicular stimulation and oocyte retrieval. In some countries, such as the U.K., this depends purely on altruism whereas in other countries donors are paid on a commercial basis. The recent introduction in the U.K. of more widespread 'eggshare' programmes has greatly enhanced the availability of donated eggs and reduced waiting time for recipients from years to several weeks.

It is possible to recover large numbers of immature oocytes from ovarian tissue without the need to administer large doses of follicular stimulants to women. However, recovery of any form of immature oocyte requires its maturation *in vitro*, which, apart from some very limited and relatively unsuccessful clinical trials, remains in the domain of priority research. (Barnes *et al.*, 1995; Russell *et al.*, 1997; Trounson *et al.*, 1994.)

There are additional problems associated with *in vitro* maturation that include hardening of the zona pellucida and the developmental competence of subsequent embryos. The former can be overcome by intracytoplasmic injection, while hatching of the blastocyst prior to implantation can be facilitated by performing assisted hatching before embryo transfer (see below).

Evidence accumulated to date suggests that few embryos develop to the blastocyst stage after maturation *in vitro*. A developmental block occurs during or subsequent to the four- to eight-cell stage (Barnes *et al.*, 1995). To date, implantation rates of transferred embryos from *in vitro* matured oocytes is <1%.

A further advantage for obtaining competent *in-vitro*-matured oocytes is in routine IVF. Should this technology become efficient, then women undergoing conventional IVF will not require follicular stimulation. A single biopsy of ovarian tissue can provide enough oocytes for an almost unlimited number of treatment cycles, as immature oocytes can be cryopreserved. Achieving successful *in vitro* maturation of primary oocytes is now an essential goal.

## Embryo culture

There is also considerable interest in the continued development of embryos *in vitro* to the blastocyst stage, before transfer; often called 'extended culture'. Advantages of this option include the removal of embryos that fail to develop thus enhancing a 'natural' selection procedure; and increasing the chances of implantation while reducing the number of multiple pregnancies. A further advantage of successful extended culture is that embryo biopsy (see below) at the blastocyst stage provides a greater number of embryonic cells for analysis. At this stage only trophoblast cells rather than embryonic cells *per se* would be required; this would be regarded as an ethical advantage in some quarters.

Conventional embryo culture medium, however, is based on a simple salt solution without any comprehensive knowledge of the requirements of the developing embryo, which may indeed be complex. Various researchers have now been examining different culture media for different stages of development which in essence is equivalent to the variable milieu existing in the female reproductive tract. Fertilization takes place in the ampullary region of the fallopian tube while the developing embryo reaches the eight-cell stage during its transport down the fallopian tube, while its eight-cell to blastocyst transition over a period of two to three days occurs during its entry into the endometrial cavity. At each stage there will be a dynamic flux and a changing composition of the immediate milieu. Hence, there is little doubt that the zygote, the intervening cleavage stages and the blastocyst have differing metabolic physiology which is not reflected by the medium used for culture *in vitro*. Using this approach and achieving blastocyst transfer has the potential to increase implantation rates and reduce multiple pregnancy (Gardner *et al*, 1998). In spite of our first reported pregnancies using blastocysts 15 years ago (Cohen *et al*., 1987) many practitioners still argue against immediate use of extended culture because of the number of patients that fail to receive embryo transfer due to developmental arrest prior to the blastocyst stage. However, our current blastocyst embryo stage ('BEST') programme yields a clinical pregnancy rate of 45–50% per embryo transfer. Clearly, further research to bring the *in vitro* development of the human embryo in line with conditions occurring *in vivo* is of significant importance to all aspects of IVF technology (Gardner *et al*., 1996).

## Assisted hatching

Before the embryo implants it must undergo the process of hatching during which the blastocyst expands and contracts eventually emerging through a breach in the zona pellucida. Various studies have indicated that *in vitro* culture causes hardening of the zona pellucida, impairing or delaying the hatching process once the embryo is returned to the uterine cavity. Cohen *et al*. (1990) suggested that artificially (by micromanipulation) inducing a breach in the zona pellucida improves the implantation rate in certain patients. Further research defined four patient groups in whom the assisted hatching process might be beneficial; these are:

1. Embryos having uniformly thick zonae.
2. Women over the age of 40.
3. Women with an elevated FSH.
4. Patients with recurrent implantation failure.

Today, the procedure is performed by ensuring a regular-sized breach, approximately 10μm, caused by the release of an acidified culture solution through a specific microneedle butted up against the zona pellucida. Data in the literature are variable and debate still exists as to the benefit of this procedure. However, in some clinics there are data indicating that the implantation rate in women falling into one of the poor prognostic groups (listed above) is similar to that of the 'control' group. Assisted hatching is still practised in many units with variable prognosis.

## Cryopreservation

Cryopreservation of mammalian tissue has been available since 1972 (Whittingham et al., 1972) and this technology has been applied to approximately 100,000 bovine embryos each year since 1980.

Cryopreservation of human zygotes and embryos is now a necessary part of the conventional IVF programme. In experienced hands it is an efficient solution to the problem of supernumerary embryos from the zygote to the blastocyst stage, offering up to 15–20% chance of delivery. The first birth from human embryos occurred in 1984 (Zielmaker et al., 1984). Freezing of mature human oocytes, in contrast, has resulted in very few successful pregnancies and even fewer live births reported (Chen, 1986; Vanuem et al., 1987). Problems with cryopreserving mature human oocytes relate to low survival and fertilization rates (the latter partially overcome by ICSI), but a high incidence of abnormal chromosomes after the freeze–thaw procedure (Hunter et al., 1991).

Embryo cryopreservation has clearly improved in recent years. Live birth rates have improved from <5% to 10–15% on a routine basis in many clinics. Attention to particular details, such as the stage of the embryo and the cryoprotectant used, optimal embryo culture conditions prior to freezing, the morphological quality of the embryo and the protocol used, are all relevant. Increases in the efficiency of embryo freezing will be beneficial to those patients who wish to increase their family years later. It is well established that the efficiency of implantation and pregnancy to term is related to the age of the woman from whom the oocyte is recovered. Therefore, women who have embryos cryopreserved when they are younger (given the statutory ten-year storage limit in the U.K.) may confer a reproductive advantage at a later stage.

Cryopreservation appears to be a safe procedure with an analysed still-birth rate of approximately 1%, major anomalies arising at around 2% (in line with the normal population, and after fresh embryo transfer), and in assessment of development in children aged between 1 and 9 years (Olivennes *et al.*, 1996; Sutcliffe *et al.*, 1995; Wada *et al.*, 1994). Data on ICSI-derived zygotes or embryos give similar results to the freezing of unmanipulated embryos (Hoover *et al.*, 1997)

### *Freezing human oocytes*

Literature on nearly a thousand frozen-thawed immature human oocytes demonstrate that between 30 and 40% can be matured *in vitro* after thawing, with up to 40% achieving fertilization using ICSI. However, despite the advantages of freezing immature oocytes, both to the patient and from a safety perspective, the prospect of clinical success remains elusive and considerable research is required before this technology can be considered a realistic option (Porcu *et al.*, 1999; Tucker *et al.*, 1996). Research efforts concentrated to overcome current difficulties will eventually provide a valuable and essential component to overcoming problems of sterility or potential sterility, such as females undergoing treatment for cancer (see below).

Recent developments have rekindled scientists' interest in the cryopreservation of mature human oocytes. Current methods ensure that at least 60% of oocytes have normal chromosome configurations with no evidence of increased frequency of cryopreservation-associated aneuploidy (Gook *et al.*, 1994; Van Blerkom and Davies, 1994). Other problems that do arise, such as a high rate of parthogenetic activation (Gook *et al.*, 1995), can be observed under the microscope (a single pronucleate development) and discarded. The introduction of ICSI to procure fertilization has dramatically improved the appalling rates of fertilization occurring with conventional IVF after oocyte cryopreservation. More recent clinical attempts (Porcu *et al.*, 1999; Tucker *et al.*, 1996) have given further hope for the introduction of this technology in the near future. Now, nearly 13 years since the first recorded birth from oocyte cryopreservation (Chen, 1986), we are beginning to understand the causes of failure and are developing technologies to overcome the difficulties.

## Preimplantation genetic diagnosis (PGD)

Preimplantation genetic diagnosis (PGD) was first undertaken on human embryos towards the end of the 1980s with the first pregnancies being reported at the beginning of the 1990s (Handyside *et al.*, 1990; Verlinsky *et al.*, 1990). PGD is an earlier stage of prenatal diagnosis that occurs at some stage between conception and the blastocyst. Most PGD occurs by removing a single cell from a four-cell embryo, or one or two cells from an eight-cell embryo (days two and day three, respectively, postconception).

PGD can be undertaken for patients with specific chromosome or single-gene defects. In couples with an autosomal or X-linked genetic disorder there is a 25–50% chance of producing an affected child. Each pregnancy carries the same risk and there is no relationship to the number of previously affected foetuses or children. Conventional prenatal diagnosis provides a result within 10–20 weeks of a pregnancy becoming established. PGD offers couples the opportunity of not embarking on a pregnancy by aborting the embryo *in vitro*. For many couples this option is ethically and morally more acceptable, and psychologically less traumatic than termination of pregnancy. The technique itself has a 30-year history, when Edwards and Gardner (1967) successfully sexed rabbit blastocysts by examining cells removed from the non-embryonic trophectoderm layer before transfer to the uterus. Current advances in PGD for clinical purposes have awaited developments in molecular biology.

Various chromosome and genetic conditions can now be examined, covering autosomal recessive and dominant disorders as well as X-linked inheritance. The commonest autosomal recessive disorder in the Caucasian population is cystic fibrosis, whilst the commonest autosomal recessive disease worldwide is β-thalassaemia. In both these disorders there are a range of significant mutations for which individual analyses is required. It is extremely important to offer genetic counselling and a detailed genetic work-up to the couple prior to embarking on IVF and PGD. With autosomal dominant disorders, only one copy of the abnormal gene needs to be present in each cell for the disease to be expressed, although many dominant disorders are not as severe or as life-threatening as those determined by recessive genes. However, there are an increasing number of requests for PGD in cases such as Huntingdon disease, Marfan Syndrome and polyposis coli.

X-linked disorders can either be recessive or dominantly inherited, but generally almost all severe cases are recessive and carried by females who themselves are unaffected (or mildly affected). Common requests for X-linked recessives include Duchenne muscular dystrophy and haemophilia. However, there are over 200 X-linked disorders, and for the vast majority the molecular basis of the disease is unknown.

In the U.K. PGD requires a specific licence from the Human Fertilisation and Embryology Authority, and licences are obtained for specific diseases. The conditions that have been successfully diagnosed using PGD are listed in Table 2.5.

A major problem in chromosome analysis of human embryos is that a large number, estimated to be up to 50%, of human conceptions fail due to the existence of chromosome abnormalities. These abnormalities appear to arise equally after conception *in vivo* or *in vitro*. Various patterns of abnormalities have been categorized (Delhanty *et al*, 1997; Harper and Delhanty, 1996), and these have been divided into four groups:

1. Uniformly diploid.
2. Uniformly abnormal (such as trisomy 21 or Turner Syndrome).
3. Mosaic (where there exists the presence of diploid nuclei and aneuploid, haploid or polyploid nuclei in different blastomeres of the same embryo).
4. Chaotic embryos, in which every nucleus has a different chromosome complement.

Therefore, assessing embryos for their chromosome status requires considerable skill and analytical ability, but even then the one or two cells removed from the embryo may not completely reflect the chromosome status of that embryo's remaining cells. In some centres, mainly in the U.S.A., PGD has been used to try to eliminate age-related aneuploidy (Munné *et al.*, 1995). In principle, this would be an extremely beneficial process given that a large proportion of miscarriage and pregnancy failure in older women is due to chromosome anomalies arising in the embryo. By tending to select the healthier embryo, improvements in the incidence of viable pregnancies might occur. Furthermore, some argue that the 0.5–1% risk of miscarriage after prenatal diagnosis is less acceptable to older women who have conceived by IVF (Reubinoff and Shushan, 1996). Nevertheless, at present the existence of chromosomal mosaicism can easily lead to a misdiagnosis, especially as only a small number (five to seven) of chromosomes can be analysed at present, there is a high likelihood that problems may exist in any of the remaining 16–18 chromosomes, and the incidence of implantation may not be greatly increased to justify the procedure. Others have taken an alternative approach by analysing the polar body of the egg (the small cytoplasmic portion of the egg that is released during its maturation, but contains half the number of chromosomes). Two polar bodies exist in the fertilized egg, one being released postfertilization. Both these polar bodies need to be analysed to provide complete information about the aneuploidies that may arise in the oocyte (Verlinsky *et al*, 1996), but this procedure will not detect postfertilization events. To maximize the opportunity for this technology we need to await further development on the availability of probes and efficient examination of these in cells from the embryo, but this technology will not become more readily available until the future.

Current research is focused on methods to detect and evaluate single-gene defects and chromosome imbalance, and to extend the range of disorders amenable to specific diagnosis. Patients who carry certain chromosome translocations can now have their embryos evaluated depending on the specific chromosome and the break points involved. Patients need to be thoroughly worked up for this procedure and the process is time consuming and expensive, but currently available. Eventually there will be a complete screen of the whole genome for aneuploidy, and there will be an increasing number of recessive and dominant single-gene disorders available for analysis.

The most recently published world data for PGD (Harper, 1996) showed an incidence of pregnancy of 28% per embryo transfer – comparable to that for routine IVF – and of the 71 babies delivered there are no reports of congenital malformations, giving confidence in the technology *per se.*

## Cytoplasmic donation and mitochondrial DNA (mDNA) transfer

Women undergo egg donation because of chromosomal or genetic disorders, ovarian dysgenesis, absence of the ovaries or as a result of nonspecific/poorly understood reasons for poor embryo quality. In recent years consideration has been given to the role of the cytoplasmic component of an oocyte, valuable contributors to which are mitochondria, messenger RNA and specific transcripts, cell cycle regulating factors and various cytoskeletal elements. For more than ten years scientists have been transferring the cytoplasm of oocytes (ooplasm) between differing oocytes and embryos. More recently, this approach has been considered to improve the quality of oocytes for women who otherwise would require egg donation (Cohen *et al.*, 1998). The first clinical trials of cytoplasmic donation involved six patients and seven treatment cycles, where each patient had a history of poor embryo development. Using micromanipulation technology a significant portion of the ooplasm (donor ooplast) was aspirated into a microinjection needle. The donor ooplast was then transferred under the zona pellucida and adjacent to the oocyte membrane (oolemma) of the recipient oocyte. The recipient oocytes were placed in a special chamber and subjected to an electrical pulse which temporarily disrupts the cell membrane and allows a fusion between the recipient cytoplasm and the donor ooplast. Twenty-one of the 22 eggs fused and standard ICSI was performed. Ten embryos were eventually transferred, but no pregnancy resulted. The authors then introduced a simplified protocol: initially, a spermatozoon was drawn into the injection pipette as if for routine ICSI, followed by the donor ooplasm. An ICSI-type procedure was then performed where approximately 5–15% of donor ooplasmic volume was transferred into the recipient oocyte. In this study four patients were treated after having implantation failure during a total of 17 cycles between them. Apparently the majority of the embryos were morphologically improved compared to control embryos and historical records. Three patients became pregnant, one miscarried early in pregnancy before a foetal heart was detected on scan, and two patients delivered normal, healthy children.

This small clinical study is insufficient evidence of the value of cytoplasmic donation. It is still difficult to understand how such a small volume of ooplasm can be significantly therapeutic to a cleaving embryo. However, a few animal model studies have supported the potential benefit of cytoplasmic donation (Levron *et al.*, 1995).

Perhaps for the future more dramatic manipulation, such as nuclear transplantation, would be beneficial both from a clinical and an ethical perspective. For example, another additional group of patients who are unable to conceive are those who carry defects in their mitochondria. Mitochondrial DNA cytopathies affect infants, children and adults with a variety of extremely severe conditions (Table 2.6). Women who carry such mitochondrial defects are unable to have children with their own oocytes. One possibility might be to exchange the nucleus from the egg of a woman affected by mDNA cytopathy and transfer this to an enucleated donor oocyte recovered from a healthy woman. From an ethical perspective, the genetic origins of the woman are preserved, but, from a biological point of view, the mitochondrial DNA – which is passed on to offspring only through the female line – will be of donor origin. The implications of this need to be further evaluated, but nuclear transplantation has succeeded in bovine for many years, albeit with poor results. Reviewing the technology of nuclear transplantation for clinical purposes might now be

Table 2.6. *Potential effects of mitochondrial DNA cytopathies*

| Infants/neonates | Children | Adults |
|---|---|---|
| Lactic acidosis | Ataxia | Deafness |
| Seizures | Diplopia | Dementia |
| Amino acidurea | Dystonia | Optic atrophy |
| Hypotonia | Psychomotor retardation | Stroke-like episodes |
| | Optic atrophy | Hereditary optic neuropathy |
| | Retinal degeneration | |
| | Myoclonic epilepsy | |
| | External opthalmoplegia and/or ptosis | |
| | Cardiomyopathy | |

appropriate and could represent an opportunity for one's own genetic offspring in certain conditions where only oocyte donation is currently appropriate.

## Fertility preservation

In Britain there are over 10,000 adult survivors of childhood cancer. This number increases by over 500 per year (Stiller, 1994). Although most survivors are fit, well and leading normal lives, one significant side-effect for a considerable number has been fertility impairment. In recent years major advances in the treatment of childhood cancers has been reported, with long-term survival being achieved in over two-thirds of children diagnosed with cancer (Miller *et al.*, 1993). Those surviving for over ten years can now be considered cured (Robertson *et al.*, 1994). Fertility potential is low down the concerns for relative quality of life during treatment for survival. As health is regained and children approach adulthood with normal life, subfertility/sterility becomes a problem and of serious concern.

A general malaise of the cancer patient can cause altered hypothalamic–pituitary function and a range of hormonal and metabolic defects related to testicular function. Hodgkin disease, for example, affects spermatogenesis with significant damage caused to germinal epithelia. Chemotherapeutic agents are cytotoxic, and their effects can be influenced by the patients' condition. The testes are highly susceptible to these toxic effects and in numerous incidences ovarian tissue can also be affected irreversibly. Similarly, radiation therapy and combinations of radiation and chemotherapy can be synergistic in providing the worst prognosis.

The inability to reproduce has major psychological consequences. The initial awareness of potential subfertility is a condition not thoroughly comprehended by a sick adolescent. Its awareness in adults and the often unrecognized but nevertheless seriously psychologically traumatic condition of being 'genetically dead' cause deep concerns, and, in a few cases, has led to suicide. In many patients that undergo treatments that have long-term sequelae of subfertility/sterility, technologies are now available to help preserve their fertility and genetic lineage before treatment. Three factors need to be considered:

1.  The presence of useable germ cells.
2.  The mode of extraction.
3.  Effective storage for later use.

The opportunity for females relates either to oocyte/follicular maturation *in vitro*, follicular maturation after xenogeneic grafting or autografting to the patient herself. (Hovatta *et al.*, 1996; Newton *et al.*, 1996; Oktay *et al.*, 1998, 2000).

Opportunities for fertility preservation now exist for males as a result of the technology developed in animal models. Cryopreserved germ cells have successfully undergone syngeneic (mouse) and xenogeneic (mouse/rat) population of sterilized immature animals using chemotherapeutic agents. Spermatogenesis has been resumed and the production of fully formed spermatozoa resulted (Avarbock *et al.*, 1996; Brinster and Avarbock, 1994). This technology offers hope for fertility preservation in boys through the removal of part of their testicular tissue before treatment. This could be cryopreserved with the eventual goal of retransplanting thawed cryopreserved tissue to achieve ipsigeneic germ-cell repopulation, to provide these patients with the chance of normal conception later in life. It would still be possible to undertake xenogeneic transplantation and, should

spermatogenesis occur, depending upon the numbers of spermatozoa obtained by either xenogeneic or ipsigeneic transplantation,
ICSI could be utilized to procure conception, if necessary. Therefore,
it is now appropriate to consider at least the removal and storage of
germ cell tissue for children about to undergo any form of treatment
whose side-effects confer subfertility/sterility. Regeneration of viable
gametes for such patients is still some time away, but these children
will have at least a generation or more of scientific development to
resolve their impending sterility.

## Conclusion

During the final quarter of the last millennium, we have witnessed
for the first time the potential of modern science to manipulate
human reproductive processes. Since the advent of assisted reproductive technologies in humans there has been a welter of ethical
debate, often obscuring the dramatic advances that have changed
the state of infertility. Many of the techniques described may seem
'Brave New World' and 'Futuristic'; this is often associated with
moral deprecation. In reality, the technologies briefly covered here
provide an opportunity to treat hitherto often immutable conditions. These new technologies can therefore improve the health and
well-being of individuals, as well as their life choices. With parallel
developments in embryo development and molecular genetics
covered more fully in the next chapter, our views on health and
disease in future generations will likewise be radically altered.

## References

Aslam, I., Fishel, S., Green, S., Campbell, A., Garratt, L., McDermott, H.,
Dowell, K., Thornton, S. (1998) Can we justify spermatid microinjection
for severe male factor infertility? *Human Reproduction Update* **4**:213–22.

Avarbock, M. R., Brinster, C. J., Brinster, R. L. (1996) Reconstitution of
spermatogenesis from frozen spermatogonial stem cells. *Nature Medicine*
**2**:693–6.

Barnes, F. L., Crombie, A., Gardner, D. K. *et al.* (1995) Blastocyst development and birth after *in vitro* maturation of human primary oocytes, intracytoplasmic sperm injection and assisted hatching. *Human Reproduction* **10**:3243–7.

Brinster, R. L., Avarbock, M. R. (1994) Germline transmission of donor haplotype following spermatogonial transplantation. *Proceedings of the National Academy of Sciences, U.S.A.* **91**:11303–7.

Chappel, S., Kelton, C., Nugent, N. (1992) Expression of human gonadotrophins by recombinant DNA methods. In: Genazzi, A. R., Petrajila, F. (eds.) *Proceedings of the Third World Congress on gynaecological endocrinology*. Carnforth, U.K.: Parthenon Press, pp.179–84.

Chen, C. (1986) Pregnancy after human oocyte cryopreservation. *The Lancet* **i**:885–6.

Cohen, J., Elsner, C., Kort, H., Malta, H. J., Massey, J., Mayer, M. P., Wiemer, K. (1990) Impairment of the hatching process following IVF in the human and improvement of implantation by assisting hatching using micromanipulation. *Human Reproduction* **5**:7–13.

Cohen, J., Scott, R., Alikani, M. *et al.* (1998) Ooplasmic transfer of immature human oocytes. *Molecular Human Reproduction* **4**:269–80.

Cohen, J., Simons, R. F., Edwards, R. G., Fehilly, C. B., Fishel, S. B. (1985) Pregnancies following the frozen-storage of expanding human blastocysts. *Journal of In Vitro Fertilization and Embryo Transfer* **21**:59–64.

Delhanty, J. D. A., Harper, J. C., Ao, A., Handyside, A. H., Winston, R. M. L. (1997) Multi-colour FISH detects frequent chromosomal mosaicism and chaotic division in normal preimplantation embryos from fertile patients. *Human Genetics* **99**:755–60.

Edwards, R. G., Gardner, R. L. (1967) Sexing of live rabbit blastocysts. *Nature* **214**:576–7.

Fishel, S. B., Lisi, F., Rinaldi, L. *et al* (1995*a*) Systematic examination of immobilising spermatozoa before intractyoplasmic sperm injection in the human. *Human Reproduction* **10**:497–500.

Fishel, S., Green, S., Bishop, M. *et al* (1995*b*) Pregnancy after intractyoplasmic injection of spermatid. *The Lancet* **345**:1641–2.

Fishel, S., Aslam, I., Tesarik, J. (1996) Spermatid conception: a stage too early, or a time too soon? *Human Reproduction* **11**:1371–5.

Gardner, D. K., Lane, M., Kalderon, I., Leeton, J. (1996) Environment of the preimplantation human embryo *in vivo*: metabolite analysis of oviduct and uterine fluids and metabolism of cumulus cells. *Fertility and Sterility* **65**:349–53.

Gardner, D. K., Vella, P., Lane, M. *et al* (1998) Culture and transfer of human blastocysts increases implantation rates and reduces the need for multiple embryo transfers. *Fertility and Sterility* **69**:84–8.

Gook D. A., Osborn, S. M., Bourne, H. *et al.* (1994) Fertilisation of human oocytes on cryopreservation; normal karyotypes and absence of stray chromosomes. *Human Reproduction* **9**:684–91.

Gook, D. A., Schieue, M. C., Osborn, S.M. *et al.* (1995) Intracytoplasmic sperm injection and embryo development of human oocytes cryopreserved using 1, 2-propanediol. *Human Reproduction* **10**:2637–41.

Handyside, A. H., Kontogialli, E. H., Hardy, K., Winston, R. M. L. (1990) Pregnancies from biopsies of human preimplantation embryos sexed by Y-specific DNA amplification. *Nature* **244**:768–70.

Harper, J. C. (1996) Preimplantation diagnosis of inherited disease by embryo biopsy. An update of the world figures. *Journal of Assisted Reproduction Genetics* **13**:90–4.

Harper, J. C., Delhanty, J. D. A. (1996) Detection of chromosomal abnormalities in human preimplantation embryos using FISH. *Journal of Assisted Reproduction and Genetics* **13**:137–9.

Hoover, L., Baker, A., Check, J.H. *et al.* (1997) Clinical outcome of cryopreserved human pronculear stage embryos resulting from intracytoplasmic sperm injection. *Fertility and Sterility* **67**:621–4.

Hovatta, O., Silye, R., Krausz, T. *et al.* (1996) Cryopreservation of human ovarian tissue using dimethyl sulphoxide and propanediol–sucrose as cryoprotectants. *Human Reproduction* **11**:1268–72.

Hull, M. G. R. (1996) Infertility: nature and extent of the problem. In: Bock, G., O'Connor, M. (eds.) *Human embryo research: yes or no?* London: CIBA Foundation, Tavistock Publications, p. 38.

Hull, M. G., Glazener, C. M., Kelly, N. J., Conway, D. I., Foster, P. A. *et al.* (1985) Population study of causes, treatment, and outcome of intertility. *British Medical Journal* **291**:1693–7.

Hunter, J. E., Bernard, A., Fuller, B. (1991) Fertilisation and development of the human oocyte following exposure to cryoprotectants, low temperatures and cryopreservation: a comparison of two techniques. *Human Reproduction* **6**:1460–5.

Johnson, G., Rolberts, D., Brown, R. *et al.* (1987) Infertile or childless of choice? A multipractice survey of women. *British Medical Journal* **294**:804–7.

Kimura, Y., Yanagimachi, R. (1995) Mouse oocytes injected with testicular spermatozoa and round spermatids can develop into normal offspring. *Development* **121**:2397–405.

Levron, J., Willadsen, S., Bertoli, M., Cohen, J. (1995) The development of mouse zygotes after fusion with synchronous and asynchronous cytoplasm. *Human Reproduction* **1**:1287–92.

Lutjen, P. J., Trounson, A. O., Leeton, F. J., Wood, C., Renou, P. (1984) The establishment and maintenance of pregnancy using *in vitro* fertilisation and embryo donation in a patient with primary ovarian failure. *Nature* **307**:174–6.

Miller, B.A. *et al.* (1993) *SEER Cancer Statistics Review: 1973–1990.* National Cancer Institute. NIH Publication No. 93–2789.

Munné, S., Daley, T., Sultan, K. M., Grifo, J., Cohen, J. (1995) The use of first polar bodies for preimplantation diagnosis of aneuploidy. *Human Reproduction* **10**:1014–20.

Newton, H., Aubard, Y., Rutherford, A. *et al.* (1996) Low temperature storage and grafting of human ovarian tissue. *Human Reproduction* **11**:1487–91.

Ogura, A., Matsuda, J., Yanagimachi, R. (1994) Birth of normal young after electrofusion of mouse oocytes with round spermatids. *Proceedings of the National Academy of Sciences, U.S.A.* **91**:7460–2.

Oktay, K., Newton, H., Mullan, J., Gosden, R. G. (1998) Development of human primordial follicles to antral stages in scid/hpg mice stimulated with follicle stimulating hormone. *Human Reproduction* **13**:1133–8.

Oktay, K., Newton, H., Gosden, R. G. (2000) Transplantation of cryo-preserved human ovarian tissue results in follicle growth initiation in SCID mice. *Fertility and Sterility* **73**:599–603.

Olivennes, F., Schneider, Z., Remy, V. *et al.* (1996) Perinatal outcome and follow-up of 82 children aged 1–9 years old conceived from cryopreserved embryos. *Human Reproduction* **11**:1565–8.

Palermo, G., Joris, H., Devroey, P. *et al* (1992) Pregnancies after intracyto-plasmic sperm injection of a single spermatozoon into an oocyte. *The Lancet* **340**:17–18.

Porcu, E., Fabbri, R., Ciotti, P. M., Petracchi, S., Seracchioli, R., Flamigni, C. (1999) Ongoing pregnancy after intracytoplasmic sperm injection of epididymal spermatazoa into cryopreserved human oocytes. *Journal of Assisted Reproduction and Genetics* **16**:283–5.

Reijo, R., Lee, T., Salo, P. *et al* (1995) Diverse spermatogenic defects in humans caused by Y chromosome deletions encompassing a novel RNA-binding protein gene. *Nature Genetics* **10**:383–93.

Reubinoff, B., Shushan, A. (1996) Preimplantation diagnosis in older patients: to biopsy or not to biopsy? *Human Reproduction* **11**:2071–8.

Robertson, C. M., Hawkins, M. M., Kingston, J. E. (1994) Late deaths and survival after childhood-cancer – implications for cure. *British Medical Journal* **309**:162–6.

Russell, J. B., Kenezevich, K. M., Fabian, K.F. *et al* (1997) Unstimulated immature oocyte retrieval: early *versus* mid follicular endometrial priming. *Fertility and Sterility* **67**:616–20.

Silber, S. J., Nagy, Z., Devroey, P. *et al* (1997) Distribution of spermatogenesis in the testicles of azoospermic men: the presence or absence of spermatid in the testes of men with germinal failure. *Human Reproduction* **12**:2422–8.

Stiller, C. A. (1994) Population-based survival rates for childhood-cancer in Britain 1980–91. *British Medical Journal* **309**:1612–16.

Sutcliffe, A. G., D'Souza, S. W., Cadman, J. *et al* (1995) Minor congenital anomalies, major congenital malformations and development in children conceived from cryopreserved embryos. *Human Reproduction* **10**:3332–7.

Tesarik, J., Mendoza, C., Testart, J. (1995) Viable embryos from injection of round spermatids into oocytes. *New England Journal of Medicine* **333**:525.

Tesarik, J., Rolet, F., Brami, C. *et al.* (1996) Spermatid injection into human oocytes. II. Clinical application in the treatment of infertility due to nonobstructive azoospermia. *Human Reproduction* **11**:780–3.

Thonneau, P., Spira, A. (1990) Prevalence of infertility; international data and problems of measurement. *European Journal of Obstetrics Gynaecological Reproductive Biology* **38**:43–52.

Trounson, A., Wood, C., Kausch, A. (1994) *In vitro* maturation and the fertilisation and development competence of oocytes recovered from untreated polycystic ovarian patients. *Fertility and Sterility* **62**:353–62.

Tucker, M. J., Wright, G., Morton, E. *et al* (1996) Preliminary experience with human oocyte cryopreservation using 1,2-propranediol and sucrose. *Human Reproduction* **11**:1513–15.

Van Blerkom, J., Davies, P. W. (1994) Cytogenetic, cellular, and developmental consequences of cryopreservation of immature and mature mouse and human oocytes. *Microscopy Research Technology* **27**:165–93.

Vanuem, J. H. F. M., Siebzehnruebl, E. R., Schuh, B., Koch, R., Trotnow, S., Lang, N. (1987) Birth after cryopreservation of unfertilised oocytes. *Lancet* **ii**:752–3.

Verlinsky, Y., Ginsberg, N., Lifchez, A., Valle, J., Moise, J., Strom, C. M. (1990) Analysis of the first polar body: preconception genetic diagnosis. *Human Reproduction* **5**:826–9.

Verlinksy, Y., Strom, C., Cieslak, J., Kuliev, A., Ivakhenko, V., Lifchez, A. (1996) Birth of healthy children after preimplantation diagnosis of common aneuploidies by polar body fluorescent *in situ* hybridisation analysis. *Fertility and Sterility* **66**:126–9.

Vogt, P., Chandley, A. C., Hargreave, T.B. *et al* (1992) Microdeletions in interval 6 of the Y chromosome of males with idiopathic sterility point to disruption of AZF, a human spermatogenesis gene. *Human Genetics* **89**:491–6.

Wada, I., Macnamee, M. C., Wick, K. *et al* (1994) Birth characteristics and perinatal outcome of babies conceived from cryopreserved embryos. *Human Reproduction* **9**:543–6.

Whittingham, D. G., Leibo, S. P., Mazur, P. (1972) Survival of mouse embryos, frozen to minus 196 °C and minus 289 °C. *Science* **174**:411–14.

Wu, J., Zhang, L., Liu, P. (1998) A new source of human oocytes: preliminary report on the identification and maturation of human pre-antral follicles from follicular aspirates. *Human Reproduction* **13**:2561–3.

Zeilmaker, G. H., Alberda, A. T., Van Geest, L. (1984) Two pregnancies following transfer of intact frozen–thawed embryos. *Fertility and Sterility* **42**:293–6.

# 3

## Genetic influences on human infertility

A. H. BITTLES AND P. L. MATSON

## Abstract

A remarkable characteristic of human reproduction is the very high prevalence of spontaneous abortion, which frequently has been associated with major chromosomal abnormalities. The various forms of maternal–fetal red cell incompatibility and their potentially adverse effects on human fertility are well understood, and during the last 15 years of the twentieth century there was vigorous debate as to whether couples who share HLA-DR and/or HLA-B alleles are subfertile.

The most common genetic disorders associated with primary infertility in females are the chromosome abnormality Turner Syndrome (monosomy X), and Stein–Leventhal Syndrome (polycystic ovarian disease) which has a more complex and somewhat poorly defined genetic aetiology. A much wider spectrum of genetic defects can cause infertility in males, including Klinefelter Syndrome, X-autosome reciprocal translocation, Y-chromosome microdeletions, congenital absence of the vas deferens, most commonly observed as part of the cystic fibrosis phenotype, and obstructive azoospermia in patients with Young Syndrome.

Successful pregnancies can be initiated in the majority of individuals with these disorders; for example, using donated oocytes or embryos in women with Turner Syndrome, and intracytoplasmic injection of sperm (ICSI) collected from men with Klinefelter Syndrome or congenital absence of the vas deferens. In some disorders, such as Y-linked microdeletions, there may be a high risk of transmission to progeny following fertilization via ICSI, which has caused concerns on dysgenic grounds. Preimplantation diagnosis has been used to monitor such embryos. However, while rapid progress in this area is under way, to date the individual cases examined are too few in number to allow firm conclusions to be drawn on the feasibility of the method, which effectively restricts risk counselling to potentially affected couples.

## Introduction

In an overview of human fertility it was estimated that about 25% of women become pregnant within one month of unprotected intercourse, 63% within six months, 75% within nine months, 80–90% within a year and only another 5% after an additional six months of exposure (Williamson and Elias, 1992). The rate of coitus is recognized as an important determining factor in achieving pregnancy, with a frequency of four times per week being optimal (MacLeod and Gold, 1953). Maximum fertility in women occurs at around 24 years of age, and thereafter it declines with increasing rapidity until by age 50 the proportion of couples who can achieve a successful natural pregnancy approaches zero (Tietze, 1957).

From a genetic perspective there is a significantly increased risk of trisomic pregnancies with advancing maternal age and several of these abnormalities, trisomy 21, 13 and 18, may proceed to term (Connor and Ferguson-Smith, 1997). Although males undergo an age-related involution of the testes, their reproductive capacity may be retained until quite advanced years. However, there is evidence of an increased frequency of autosomal dominant disorders, such as achondroplasia (Penrose, 1955) and Apert Syndrome (Erickson, 1974), among the progeny of older fathers suggesting an increased rate of germ cell mutation in these individuals.

## The prevalence of infertility in humans

Although primary infertility is relatively rare in humans, affecting as indicated above some 5–8% of couples in developed countries

(Macfarlane and Mugford, 1984), early pregnancy loss is thought to be very common. Thus, in a study based on the examination of early abortuses, it was estimated that in any one month and under optimal conditions 15% of oocytes failed to become fertilized, 10–15% cleaved but failed to implant, and of those fertilized ova that did implant only 42% were of sufficient viability as to result in suppression of the next menstrual period (Hertig, 1967). Furthermore, in pregnancies followed from week four of gestation, 24% ended in loss of the conceptus (French and Bierman, 1962).

Subsequent work has suggested that these figures could perhaps best be regarded as lower level estimates and, for example, in a theoretical summation of total pre- and postimplantation pregnancy losses it was calculated that 78% of conceptions ended in spontaneous abortion or miscarriage (Roberts and Lowe, 1975). At the time of publication this figure was quite widely regarded as exaggerated; however, prospective studies based on the monitoring of human chorionic gonadotrophin (hCG) levels, which increase immediately after implantation, have produced results that suggest it may have been quite realistic. Thus, urine or serum analysis of hCG levels in volunteer subjects who wished to conceive recorded postimplantation losses of 43% (Miller *et al.*, 1980) and 31% (Wilcox *et al.*, 1988) respectively. With improvements in the sensitivity of the assay system, the most recent hCG-based studies, which employed urine testing of female volunteers every third day throughout the menstrual cycle, suggested a postimplantation loss rate of 45% among women in the optimum reproductive ages, rising to over 90% as the subjects approached menopause (Holman *et al.*, 2000).

Cytogenetic examination of embryos and fetuses from spontaneous abortions have revealed a high level of chromosomal anomalies, with initial estimates ranging from 21.5% (Carr, 1971) to 51.3% (Boué and Boué, 1970). In most cases, the observed anomalies were numerical defects. Later studies showed that the prevalence of chromosomal anomalies was highest in conceptuses lost early in pregnancy, with an estimated 66.0% abnormality among fetuses aborted between weeks two and seven of gestation, by comparison with 23.1% at weeks 8–12 (Boué *et al.*, 1985). A review of chromosomal anomalies in six studies of spontaneous abortion (Chandley, 1981) indicated that the most common forms of abnormality were autosomal trisomies (50.9%), monosomy X (19.9%), triploidies (16.5%), tetraploidies (6.3%), structural anomalies (3.9%) and mosaicism (2.0%). However, as will be discussed later, it can be predicted that technical improvements in cytogenetic analysis will alter the spectrum of chromosomal defects identified in future surveys, resulting in an increased proportion of previously unrecognized structural anomalies.

With advancing maternal age there appears to be an increase in the risk of early pregnancy loss, which in turn reflects an accumulation of chromosomal damage that is mostly attributable to non-disjunction during meiosis (Boué *et al.*, 1985). In studies of trisomy 16, which is the most common human trisomy and occurs in approximately 1% of all clinically recognized pregnancies, the association between maternal age and trisomy was shown to be due to diminished recombination (Hassold *et al.*, 1995). However, it has been postulated that the increased rates of trisomy 21 and other trisomies with advancing maternal age may result from declining efficiency in an unidentified maternal screening process which operates between fertilization and the clinical recognition of pregnancy, i.e. less than 28 days after the last menstrual period (Stein *et al.*, 1986). According to this hypothesis, the most probable stage at which the proposed screening process operates is during the first mitotic division of the zygote.

## Infertility due to maternal–fetal red cell compatibility

Maternal–fetal red cell incompatibility has been extensively described as a genetic cause of infertility. ABO incompatibility between mother and fetus is relatively frequent, but it is usually quite mild in effect since the causative anti-A and/or anti-B antibodies are predominantly IgM and so they cannot cross the placenta. Nevertheless, studies have indicated that ABO maternal–fetal incompatibility appears to be associated both with a higher rate of spontaneous abortion and increased childlessness (Matsunaga and Itoh, 1958) and stillbirths (Reed and Lowell, 1958), although the extent of the effect is relatively slight (Morton *et al.*, 1966) and the precise pattern and timing is variable (Schaap *et al.*, 1984).

By comparison, haemolytic disease due to Rhesus (Rh) incompatibility is less common because of the low frequency of Rh–ve alleles in most populations, but it is usually severe as the anti-D antibodies are IgG which can readily cross the placenta and cause large-scale red cell destruction. The condition arises following the escape of Rh+ve red cells from a fetus into the maternal circulation, resulting in the formation of maternal anti-Rh(D) antibody if the mother is Rh–ve. This situation may arise at parturition or, less commonly, following an abortion or some form of prenatal testing, e.g. amniocentesis or chorionic villus sampling (Connor and Ferguson-Smith, 1997).

In the past, Rh incompatibility became especially critical in the second and later pregnancies when maternal anti-Rh antibodies crossed the placenta, and the condition could result in death due to *erythroblastosis fetalis*. Following the introduction of anti-D immunoglobulin therapy to remove fetal red cells before they could provoke maternal anti-Rh antibody production, in the U.K. fetal deaths attributed to Rh incompatibility were reduced in frequency from 46/100,000 prior to 1969 to 1.6/100,000 in 1990 (Mollinson *et al.*, 1997). Nevertheless, RhD alloimmunization continues to occur, with RhD antibodies detected in 0.23–1.8% of RhD–ve pregnant women (National Blood Transfusion Service Immunoglobulin Working Party, 1991). Since most of these cases appear to have arisen because of immunization during a pregnancy in which there has been no overt sensitizing event, it has been proposed that all women should receive anti-D immunoglobulin during pregnancy at 28–34 weeks gestation (Robson *et al.*, 1998). Interestingly, prior to the availability of anti-D therapy, it had been recognized that maternal–fetal ABO incompatibility could prevent the establishment of Rh sensitization by rapidly removing fetal red cells from the maternal circulation, thus acting in a protective manner (Clarke *et al.*, 1958; Levine, 1958).

In approximately 1 in 1500 births, maternal–fetal platelet incompatibility occurs (Connor and Ferguson-Smith, 1997).

Table 3.1. *Parental HLA sharing and recurrent spontaneous abortion*

| Increased parental sharing | No association | Source |
|---|---|---|
| HLA-A,B | | Komlos *et al.* (1997) |
| HLA-DR | HLA-A,B,C | Reznikoff-Etievant *et al.* (1984) |
| HLA-A | HLA-B,DR | Schacter *et al.* (1984) |
| | HLA-A,B,DR | Oksenberg *et al.* (1984) |
| | HLA-A,B,DR | Thomas *et al.* (1985) |
| HLA-DQ,DR | HLA-B | *Coulam *et al.* (1987) |
| HLA-A | HLA-B | Gerencer *et al.* (1988) |
| HLA-A,DQ | HLA-B,C,DR | *Ho *et al.* (1990) |
| | HLA-DQ,DR | Laitinen *et al.* (1993) |
| HLA-DR | HLA-A,B,DQ | Jin *et al.* (1995) |

\* Primary aborters only.

As the mother is only rarely sensitized to produce IgG, thrombo-cytopenia in the fetus seldom becomes a recurrent problem for such couples in succeeding pregnancies.

## Infertility associated with maternal– fetal HLA compatibility

During the last 15 years of the twentieth century there was vigorous debate as to whether couples who share HLA alleles exhibit some degree of subfertility. As indicated in Table 3.1, no clear-cut answer is yet forthcoming, with both positive and negative findings reported. At least in part these discrepancies can be ascribed to the nonuniformity of study design, and to methodological differences between groups of investigators. Problems also arise in the selection of subjects. In some studies, couples who reported recurrent spontaneous abortions were investigated separately from those who had unexplained infertility and, in the former category, couples who had never experienced a successful pregnancy were differentiated from those who had one or two successful pregnancies before multiple abortions. By comparison, in other investigations these categories were collapsed.

Studies of highly endogamous communities, such as the Hutterites in the U.S.A., have suggested that genes at the HLA-DR and HLA-B loci are important in determining the ability to initiate a pregnancy and in fetal losses respectively (Ober et al., 1992). Two points are worthy of consideration. First, the infertility associated with HLA-DR sharing in the Hutterites could most appropriately be described as relative in its effect. Some couples who share HLA-DR alleles experience no spontaneous abortions despite ten or more pregnancies (Ober et al., 1985) and, although longer birth intervals were observed, on average the completed family size of HLA-DR-compatible couples was 6.5 by comparison with 9.0 in those who did not share alleles at the HLA-DR locus (Ober et al., 1988). Second, the Hutterite study community was descended from a maximum of 68 ancestors with a resulting paucity of HLA alleles and haplotypes (Dawson et al., 1995). Therefore, the extent to which data derived from the Hutterites, or any other genetic isolate, could be applied to other major human populations may be limited. Despite these reservations, a study conducted in Japan on males with unexplained azoospermia has indicated a significant excess of several class 1 HLA alleles, in particular HLA-B44 which is often involved in processes such as allograft rejection (Miura et al., 1998).

From a contrary perspective, it is noteworthy that in marriages between close biological relatives, for example at first cousin level where the partners would be expected to have one-eighth of their genes in common, there is no evidence of a significant increase in fetal loss rates (Böök, 1957; Jaber et al., 1997; Shami et al., 1991; Warburton and Fraser, 1964). However, data on early pregnancy losses can be notoriously unreliable, especially when the information is collected by retrospective survey (Wilcox and Horney, 1984) and these difficulties may be exacerbated if the topic is regarded as culturally sensitive within the study population.

There is evidence to suggest that recurrent spontaneous abortions can occur as a familial trait (Mowbray et al, 1991). More recent reports have concentrated on the hypothesis that the sharing of HLA antigens is not the primary cause of failure to initiate a pregnancy or of pregnancy losses. Rather, it is suggested that responsibility both for the infertility problems and increased susceptibility to a range of genetically determined defects mainly can be ascribed to the expression of detrimental recessive genes, as yet unidentified, located on chromosome 6 and in tight linkage disequilibrium with the HLA -B and HLA-DR loci (Gill, 1992; Jin *et al.*, 1995).

Despite the considerable degree of uncertainty surrounding the nature, and even the existence, of the putative association between HLA compatibility and infertility, purified lymphocytes prepared from their male partner have been administered to females who have experienced recurrent spontaneous abortion (Beer *et al.*, 1981). In one such trial, successful pregnancies were claimed in 17 of 22 women immunized with their partner's cells, as opposed to 10 of 27 women who had been injected with their own lymphocytes (Mowbray *et al.*, 1985). Although additional positive findings have been reported (reviewed in Clark and Daya, 1991), other workers have recorded no specific advantage following passive immunization and instead have indicated that there may be a significant placebo effect (Cauchi *et al.*, 1991; Ho *et al.*, 1991).

## Specific genetic disorders causing primary infertility

As discussed above, evidence to date suggests that the large majority of spontaneous abortions are the result of major chromosomal defects in the fetus, possibly complicated by additional maternal implantation problems and/or placental insufficiency. However, as indicated in Table 3.2, compiled from a study conducted in the Canadian province of British Columbia, some 5% of liveborns have a genetic disorder expressed during childhood or early adulthood, the large majority of which are multifactorial in origin (Baird *et al.*, 1988). Within this spectrum of genetic disease involving the nuclear genome there is a wide range of disorders that have been causatively implicated in human infertility (Williamson and Elias, 1992).

Table 3.2. *Prevalence of genetic disorders in childhood and early adulthood*

| Single gene disorders | Prevalence |
|---|---|
| Autosomal dominant | 1.4/1000 |
| Autosomal recessive | 1.7 |
| X-linked recessive | 0.5 |
| Chromosomal anomalies | 1.8 |
| Multifactorial disorders | 46.4 |
| Other disorders of uncertain aetiology | 1.2 |

Total >53/1000.
*Source*: Baird *et al.* (1988).

Table 3.3. *Chromosomal abnormalities associated with infertility*

Male infertility
  Numerical
  47,XXY (Klinefelter Syndrome)
  45,X/46,XY mosaicism (male pseudohermaphroditism)
  Structural
  46,XX males
  Y-chromosome deletions
  X- and Y-autosome reciprocal translocations
Female infertility
  Numerical
  45,X (Turner Syndrome)
  45,X/46,XX mosaicism
  Structural
  X-structural rearrangements
  Y-structural rearrangements
  X-autosome rearrangements

## Chromosomal disorders

This category includes gross chromosomal disorders, both numerical and structural, and may affect the autosomes and sex chromosomes. Disorders of this nature often may be revealed only after
cases of unexplained infertility are subjected to cytogenetic investigation, when either a numerical or a structural defect is diagnosed
(Table 3.3). In a study in which 1000 spermatozoa from 33 normal

men were examined for chromosomal anomalies, 5.2% were aneuploid and 3.3% had a structural abnormality, mainly occurring in the form of chromosome breaks (Martin *et al.*, 1983*a*). A follow-up study of six men heterozygous for a chromosome translocation or inversion showed that the frequency of chromosomally un-balanced sperm was 77%, 32% and 19% respectively in the three cases of reciprocal translocation, 13% in a subject with a robertson-ian translocation and zero in the two individuals with inversions (Martin *et al.*, 1983*b*).

On the basis of these studies it would appear that while chromo-some anomalies are found in the sperm of phenotypically normal males and so may explain a proportion of spontaneous pregnancy losses, their frequency generally is greater in persons with a known chromosomal defect. This frequency may however vary to a significant extent, depending on the nature of the abnormality. For these reasons, Chandley (1981) suggested that human chromosomal anomalies could usefully be subdivided into four categories with respect to survival and fertility: viable sterile, viable semisterile, viable nonreproductive and viable fertile.

## Numerical disorders

The most common chromosomal disorder associated with primary infertility in females is Turner Syndrome (monosomy X). Although germ cells are present in the ovaries of human 45X fetuses, their loss begins in fetal life. By birth, few oocytes remain and at puberty virtually all of the oocytes have degenerated (Chandley, 1981). In persons who are Turner mosaic (45X/46XX) there may be a proportion of oocytes capable of fertilization, and in such cases pregnancies have been reported with the success rate largely dependent on the individual's relative proportions of the two chromosome types.

A much wider spectrum of genetic defects can cause infertility in males, including Klinefelter Syndrome, 47,XXY, in which there may be an increased prevalence of sex chromosome aneuploidies (Foresta *et al.*, 1998), and X-autosome reciprocal translocation (Chandley, 1997). In Down Syndrome (trisomy 21), spermatozoa have been reported in the ejaculate of some affected individuals, but male subjects with the disorder are generally believed to be impotent. By comparison, there have been a number of reports of successful pregnancies in females with trisomy 21, with approximately equal numbers of chromosomally normal and trisomic progeny born (Chandley, 1981).

*Structural disorders*

Female carriers of a balanced reciprocal X-autosome translocation may exhibit infertility in a proportion of cases, caused by gonadal dysfunction (Chandley, 1981). The problem appears to be restricted to women with a breakpoint between bands Xq13 and Xq27, who in most cases present with primary amenorrhoea. In an analogous manner, men with an X- or Y-autosome reciprocal translocation are infertile because of spermatogenic arrest. In purely autosomal reciprocal translocations there is a poor prognosis for fertility when one point of exchange is close to a centromere and the other is distal on the chromosome involved, and an acrocentric chromosome is frequently involved in these forms of male-sterile autosomal translocations (Chandley, 1981). The adverse effects of autosomal reciprocal translocations appear to be limited to male heterozygotes as, in familial cases of translocation, sterility and azoospermia have been observed in males but gamete production in the females appears to be unaffected. Thus the defect seems to be caused by disturbed meiotic function that can be accommodated in female but not in male meiosis (Chandley, 1981).

With advances in cytogenetic analysis, in particular fluorescence *in situ* hybridization (FISH), previously unrecognized structural aberrations have been described in cases of infertility. For example, it has been estimated that some 14% of men with azoospermia and a further 9% with severe oligospermia (defined as a total sperm count in the ejaculate of less than five million) have deletions in the Azoospermia Factor (AZF) on the long arm of the Y-chromosome at Yq11 (Patrizio, 1997). On the assumption that about 1 in 1000 males is azoospermic, some 12–15% of whom will have Y-chromosome microdeletions, the frequency of this genetic defect is currently estimated to be 1 in 8000 to 1 in 10,000 births.

Table 3.4. *Single gene disorders associated with infertility*

| Pattern of inheritance | Disorder | Chromosomal location |
|---|---|---|
| Autosomal dominant | Noonan Syndrome | 12q22-qter |
| | Myotonic dystrophy | 19p13.2-19cen |
| Autosomal recessive | Cystic fibrosis | 7q31.2 |
| | 5α-Reductase deficiency | 2p23 |
| X-linked recessive | Spinal and bulbar muscular atrophy | Xq11-q12 |
| | Reifenstein Syndrome | Xq11-q12 |

## Single gene disorders

In functional terms, genetic disorders which predispose to subfertility can be subdivided into three categories: mutations that are restricted to the germ line, mutations in genes that are involved in gonadal development, and pleiotropic mutations affecting both gonadal and nongonadal cells, associated with diseases such as cystic fibrosis and myotonic dystrophy (Vogt, 1995). Within these categories, disorders with autosomal dominant, autosomal recessive and X-linked recessive modes of inheritance have been described, and some of the more common conditions are listed in Table 3.4.

To preclude possible ambiguity in descriptions of the single gene disorders that are associated with infertility, in this chapter the cataloguing system devised by Victor McKusick of Johns Hopkins University has been adopted, with a specific, six-digit number given to each individual disease. In this system, disorders with an autosomal dominant mode of inheritance have an identifying number beginning with one, while for autosomal recessive and X-linked disorders the identifying numbers commence with two and three, respectively. Further details are contained in the on-line version of the system (OMIM, 1997).

### Autosomal dominant disorders

Thirteen dominantly inherited diseases have been identified as associated with problems of reduced fertility (Vogt, 1995). Two of the more common diseases in this group are Noonan Syndrome and myotonic dystrophy. The main factors contributing to the impairment of fertility in males with Noonan Syndrome (McKusick 163950) are bilateral testicular maldescent and cryptorchidism (Elsawi *et al.*, 1994), although affected individuals may present with a variety of additional symptoms, including failure to thrive in infancy, motor developmental delay, learning disability, language delay, mild hearing loss and mild mental retardation (Allanson, 1987).

Myotonic dystrophy (McKusick 160900) is one of the growing number of genetic diseases characterized by anticipation and the expansion of a trinucleotide repeat, in this case CTG. Normal individuals usually have 5–30 CTG triplet repeat copies, mildly affected persons 50–80 copies, and severely affected persons 2000 copies (OMIM, 1997). The disease appears to be a true dominant, with the mutation fully expressed in heterozygotes (Zlotogora, 1997). The progression of myotonic dystrophy is quite different to that of Noonan Syndrome. Although the disease phenotype includes hypogonadism with symptoms typically becoming evident from the second decade but more usually in middle life, a case–control study conducted in Saguenay-Lac-St. Jean, Quebec on 373 affected persons marrying between 1853 and 1971 indicated no reduction in their overall fertility (Dao *et al.*, 1992). Obstetric difficulties may however be encountered and so some degree of reduction in fertility can be expected.

### Autosomal recessive disorders

Cystic fibrosis (McKusick 219700) is the most common autosomal recessive disease in persons of North European ancestry, and the frequency of approximately 1/2500 to 1/3000 indicates that approximately 4% of the population in these countries is heterozygous for the disorder. Cystic fibrosis (CF) was the first genetic disorder to be identified via the process of positional cloning (reverse genetics), i.e. on the basis of its chromosomal location. The gene was mapped to the long arm of chromosome 7 (Riordan *et al.*, 1989), and the precise location later identified as 7q31.2. In the populations initially investigated it was shown that approximately 70% of the causative mutations in patients with CF were due to the specific deletion of three base pairs, which resulted in the loss of a phenylalanine residue at amino acid position 508 (delF508) of the putative CF gene product (Kerem *et al.*, 1989). Subsequent population studies have revealed a wide and often population-specific distribution of CF mutations with, for example, 87% delF508 in persons of pure Basque descent as opposed to 58% delF508 among persons of mixed Basque origin (Casals *et al.*, 1992), suggesting the operation of founder effect and random genetic drift.

The high prevalence of CF in populations of Northern European origin has led to the assumption that a common CF mutation such as delF508 must be maintained via heterozygote advantage, with carriers for the disorder showing resistance to one or more virulent infectious agents. Although many such organisms have been suggested, in general the reports have seldom been supported by credible experimental evidence. A recent exception is a study based on the premise that persons heterozygous for the delF508 mutation are less likely to be infected by *Salmonella typhi*, the human pathogen causing typhoid fever. It is believed that *S. typhi* initiates infection by entry into the epithelial cells of the gastrointestinal tract via the cystic fibrosis transmembrane conductance regulator (CFTR) gene product, and as the name suggests the CFTR gene is the causative locus of CF. As a result of the delF508 mutation in one of their two CFTR alleles, individuals who are carriers for CF are effectively protected during outbreaks of typhoid fever because *S. typhi* is largely prevented from entering the gastrointestinal tract. Individuals who are CF heterozygotes are thus at a selective advantage in evolutionary terms, which in turn results in maintenance of the CF mutation at high frequency (Pier *et al.*, 1998).

From a genetic perspective cystic fibrosis is extremely heterogeneous, with over 800 mutations so far described in the CFTR gene. Infertility is a common feature of CF in males (Rigot *et al.*, 1991), and to a lesser extent females. It has been proposed that the CFTR protein may be involved in the process of spermatogenesis or sperm maturation, as well as playing a critical role in the development of the epididymal glands and the vas deferens (van der Ven *et al.*, 1996). Clinically affected males can however exhibit a spectrum of genital phenotypes ranging from normal fertility to congenital bilateral absence of the vas deferens (van der Ven *et al.*, 1996).

Congenital bilateral absence of the vas deferens (CBAVD) affects approximately 1 in 1000 male subjects (Bienvenu *et al.*, 1997). Affected individuals are either compound heterozygotes, with different mutations in each of their CFTR alleles, or more commonly they have a mutation in only one copy of the CFTR gene with an intron 8 polypyrimidine 5T splice variant, associated with low levels of functional CFTR protein, in the second allele (Bienvenu *et al.*, 1997; Chillon *et al.*, 1995; Lissens *et al.*, 1996). In 20–30% of persons with CBAVD but otherwise in good health, there was no evidence of either CFTR mutations or the 5T allele (Bienvenu *et al.*, 1997; Donat *et al.*, 1996). These findings indicate the possible presence of as yet unidentified mild CFTR mutations (Costes *et al.*, 1995), or other forms of renal malformations that are unconnected to CF (Augarten *et al.*, 1994).

There was just 7% concordance for CBAVD in the brothers of CBAVD individuals, which has been interpreted as indicating incomplete penetrance for the CBAVD phenotype after inheritance of a CFTR mutation (Shin *et al.*, 1997). An additional factor to be considered is that the tissue-specific disease phenotypes observed in individuals with CBAVD may correlate with differences in the proportion of CFTR transcripts lacking exon 9 sequences, caused by alternative splicing at that site (Teng *et al.*, 1997). Infertile males with congenital unilateral absence of the vas deferens (CUAVD) have been found to be both clinically and anatomically heterogeneous with respect to a mutation in the CFTR gene, with no evidence of a CF mutation in those who had an anatomically complete vas deferens on one side (Mickle *et al.*, 1995).

Steroid 5α-reductase-2 deficiency (pseudovaginal perineoscrotal hypospadias, McKusick 264600) is an autosomal recessive disorder affecting the steroid 5α-reductase-2 gene, which in normal males is responsible for the conversion of testosterone to dihydrotestosterone, the intracellular mediator of many androgenic actions. The effect of the mutation is thus to prevent normal male genital development and instead to permit the development of a female phenotype, which in humans acts as the 'default' phenotype. The majority of defects so far described are point mutations, and they are mainly homozygous in nature but with some compound heterozygotes (Griffin *et al.*, 1995).

Affected individuals are 46,XY males with an external female phenotype at birth and so they are often raised as females. They have histologically normal testes with normal testosterone and oestrogen levels and can produce semen, but they have a small prostate. In a number of case studies there was a strong family history of consanguinity and, for example, Simpson *et al.* (1971) reported three affected brothers born to parents who were double first cousins. In these individuals no breast development or menstruation occurred at puberty and instead normal masculinization was observed. Similarly, three brothers at first thought to be girls were born to a family in which the parents and grandparents on one side were first cousins and the great-grandparents also were related (De Vaal, 1955). In both families founder effect would appear to be operating, as is the case in three large clusters of the disorder occurring as geographical isolates in the Dominican Republic, Turkey and Papua New Guinea (Griffin *et al.*, 1995).

Men with spinal and bulbar muscular atrophy (McKusick 313200), which has an age at onset of 30–40 years, are infertile because of a mutation in exon 1 of the androgen receptor gene at Xq11-q12 (Patrizio, 1997). As with myotonic dystrophy, this disorder is associated with an abnormal triplet repeat number (CAG), and subjects have a hypothalamic defect with androgen deficiency and oestrogen excess that results in symptoms of impotence, sterility and testicular atrophy. However, in an extended family of four males who were related as first cousins, while all four had gynaecomastia and impotence, they each had fathered children (Guidetti *et al.*, 1986).

Reifenstein Syndrome (androgen insensitivity, partial, McKusick 312300) is a second X-linked recessive androgen receptor disorder located at Xq11-q12 which causes a form of male pseudohermaphroditism. Persons with the disorder have a normal 46,XY karotype but they exhibit symptoms which include gynaecomastia, a microphallus, hypospadias and absent vas deferens. They have high testosterone levels and elevated follicle-stimulating hormone

(FSH) levels secondary to their androgen insensitivity, but are infertile and no spermatozoa are detectable on testis biopsy (OMIM, 1997).

A number of additional, clinically distinct X-linked disorders have been described which arise from defects in the androgen receptor gene, e.g. androgen insensitivity syndrome (McKusick 313700). These disorders result in phenotypes that are similar in their spectrum of effects but they vary in the extent to which the symptoms are expressed, ranging from complete testicular feminization to the undervirilized, fertile male (Griffin et al., 1995; OMIM, 1997). In the counselling of such conditions, it is important to discriminate between disorders that affect the androgen receptor gene and so are inherited as an X-linked recessive with a one in two recurrence for male children, and steroid 5α-reductase-2 deficiency which as a male-limited autosomal recessive has an overall recurrence risk of one in eight.

### Disorders with a currently indeterminate pattern of inheritance

A number of single gene disorders that cause infertility in humans have a poorly defined or complex mode of inheritance (Table 3.5). Stein–Leventhal Syndrome (polycystic ovarian disease, familial, McKusick 184700) has been widely described as an autosomal dominant disorder, but more extensive investigation has suggested a complex genetic aetiology, with the probability that the pattern of inheritance is heterogeneous and may result from the interaction of a small number of genes with environmental/nutritional factors (Franks et al., 1997). Patients with the disorder have abnormal hormone profiles, with elevated androstanedione, testosterone and luteinizing hormone, and low oestradiol and FSH levels, resulting in oligomenorrhoea and amenorrhoea.

In Young Syndrome (McKusick 279000), patients present with chronic suppurating respiratory disease, due to reduced mucus clearance by the cilia in the respiratory tract. Although the spermatozoa are normal, about 50% of cases have abnormal vas deferens and obstructive azoospermia. It has been suggested that

Table 3.5. *Single gene defects associated with infertility: pattern of inheritance uncertain*

| Disorder | Pattern of inheritance | Symptoms |
|---|---|---|
| Stein–Leventhal Syndrome | AD, but probably heterogeneous | Multiple ovarian cysts, oligomenorrhoea, amenorrhoea |
| Young Syndrome | AR | Chronic respiratory disease with obstructive azoospermia |
| Kartagener Syndrome | AR | Bronchiectasis, reduced sperm mobility |
| Acrosome malformation of spermatozoa | AD versus X-linked or polygenic | Congenital disorder, round-headed sperm (globozoospermia) |

AD, autosomal dominant; AR, autosomal recessive.

Young Syndrome may be equivalent in prevalence to Klinefelter Syndrome as a cause of male infertility (Handelsman *et al.*, 1984). Despite the similar clinical pictures, no CFTR mutations have been found in patients with Young Syndrome, and so the condition must be regarded as a separate clinical entity with the probability that it is acquired rather than congenital (Le Lannou *et al.*, 1995).

Kartagener Syndrome (McKusick 244400) is a rare congenital disorder presenting as a triad of situs inversus totalis, bronchiectasis and recurrent sinusitis, and it affects an estimated 1 in 20,000 males (Gagnon, 1997). The patients are infertile because the axonemes of their spermatozoa lack the dynein arms responsible for microtubule sliding. In turn, this causes a very marked reduction in sperm velocity and flagellar beating frequency, leading to sperm immobility and failure to penetrate the cervical mucus. Since the sperm are normal, they are however capable of fusing with the oocyte membrane and fertilizing the egg via micromanipulation (OMIM, 1997). While the syndrome was originally described as an autosomal recessive, other patterns of inheritance, including autosomal dominant and X-linked recessive, also appear possible (Gagnon, 1997).

Acrosome malformation of spermatozoa (globozoospermia, McKusick 102530) is a rare congenital disease with a pattern of inheritance that variously has been described as autosomal dominant, X-linked or polygenic. It is characterized by spermatozoa that are round-headed and totally lack the acrosomal sac. Although normally motile, the sperm are unable to penetrate the ovum and bind to the zona pellucida, and they may be deficient in oocyte-activating factors (Gagnon, 1997).

## Mutations of mitochondrial DNA

The mitochondria are subcellular organelles responsible for aerobic energy production in humans and many other species. During the last ten years there has been considerable interest displayed in the possible causative role of mitochondria in ageing. Elevated levels of mitochondrial DNA (mtDNA) deletions and other mutations have been observed with advancing age in a wide variety of tissues, including heart, brain, liver, kidney, spleen and skeletal muscle (reviewed in Bittles, 1997). The best described of these mutations is a 4997-base-pair deletion involving genes encoding essential components of the energy-producing functions of the mitochondria, and accounting for approximately one-third of the mitochondrial genome (Cortopassi and Arnhem, 1990). In addition to these age-related changes, it has been suggested that there may be an elevated prevalence of mtDNA deletions in some cases of male infertility, specifically associated with ischaemic disorders of the testis (Cummins, 1997).

## Treatment of individuals with genetically determined infertility

Initially, *in vitro* fertilization and embryo transfer were used to circumvent specific forms of human infertility. However, in a large proportion of cases it became clear that part of the reason for the high failure rates of implantation after replacing the abnormal embryo in the mother was the presence of chromosomal anomalies (Angell *et al.*, 1983). Even in normally androgenized infertile males, chromosomal abnormalities were found in 17.3% of azoospermic individuals, and in 10.6% of those with oligozoospermia, but in none with normozoospermia (Bonaccorsi *et al.*, 1997).

Pregnancies can be initiated in females who have infertility of a genetic origin. For example, in women with Turner Syndrome this can be achieved via stimulation of the endometrium by treatment with exogenous steroids and donated oocytes or embryos (Khastgir *et al.*, 1997). There is a significantly lower rate of deliveries per pregnancy, with evidence to suggest that women who have complete or partial deficiency of an X-chromosome may have some form of additional, inherent endometrial abnormality that results in early implantation failure (Yaron *et al.*, 1996).

In males with Klinefelter Syndrome, and more especially those who are mosaic for the disorder (46,XY/47,XXY), sperm can be collected by testicular biopsy (Tournaye *et al.*, 1996) and successful pregnancies produced using intracytoplasmic injection of sperm (ICSI) into oocytes (Bourne *et al.*, 1997; Hinney *et al*, 1997). Similarly, surgical recovery of sperm by microscopic epididymal aspiration in cases of CBAVD enables pregnancies to be achieved (Oates *et al.*, 1992). Among males with CBAVD as part of the CF phenotype the presence of detectable CFTR mutations does not adversely affect rates of fertilization or pregnancy when IVF and micromanipulation are used (Schlegel *et al.*, 1995), possibly because of the reduced penetrance of the CBAVD phenotype in CF. If this proves to be the case, it may lower the risk of having a child with CBAVD for couples who are undergoing sperm retrieval and assisted reproductive techniques (Shin *et al.*, 1997). With such couples, as a precautionary measure it would be appropriate to screen the partners of CBAVD males for the presence of CFTR mutations which, if present, could result in their progeny being exposed to the risk of inheriting CBAVD and/or CF (Lissens *et al.*, 1996).

## *Potential dysgenic consequences of ICSI*

For men with chromosomal anomalies in their somatic karyotype who opt for pregnancy initiation via ICSI, there is a high risk that

Table 3.6. *Disorders associated with specific, potential dysgenic outcomes of intracytoplasmic sperm injection (ICSI)*

1.   Sex chromosome numerical anomalies, e.g. 45X, 47XXY
2.   Y-chromosome microdeletions
3.   Males with undiagnosed cystic fibrosis
4.   Females with diagnosed cystic fibrosis

the postmeiotic cells, i.e. the spermatids and spermatozoa, will carry a chromosomal rearrangement (Chandley, 1997). This high risk of a chromosomal rearrangement may however also apply to infertile men with no currently detectable form of chromosomal abnormality because, using FISH with chromosome-specific DNA probes, infertile individuals with apparently normal karyotypes have been shown to have an increased risk of aneuploidy and polyploidy in their spermatozoa (Martin *et al.*, 1997).

As indicated in Table 3.6, findings of this nature have resulted in more general concerns being expressed with regard to the possible dysgenic outcomes of pregnancies undertaken by infertile persons who have known or suspected chromosomal abnormalities (de Kretser, 1997). Currently, the main risks to be considered would be, for example, that progeny born after ICSI will display the same sex chromosome abnormalities as a male parent with Klinefelter Syndrome, who otherwise would have been incapable of initiating a pregnancy. Thus it could be claimed that ICSI permits the transmission of a genetic defect which previously would have been effectively eliminated from the gene pool. Genetically determined infertility in sons who were born following ICSI likewise could be ascribed to use of the technique (Tournaye *et al.*, 1997).

A similar situation applies to Yq deletions and, in a study of 32 couples who produced children via ICSI, three male progeny had Yq deletions even though the same deletion was present in only one of the fathers (Kent-First *et al.*, 1996). The conclusion drawn was that demonstration of an intact Y-chromosome in the father could not be taken as any guarantee that a child would not be born with a Yq deletion. Conversely, the presence of a Yq deletion in a male wishing to undergo ICSI would be taken as indicative of transmission should the same deletion be detected in the Y-chromosome of any son born to the couple. While it could be argued that in such an eventuality ICSI could again be employed to assist the son should he wish to have children at some future stage, given the current incomplete state of knowledge with respect to Y-chromosome deletions this outcome could not be guaranteed. There is the additional possibility that in the next generation the deletion might result in azoospermia rather than oligospermia (de Kretser *et al.*, 1997). To circumvent such a possibility, where an infertile male had a deletion in Yq11, a couple might opt to transfer only female embryos following a preimplantation genetic diagnosis, but a solution of this nature might not be acceptable in societies where male children are especially prized.

In all of these cases, the ultimate ethical argument arises as to whether life in any form, however truncated or disadvantaged, is superior to the effective denial of the possibility of existence. Debate of this nature is at best convoluted and contentious, and its resolution depends mainly on the personal beliefs of those directly engaged in this form of discourse. Nevertheless, it can be anticipated that ethical concerns increasingly will have to be addressed, and that they will play a central role in the deliberations of the national bodies that have been established to regulate work in the area of assisted reproduction.

Although somewhat different in character, similarly complex considerations apply to women with CF who, as a result of improved support therapy, have a greater life expectancy and so might increasingly wish to undertake a pregnancy (Hilman *et al.*, 1996; Kotloff *et al.*, 1992). Studies have indicated that women with CF have a comparable rate of sexual activity to age-matched non-CF controls. Yet they are less likely to be using contraception because of a belief that their fertility is reduced. In general, women with CF were found to have a poor appreciation of the potentially deleterious effects of pregnancy (Sawyer *et al.*, 1995), despite indications that especially in severe cases of CF both maternal and fetal complications may arise (Kotloff *et al.*, 1992).

### Preimplantation diagnosis

As indicated in the previous chapter by S. Fishel *et al.*, preimplantation diagnosis (PGD) has been developed in part as a means of monitoring embryos conceived using techniques such as ICSI (Staessen *et al.*, 1996), with the intent of alleviating at least some of the concerns that are outlined above. While rapid progress in this area is being made, to date the cases examined have been too few in number and diverse in their nature to allow firm conclusions to be drawn on the feasibility of PGD for this purpose (Harper, 1996; Soussis *et al.*, 1996; Verlinsky, 1996). From a genetic perspective, what has been interesting is the relatively high level of autosome and sex chromosome mosaicism, and other more significant chromosomal anomalies found in human embryos under investigation in a programme for the preimplantation diagnosis of X-linked disease (Harper *et al.*, 1995).

### Potential problems of inbreeding associated with sperm donation

Since the introduction of donor insemination, where the male partner is infertile or is known to be at high risk of transmitting a detrimental genetic disorder, there has been concern that persons fathered by the same anonymous donor might at some future stage meet and decide to have a child of their own, thus raising the possibility of an inadvertent mating between half-sibs (Curie-Cohen, 1980). The regulation of such a form of accidental inbreeding tends to differ from country to country and, for example, while in The Netherlands 25 children per donor are permitted, in Norway a maximum of ten children per donor is accepted as safe clinical practice (de Boer *et al.*, 1995, 1997; Egeland *et al.*, 1997).

A factor that to date appears to have been substantially overlooked is the large numbers of individuals and families who within the last 40 years have migrated to Western Europe, North and South America, and Australasia from countries where close kin marriage is preferential, and some 20% to 50+% of marital unions are between persons related as second cousins or closer (Bittles, 1994; Nelson *et al.*, 1997). Furthermore, since in these societies the preference for a consanguineous union is a long-standing tradition, not only are many persons in the current generation married as first cousins with a predicted one-eighth of their genes in common, but they themselves may be the progeny of multiple generations of such marriages and so share a significantly higher proportion of genes inherited from common ancestors (Hussain and Bittles, 1998).

Under these circumstances, and in the absence of a complete multigeneration pedigree, it would be difficult to devise a method to calculate the precise level of inbreeding for any given pair of individuals and hence the consanguinity-associated risks faced by their progeny. For the children of a first cousin union, in whom $F = 0.0625$, excess mortality from the late prenatal phase to approaching puberty has been calculated as 44/1000 (Bittles and Neel, 1994), and from this figure it should be possible to calculate equivalent risk estimates for other types of consanguineous union, such as uncle–niece or double first cousin (in both cases $F = 0.0125$) or first cousins once removed ($F = 0.0313$). However, it is unclear how this knowledge could be practically applied in calculating the permissible number of children per semen donor within a migrant community, where consanguinity is historically strongly preferential, the number of potential donors is small, and additional ethnic constraints to marriage may coexist.

## Conclusions

To some extent it could be argued that, given the apparent efficiency of the process whereby chromosomally abnormal embryos and fetuses are eliminated by spontaneous abortion, genetic disorders play a relatively unimportant role as determinants of human infertility, especially with the quite small percentage of persons who have been identified with a genetic defect (Table 3.2). Given the current, imperfect state of our knowledge as to the nature and structure of the human genome, any such judgement could very rapidly prove incorrect. Rather, as the Human Genome Project progresses, so our understanding of how and why specific genetic disorders interfere with many aspects of human reproduction should improve, and our ability to overcome these difficulties become concomitantly more focused.

In this respect, apoptosis or programmed cell death is a topic that appears likely to increase in importance in the near future and, for example, it is argued that the infertility which accompanies cryptorchidism in Noonan Syndrome and the atresia of follicles in Stein–Leventhal Syndrome may be apoptosis-related (Izawa and Yeh, 1997). Another area of fundamental interest is the apparent under-representation of homozygotes revealed by DNA microsatellite studies of highly inbred communities, which raises the possibility that in human populations there is prenatal selection against excessive levels of homozygosity, possibly monitored at gene loci involved in early development (Bittles *et al.*, 2000; Wang *et al.*, 2000). A mechanism of this nature might provide at least a partial explanation as to why infertile consanguineous couples appear to have higher miscarriage rates in pregnancies achieved by assisted reproductive technology (Egbase *et al.*, 1996).

At the same time, it is recognized that much work needs to be undertaken in the areas of counselling and bioethics, and in an examination of the many highly complex legal issues that have arisen as a result of successful fertility-based interventions. For example, while pregnancies can be achieved in patients with disorders such as Klinefelter Syndrome, the techniques involved, which include multiple testicular biopsies from hypogonadal testes, ICSI and preimplantation diagnosis by FISH, are complex and may entail significant emotional and physical cost to the individual/couple who have requested such treatment (Tournaye *et al.*, 1996). As a first step, it should be regarded as obligatory that appropriately comprehensive and informative counselling services are in place prior to the commencement of any such treatment protocol.

Related concerns apply to diseases such as CF, especially as such a large proportion of persons who are of Northern European origin are asymptomatic carriers of the mutant gene in one or other of its many forms. The relationship between CF and CBAVD is currently unclear, which makes genetic counselling both difficult and uncertain, since CBAVD individuals in whom no CFTR defect has been detected may have mild, unidentified mutations (Costes *et al.*, 1995). There is also the problem of counselling women with CF who intend to have a child. This counselling should include not only the maternal and fetal risks of pregnancy, and the genetic risks for the child but, given the current mean life expectancy for CF patients of 31 years, the vexed question of who will raise the child in the event of maternal mortality (Hilman *et al.*, 1996).

Finally, there is the question of whether a child conceived via a technique such as ICSI will develop and mature in a manner and at a rate comparable to that of children who are naturally conceived. It has been argued that, by using ICSI, selective barriers developed during evolution are effectively by-passed, especially when immature sperm and spermatids from the epididymis or testis are used. Although the technique was never tested experimentally before its introduction, partly because animal models were thought to be unsuitable and also because of its apparent success in achieving pregnancies despite severe male infertility, to date tens of thousands of babies are thought to have been born following ICSI (te Veide *et al.*, 1998).

A recent study from Australia reported that at one year of age, ICSI children had a mean deficit in their Mental Development Index (MDI) of some six points when compared to those conceived either naturally or via conventional IVF, with greater developmental delays observed in boys than girls. The ICSI children exhibited mild or significantly delayed mental development in 17% of cases, as opposed to 2% for children conceived by IVF and 1% for naturally conceived children (Bowen *et al.*, 1998). These findings were interpreted as indicating the possible operation either of factors related to genetic abnormalities in the sperm, or to problems directly associated with the ICSI procedure. At the same time, a study conducted in Belgium on ICSI children at approximately two years of age concluded that there was no overall indication that ICSI children displayed slower mental development than the general population (Bonduelle *et al.*, 1998).

Methodological and demographic limitations have been identified in both studies, and there is the basic question of whether the application of the specific test protocol adopted by both sets of researchers was appropriate, since its norms had been developed against a U.S. population which may have had a different ethnic composition than either the Australian or Belgium sample groups (te Veide *et al.*, 1998). For these reasons, confirmatory investigations at later ages and in different regions are needed, even though studies of this nature may have to be extended at least into the postpubertal period. However, until resolved, it would appear appropriate that before further assisted reproduction techniques are introduced into routine use, they should be extensively pretested in animal and human embryo models, complemented by clinical trials during which the children would be subject to long-term monitoring (te Viede *et al.*, 1998).

Despite these provisos, given the enormous social pressures felt by many childless couples, it seems improbable that there will be any future decline in the demand for treatment of infertility, and it further can be predicted that genetic disorders that include infertility in their phenotype will be prime targets for intervention. Given this scenario, it is critical that future improvements in treatment are accompanied by a greater appreciation of the related social, psychological, ethical, legal and genetic imperatives, so that a problem apparently resolved in this generation does not re-emerge in an amplified form at some future time.

## Acknowledgements

Generous financial support to A.H.B. from the Australian Research Council, grant number A09701345, is acknowledged with gratitude. During the preparation of the paper A.H.B. was a By-Fellow of Churchill College, University of Cambridge and a Visiting Fellow in the University Department of Biological Anthropology.

# References

Allanson, J. E. (1987) Noonan Syndrome. *Journal of Medical Genetics* **24**:9–13.

Angell, R. R., Aitken, R. J., van Look, P. F. A., Lumsden, M. A., Templeton, A. A. (1983) Chromosome abnormalities in human embryos after *in vitro* fertilization. *Nature* **303**:336–8.

Augarten, A., Yahav, Y., Kerem, B. S., Halle, D., Laufer, J., Szeinberg, A. *et al.* (1994) Congenital absence of vas deferens in the absence of cystic fibrosis. *The Lancet* **344**:1473–4.

Baird, P. A., Anderson, T. W., Newcombe, H. B., Lowry, R. B. (1988) Genetic disorders in children and young adults: a population study. *American Journal of Human Genetics* **42**:677–93.

Beer, A. E., Quebbeman, J. F., Ayers, J. W. T., Haines, R. F. (1981) Major histocompatibility complex antigens, maternal and paternal immune responses, and chronic habitual abortion in humans. *American Journal of Obstetrics and Gynecology* **141**:987–97.

Bienvenu, T., Adjiman, M., Thiounn, N., Jeanpierre, M., Hubert, D., Lepercoq, J. *et al.* (1997) Molecular diagnosis of congenital bilateral absence of the vas deferens: analyses of the CFTR gene in 64 French patients. *Annals of Genetics* **40**:5–9.

Bittles, A. H. (1994) The role and significance of consanguinity as a demographic variable. *Population and Development Review* **20**:561–84.

Bittles, A. H. (1997) Biological aspects of human ageing. In: Jacoby R., Oppenheimer, C. (eds.) *Psychiatry in the elderly*, 2nd edn. (pp. 3–24). Oxford: Oxford University Press.

Bittles, A. H., Neel, J. V. (1994) The costs of human inbreeding and their implications for variations at the DNA level. *Nature Genetics* **8**:117–21.

Bittles, A. H., Savithri, H. S., Venkatesha Murthy, H. S., Bhaskaran, G., Cahill, J., Wang, W., Appaji Rao, N. (2000) Human inbreeding: a predictable story full of surprises. In: Macbeth H., Shetty, P. (eds.) *Ethnicity and health*. London: Taylor & Francis, in press.

Bonaccorsi, A. C., Martins, R. R., Vargas, F., Franco junior, J. G., Botler, J. (1997) Genetic disorders in normally androgenized infertile men and the use of intracytoplasmic sperm injection as a way of treatment. *Fertility and Sterility* **67**:928–31.

Bonduelle, M., Joris, H., Hofmans, K., Liebaers, I., Van Steirteghen, A. (1998) Mental development of 201 ICSI children at 2 years of age. *The Lancet* **351**:1553.

Böök, J. A. (1957) Genetical investigations in a north Swedish population. The offspring of first-cousin marriages. *Annals of Human Genetics* **21**:191–223.

Boué, J.-G., Boué, A. (1970) Les aberrations chromosomiques dans les avortements spontanés humains. *La Presse Médicale* **78**:635–41.

Boué, A., Boué, J., Gropp, A. (1985) Cytogenetics of pregnancy wastage. *Advances in Human Genetics* **14**:1–57.

Bourne, H., Stern, K., Clarke, G., Pertile, M., Speirs, A., Baker, H. W. (1997) Delivery of normal twins following the intracytoplasmic injection of spermatozoa from a patient with 47,XXY Klinefelter's Syndrome. *Human Reproduction* **12**:2447–50.

Bowen, J. R., Gibson, F. L., Leslie, G. I., Saunders, D. M. (1998) Medical and developmental outcome at 1 year for children conceived by intracytoplasmic sperm injection. *The Lancet* **351**:1529–34.

Carr, D. H. (1971) Chromosomes and abortion. *Advances in Human Genetics* **2**:210–57.

Casals, T., Vazquez, C., Lazaro, C., Girbau, E., Gimenez, F. J., Estivill, X. (1992) Cystic fibrosis in the Basque country: high frequency of mutation delF508 in patients of Basque origin. *American Journal of Human Genetics* **50**:404–10.

Cauchi, M. N., Lim, D. E., Young, D. E., Kloss, M., Pepperell, R. J. (1991) Treatment of recurrent aborters by immunization with paternal cells – controlled trial. *American Journal of Reproductive Immunology* **25**:16–17.

Chandley, A. C. (1981) The origin of chromosomal aberration in man and their potential for survival and reproduction in the adult human population. *Annales de Génétique* **24**:5–11.

Chandley, A. C. (1997) Karotype and infertility. In: Barratt, C., De Jonge, C., Mortimer, D., Parinaud, J. (eds.) *Genetics of human male fertility* (pp. 111–22). Paris: Editions E. D. K.

Chillon, M., Casals, T., Mercier, B., Bassas, L., Lissens, W., Silber, S. *et al.* (1995) Mutations in the cystic fibrosis gene in patients with congenital absence of the vas deferens. *New England Journal of Medicine* **332**:1475–80.

Clark, D. A., Daya, S. (1991) Trials and tribulations in the treatment of recurrent spontaneous abortion. *American Journal of Reproductive Immunology* **25**:18–24.

Clarke, C. A., Finn, R., McConnell, R. B., Sheppard, P. M. (1958) The protection afforded by ABO incompatibility against erythroblastosis due to Rhesus anti-D. *International Archives of Allergy* **13**:380.

Connor, M., Ferguson-Smith, M. (1997) *Medical genetics*, 5th edn., Oxford: Blackwell Science.

Cortopassi, G. A., Arnheim, N. (1990) Detection of a specific mitochondrial DNA deletion in tissues of older humans. *Nucleic Acids Research* **18**:6927–33.

Costes, B., Girodon, E., Ghanem, N., Flori, E., Jardin, A., Sufir, J. C. (1995) Frequent occurrence of the CFTR intron 8 (TG)n 5T allele in men with congenital bilateral absence of the vas deferens. *European Journal of Human Genetics* **3**:285–93.

Coulam, C. B., Moore, S. B., O'Fallon, W. M. (1987) Association between major histocompatibility antigen and reproductive performance. *American Journal of Reproductive Immunology and Microbiology* **14**:54–8.

Cummins, J. M. (1997) Mitochondrial DNA: implications of the genetics of human male fertility. In: Barratt, C., De Jonge, C., Mortimer, D., Parinaud, J. (eds.) *Genetics of human male fertility* (pp. 287–307). Paris: Editions E. D. K.

Curie-Cohen, M. (1980) The frequency of consanguineous matings due to multiple use of donors in artifical insemination. *American Journal of Human Genetics* **32**:589–600.

Dao, T.-N., Mathieu, J., Bouchard, J.-P., De Braekeleer, M. (1992) Fertility in myotonic dystrophy in Sagueney-Lac-St. Jean: a historical perspective. *Clinical Genetics* **42**:234–9.

Dawson, D. V., Ober, C., Kostyu, D. D. (1995) Extended HLA profile of an inbred isolate: the Schmiedeleut Hutterites of South Dakota. *Genetic Epidemiology* **12**:47–62.

de Boer, A., Oosterwijk, J. C., Rigters-Aris, C. A. E. (1995) Determination of a maximum number of artificial inseminations by donor children per sperm donor. *Fertility and Sterility* **63**:419–21.

de Boer, A., Oosterwijk, J. C., Rigters-Aris, C. A. E. (1997) Excessive use of single donor and inadvertent consanguinity. *Fertility and Sterility* **67**:1182–3.

de Kretser, D. M. (1997) Ethical issues in the use of assisted reproduction technologies in the treatment of male infertility. In: Barratt, C., De Jonge, C., Mortimer, D., Parinaud, J. (eds.) *Genetics of human male fertility* (pp. 235–43). Paris: Editions E. D. K.

de Kretser, D. M., Mallidis, C., Ma, K., Bhasin, S. (1997) Y chromosome deletions and male infertility. *Reproductive Medicine Review* **6**:37–53.

De Vaal, O. M. (1955) Genetic intersexuality in three brothers, connected with consanguineous marriages in the previous generations. *Acta Paediatrica* **44**:35–9.

Donat, R., McNeill, A. S., Fitzpatrick, D. R., Hargreave, T. B. (1996) The incidence of cystic fibrosis gene mutations in patients with congenital bilateral absence of the vas deferens in Scotland. *Journal of Urology* **79**:74–7.

Egbase, P. E., Al-Sharhan, M., Al-Othman, S., Al-Mutawa, M., Grudzinkas, J. G. (1996) Outcome of assisted reproduction technology in infertile couples of consanguineous marriage. *Journal of Assisted Reproduction and Genetics* **13**:279–81.

Egeland, T., Hoff-Olsen, P., Magnus, O. (1997) Excessive use of single donor and inadvertent consanguinity. *Fertility and Sterility* **67**:1181–2.

Elsawi, M. M., Pryor, J. P., Klufio, G., Barnes, C., Patton, M. A. (1994) Genital tract function in men with Noonan Syndrome. *Journal of Medical Genetics* **31**:468–70.

Erickson, J. D. (1974) A study of parental age effects on the occurrence of fresh mutations for the Apert Syndrome. *Annals of Human Genetics* **38**:89–96.

Foresta, C., Galeazzi, C., Bettella, A., Stella, M., Scandellari, C. (1998) High incidence of sperm sex chromosome aneuploidies in two patients with Klinefelter's Syndrome. *Journal of Clinical Endocrinology and Metabolism* **83**:203–5.

Franks, S., Gharani, N., Waterworth, D., Batty, S., White, D., Williamson, R. *et al.* (1997) The genetic basis of polycystic ovary Syndrome. *Human Reproduction* **12**:2641–8.

French, F. E., Bierman, J. M. (1962) Probabilities of fetal mortality. *Public Health Reports* **77**:835–47.

Gagnon, C. (1997) Genetic aspects of flagellar dyskinesia, globozoospermia. In: Barratt, C., De Jonge, C., Mortimer, D., Parinaud, J. (eds.) *Genetics of human male fertility* (pp. 76–97). Paris: Editions E. D. K.

Gerencer, M., Singer, Z., Pfeifer, S., Tomaskovic, M., Humar, I., Mezulic, V. *et al.* (1988) HLA and red blood group antigens in pregnancy disorders. *Tissue Antigens* **32**:130–8.

Gill, T. J. (1992) Influence of MHC and MHC-linked genes on reproduction. *American Journal of Human Genetics* **50**:1–5.

Griffin, J. E., McPhaul, M. J., Russell, D. W., Wilson, J. D. (1995) The androgen resistance syndromes: steroid 5α-reductase-2 deficiency, testicular feminization, and related disorders. In: Scriver, C. R., Beaudet, A. L., Sly, W. S., Valle, D. (eds.) *The metabolic and molecular basis of medicine*, 7th edn. (pp. 2967–98). New York: McGraw-Hill.

Guidetti, D., Motti, L., Marcello, N., Vescovini, E., Marbini, A., Dotti, C. *et al.* (1986) Kennedy disease in an Italian kindred. *European Neurology* **25**:188–96.

Handelsman, D. J., Conway, A. J., Boylan, L. M., Turtle, J. R. (1984) Young's Syndrome. Obstructive azoozpermia and chronic sinopulmonary infections. *New England Journal of Medicine* **310**:3–9.

Harper, J. C. (1996) Preimplantation diagnosis of inherited disease by embryo biopsy: an update of the world figures. *Journal of Assisted Reproduction and Genetics* **13**:90–5.

Harper, J. C., Cooenen, E., Handyside, A. H., Winston, R. M., Hopman, A. H., Delhanty, J. D. (1995) Mosaicism of autosomes and sex chromosomes in morphologically normal, monospermic preimplantation human embryos. *Prenatal Diagnosis* **15**:41–9.

Hassold, T., Merrill, M., Adkins, K., Freeman, S., Sherman, S. (1995) Recombination and maternal age-dependent nondisjunction: molecular studies of trisomy 16. *American Journal of Human Genetics* **57**:867–74.

Hertig, A. T. (1967) The overall problem in man. In: Benirschke, K. (ed.) *Comparative aspects of reproductive failure* (pp. 11–41). Berlin: Springer-Verlag.

Hilman, B. C., Aitken, M. L., Constantinescu, M. (1996) Pregnancy in patients with cystic fibrosis. *Clinical Obstetrics and Gynecology* **39**:70–86.

Hinney, B., Guttenbach, M., Schmid, M., Engel, W., Michelmann, H. W.

(1997) Pregnancy after intracytoplasmic sperm injection with sperm from a man with a 47,XXY Klinefelter's karotype. *Fertility and Sterility* **68**:718–20.

Ho, H.-N., Gill, T. J., Hsieh, H.-J., Jiang, J.-J., Lee, T.-Y., Hsieh, C.-Y. (1991) Immunotherapy for recurrent spontaneous abortions in a Chinese population. *American Journal of Reproductive Immunology* **25**:10–15.

Ho, H.-N., Gill, T. J., Nsieh, R.-P., Hsieh, H.-J., Lee, T.-Y. (1990) Sharing of human leukocyte antigens in primary and secondary recurrent spontaneous abortions. *American Journal of Obstetrics and Gynecology* **163**:178–88.

Holman, D. J., O'Connor, K. A., Wood, J. W. (2000) Age and female reproductive function: identifying the most important determinants. In: Sauvain-Dugerdil, C., Leridon, H., Mascie-Taylor, C. G. N. (eds.) *Ageing – from culture to nature*, Oxford: Clarendon Press, in press.

Hussain, R., Bittles, A. H. (1998) The prevalence and demographic characteristics of consanguineous marriage in Pakistan. *Journal of Biosocial Science* **30**:261–79.

Izawa, M., Yeh, J. (1997) Apoptosis in human reproductive tissues: emerging concepts. *Reproductive Medicine Review* **6**:23–36.

Jaber, L., Merlob, P., Gabriel, R., Shohat, M. (1997) Effects of consanguineous marriage on reproductive outcome in an Arab community in Israel. *Journal of Medical Genetics* **34**:1000–2.

Jin, K., Ho, H.-N., Speed, T. P., Gill, T. J. (1995) Reproductive failure and the major histocompatibility complex. *American Journal of Human Genetics* **56**:1456–67.

Kent-First, M. G., Kol, S., Muallem, A., Ofir, R., Manor, D., Blazer, S. *et al.* (1996) The incidence and possible relevance of Y-linked microdeletions in babies born after intracytoplasmic sperm injection and their infertile fathers. *Molecular Human Reproduction* **2**:943–50.

Kerem, B., Rommens, J. M., Buchanan, J. A., Markiewicz, D., Cox, T. K., Chakravarti, A. *et al.* (1989) Identification of the cystic fibrosis gene: genetic analysis. *Science* **245**:1073–80.

Khastgir, G., Abdalla, H., Thomas, A., Korea, L., Latarche, L., Studd, J. (1997) Oocyte donation in Turner's Syndrome: an analysis of the factors affecting the outcome. *Human Reproduction* **12**:279–85.

Komlos, L., Zamir, R., Joshua, H., Halbrecht, I. (1977) Common HLA antigens in couples with repeated abortions. *Clinical Immunology and Immunopathology* **7**:330–5.

Kotloff, R. M., Fitzsimmons, S. C., Fiel, S. B. (1992) Fertility and pregnancy in patients with cystic fibrosis. *Clinical Chest Medicine* **13**:623–35.

Laitinen, T., Koskimies, S., Westman, P. (1993) Foeto–maternal compatibility in HLA-DR, -DQ, and -DP loci in Finnish couples suffering from recurrent spontaneous abortions. *European Journal of Immunogenetics* **20**:249–58.

Le Lannou, D., Jezequel, P., Blayau, M., Dorval, I., Lemoine, P., Dabadie, A.

*et al.* (1995) Obstructive azoospermia with agenesis of vas deferens or with bronchiectasia (Young's Syndrome): a genetic approach. *Human Reproduction* **10**:338–41.

Levine, P. (1958) The influence of the ABO system on Rh haemolytic disease. *Human Biology* **30**:14–28.

Lissens, W., Mercier, B., Tournaye, H., Bonduelle, M., Ferec, C., Seneca, S. (1996) Cystic fibrosis and infertility caused by congenital bilateral absence of the vas deferens and related clinical entities. *Human Reproduction* **11** [Suppl. 4]:55–78.

Macfarlane, A., Mugford, M. (1984) *Birth counts: statistics of pregnancy and childbirth*. London: Her Majesty's Stationery Office.

MacLeod, J., Gold, R. Z. (1953) The male factor in fertility and sterility. *Fertility and Sterility* **4**:10–33.

Martin, R. H., Balkan, W., Burns, K., Rademaker, A. W., Lin, C. C., Rudd, N. L. (1983*a*) The chromosome constitution of 1000 human spermatozoa. *Human Genetics* **63**:305–9.

Martin, R. H., Balkan, W., Burns, K. (1983*b*) Analysis of sperm chromosome complements in males heterozygous for structural chromosomal rearrangements. *American Journal of Human Genetics* **35**:143A.

Martin, R. H., Spriggs, E., Moosani, N., Rademaker, A., Barclay, L., Ko, E. (1997) In: Barratt, C., De Jonge, C., Mortimer, D., Parinaud, J. (eds.) *Genetics of human male fertility* (pp. 164–81). Paris: Editions E. D. K.

Matsunaga, E., Itoh, S. (1958) Blood groups and fertility in a Japanese population, with special reference to intrauterine selection due to maternal–foetal incompatibility. *Annals of Human Genetics* **22**:111–31.

Mickle, J., Milunsky, A., Amos, J. A., Oates, R. D. (1995) Congenital unilateral absence of the vas deferens: a heterogeneous disorder with two distinct subpopulations based upon aetiology and mutational status of the cystic fibrosis gene. *Human Reproduction* **10**:1728–35.

Miller, J. F., Williamson, E., Glue, J., Gordon, Y. B., Grudzinkas, J. G., Sykes, A. (1980) Fetal loss after implantation. *The Lancet* **II**:554–6.

Miura, H., Tsuijimura, A., Nishimura, K., Kitamura, M., Kondoh, N., Takeyama, M. *et al.* (1998) Susceptibility to idiopathic azoospermia in Japanese men is linked to HLA class I antigen. *Journal of Urology* **159**:1939–41.

Mollinson, P. L., Engelfreit, C. P., Contreras, M. (1997) Haemolytic disease of the fetus and newborn. In: *Blood transfusion in clinical medicine* (pp. 543–91). Oxford: Blackwell Science.

Morton, N. E., Krieger, H., Mi, M. P. (1966) Natural selection on polymorphisms in northeastern Brazil. *American Journal of Human Genetics* **18**:153–71.

Mowbray, J. F., Gibbings, C., Liddell, H., Reginald, P. W., Underwood, J. L., Beard, R. W. (1985) Controlled trial of treatment of recurrent spontaneous abortion by immunisation with paternal cells. *The Lancet* **I**:941–3.

Mowbray, J. F., Underwood, J., Gill, T. J. (1991) Familial recurrent spontaneous abortion. *American Journal of Reproductive Immunology* **26**:17–18.

National Blood Transfusion Service Immunoglobulin Working Party (1991) Recommendations for the use of anti-D immunoglobulin. *Prescribers' Journal* **31**:137–45.

Nelson, J., Smith, M., Bittles, A. H. (1997) Consanguineous marriage and its clinical consequences in migrants to Australia. *Clinical Genetics* **52**:142–6.

Oates, R. D., Honig, S., Berger, M. J., Harris, D. (1992) Microscopic epididymal sperm aspiration (MESA): a new option for treatment of the obstructive azoospermia associated with cystic fibrosis. *Journal of Assisted Reproduction and Genetics* **9**:36–40.

Ober, C., Hauck, W. W., Kostyu, D. D., O'Brien, E., Elias, S., Simpson, J. L. *et al.* (1985) Adverse effects of human leukocyte antigen-DR sharing on fertility: a cohort study in a human isolate. *Fertility and Sterility* **44**:227–32.

Ober, C., Elias, S., O'Brien, E., Kostyu, D. D., Hauck, W. W., Bombard, A. (1988) HLA sharing and fertility in Hutterite couples: evidence for prenatal selection against compatible fetuses. *American Journal of Reproductive Immunology* **18**:111–15.

Ober, C., Elias, S., Kostyu, D. D., Hauck, W. W. (1992) Decreased fecundability in Hutterite couples sharing HLA-DR. *American Journal of Human Genetics* **50**:6–14.

Oksenberg, J. R., Persitz, E., Amar, A., Brautbar, C. (1984) Maternal–paternal histocompatibility: lack of association with habitual abortions. *Fertility and Sterility* **42**:389–95.

OMIM (1997) Online Mendelian Inheritance in Man. Center for Medical Genetics, Johns Hopkins University (Baltimore, MD) and National Center for Biotechnology Information, National Library of Medicine (Bethesda, MD) World Wide Web URL: http://www.ncbi.nlm.nih.gov/omim/.

Patrizio, P. (1997) Mapping of the Y chromosome and its clinical consequences. In: Barratt, C., De Jonge, C., Mortimer, D., Parinaud, J. (eds.) *Genetics of human male fertility* (pp. 25–42). Paris: Editions E. D. K.

Penrose, L. S. (1955) Parental age and mutation. *The Lancet* **II**:312–13.

Pier, G. B., Grout, M., Zaidi, T., Meluleni, G., Mueschenborn, S. S., Banting, G. *et al.* (1998) *Salmonella typhi* uses CFTR to enter intestinal epithelial cells. *Nature* **393**:79–82.

Reed, T. E., Lowell, E. L. (1958) The completed reproductive performance of 161 couples selected before marriage and classified by ABO blood group. *Annals of Human Genetics* **22**:165–81.

Reznikoff-Etievant, M. F., Edelman, P., Muller, J. Y., Pinon, F., Sureau, C. (1984) HLA-DR locus and maternal–foetal relation. *Tissue Antigens* **24**:30–4.

Rigot, J. M., Lafitte, J. J., Dumur, V., Gervais, R., Manouvrier, S., Biserte, J. *et al.* (1991) Cystic fibrosis and congenital absence of the vas deferens. *New England Journal of Medicine* **325**:54–5.

Riordan, J. R., Rommens, J. M., Kerem, B., Alon, N., Rozmahel, R., Grzelczak, Z. *et al.* (1989) Identification of the cystic fibrosis gene: cloning and characterization of complementary DNA. *Science* **245**:1066–73.

Roberts, C. J., Lowe, C. R. (1975) Where have all the conceptions gone? *The Lancet* **I**:498–9.

Robson, S. C., Lee, D., Urbaniak, S. (1998) Anti-D immunoglobulin in RhD prophylaxis. *British Journal of Obstetrics and Gynaecology* **105**:129–34.

Sawyer, S. M., Phelan, P. D., Bowes, G. (1995) Reproductive health in young women with cystic fibrosis: knowledge, behavior and attitudes. *Journal of Adolescent Health* **17**:46–50.

Schaap, T., Shener, R., Palti, Z., Sharon, R. (1984) ABO incompatibility and reproductive failure. 1. Prenatal selection. *American Journal of Human Genetics* **36**:143–51.

Schacter, B., Weitkamp, L. R., Johnson, W. E. (1984) Parental HLA compatibility, fetal wastage and neural tube defects: evidence for a T/t–like locus in humans. *American Journal of Human Genetics* **36**:1082–91.

Schlegel, P. N., Cohen, J., Gpolstein, M., Alikani, M., Adler, A., Gilbert, B. R. *et al.* (1995) Cystic fibrosis gene mutations do not affect sperm function during *in vitro* fertilization with micromanipulation for men with bilateral congenital absence of vas deferens. *Fertility and Sterility* **64**:421–6.

Shami, S. A., Schmitt, L. H., Bittles, A. H. (1991) Consanguinity, spousal age at marriage and fertility in seven Pakistani Punjabi cities. *Annals of Human Biology* **17**:97–105.

Shin, D., Gilbert, F., Goldstein, M., Schlegel, P. N. (1997) Congenital absence of the vas deferens: incomplete penetrance of cystic fibrosis gene mutations. *Journal of Urology* **158**:1794–8.

Simpson, J. L., New, M., Peterson, R. E., German, J. (1971) Pseudovaginal perineoscrotal hypospadias (PPSH) in sibs. *Birth Defects Original Article Series* **6**:140–4.

Soussis, I., Harper, J. C., Handyside, A. H., Winston, R. M. (1996) Obstetric outcome of pregnancies resulting from embryos biopsied for pre-implantation diagnosis of inherited disease. *British Journal of Obstetrics and Gynaecology* **103**:784–8.

Staessen, C., Coonen, E., Van Assche, E., Tournaye, H., Joris, H., Devroey, P. *et al.* (1996) Preimplantation diagnosis for X and Y normality in embryos from three Klinefelter patients. *Human Reproduction* **11**:1650–3.

Stein, Z., Stein, W., Susser, M. (1986) Attrition of trisomies as a maternal screening device. *The Lancet* **I**:944–7.

te Veide, E. R., van Baar, A. L., van Kooij, R. J. (1998) Concerns about assisted reproduction. *The Lancet* **351**:1524–5.

Tietze, C. (1957) Reproductive span and rate of conception among Hutterite women. *Fertility and Sterility* **8**:89–97.

Teng, H., Jorissen, M., Von Poppel, H., Legius, E., Cassiman, J.-J., Cuppens,

H. (1997) Increased proportion of exon 9 transcripts in vas deferens compared with nasal epithelial cells. *Human Molecular Genetics* **6**:85–90.

Thomas, M. L., Harger, J. H., Wagener, D. K., Rabin, B. S., Gill, T. J. (1985) HLA sharing and spontaneous abortion in humans. *American Journal of Obstetrics and Gynecology* **151**:1053–8.

Tournaye, H., Staessen, C., Liebaers, I., Van Assche, E., Devroey, P., Bonduelle, M. *et al.* (1996) Testicular sperm recovery in nine 47,XXY Klinefelter patients. *Human Reproduction* **11**:1644–9.

Tournaye, H., Lissens, W., Liebaers, I., Van Assche, E., Bonduelle, M., Fastenaekels, V. *et al.* (1997) Heritability of sterility: clinical implications. In: Barratt, C., De Jonge, C., Mortimer, D., Parinaud, J. (eds.) *Genetics of human male fertility* (pp. 123–44). Paris: Editions E. D. K.

van der Ven, K., Messer, L., van der Ven, H., Jeyendran, R. S., Ober, C. (1996) Cystic fibrosis mutation screening in healthy men with reduced sperm quality. *Human Reproduction* **11**:513–17.

Verlinsky, V. (1996) Preimplantation genetic diagnosis. *Journal of Assisted Reproduction and Genetics* **13**:87–9.

Vogt, P. H. (1995) Genetic aspects of artificial fertilization. *Human Reproduction* **10** [Suppl. 1]:128–37.

Wang, W., Sullivan, S. G., Ahmed, S., Chandler, D., Zhivotovsky, L. A., Bittles, A. H. (2000) A genome-based study of consanguinity in three co-resident endogamous Pakistan communities. *Annals of Human Genetics* **64**:41–49.

Warburton, D., Fraser, F. C. (1964) Spontaneous abortion risks in man: data from reproductive histories collected in a medical genetics unit. *Human Genetics* **16**:1–25.

Wilcox, A. J., Horney, L. F. (1984) Accuracy of spontaneous abortion recall. *American Journal of Epidemiology* **120**:727–33.

Wilcox, A. J., Weinberg, C. R., O'Connor, J. F., Baird, D. D., Schlatterer, J. P., Canfield, R. E. *et al.* (1988) Incidence of early loss of pregnancy. *New England Journal of Medicine* **319**:189–94.

Williamson, R. A., Elias, S. (1992) Infertility and pregnancy loss. In: King, R. A., Rotter, J. I., Motulsky, A.G (eds.) *The genetic basis of common diseases* (pp. 577–95). New York: Oxford University Press.

Yaron, Y., Ochshorn, Y., Amit, A., Yovel, I., Kogosowki, A., Lessing, J. B. (1996) Patients with Turner's Syndrome may have an inherent endometrial abnormality affecting receptivity in oocyte donation. *Fertility and Sterility* **65**:1249–52.

Zlotogora, J. (1997) Dominance and homozygosity. *American Journal of Medical Genetics* **68**:412–16.

# PART II:

# Environmental influences on fertility

# 4

## Environmental pollutants and fertility

G. R. BENTLEY

## Abstract

In the past decade, two popular science books, numerous articles and at least one television documentary have focused on environmental pollutants that are suggested to affect human reproductive potential. For example, xenoestrogens – substances present in many human-made products, such as plastics – have been linked to apparent dramatic declines in human sperm counts. They have also been blamed for recent increases in reproductive developmental abnormalities as well as rates of cancer of the reproductive tract. This chapter examines the relevant data as well as proponents' and critics' arguments for changes in male and female reproductive function and physiology in relation to manufactured environmental agents. In addressing these topics, the chapter takes an explicitly ecological approach to human fertility. It stresses the issue of natural variation both within and between human populations that may arise from a variety of environmental, genetic, temporal and even behavioural factors, and that may obscure our understanding of any single environmental factor suspected to affect human reproduction adversely. At present there is insufficient evidence to support the theory that environmental pollutants are primarily responsible for such adverse changes. We should, however, continue to monitor carefully the potentially harmful effects of these polluting agents.

## Introduction

Beginning with the publication of Rachel Carson's *Silent spring* in 1962, environmental pollution and its consequences for human health has become an issue of increasing public concern. Recently, however, the effects of chemical pollutants on reproductive health have made media headlines following a report published in 1992 by Danish scholars that human sperm counts had declined dramatically during the previous 50 years (Carlsen *et al.*, 1992). This paper will be referred to henceforth as the Danish Study.

The impact of the Danish Study was such that numerous follow-up papers on sperm production were published and continue to appear in the scholarly journals, as well as several critiques. The Danish Study specifically pointed to a group of chemical substances, generally referred to as xenoestrogens, as the cause of the apparent decrease in sperm counts. This and other studies, primarily by the same group of scholars, speculate that exposure to xenoestrogens *in utero* have led to pathological alterations in reproductive tract development with a resulting loss in spermatogenesis (Giwercman *et al.*, 1993; Jensen *et al.*, 1995; Kelce and Wilson, 1997; Sharpe, 1993; Sharpe and Skakkebaek, 1993; Skakkebaek *et al.*, 1998; Toppari *et al.*, 1996; cf. Safe, 1995; Turner and Sharpe, 1997).

Xenoestrogens fall under a general class of artificially produced substances known as xenobiotics that are known to interfere with normal biological functions in living organisms. Xenoestrogens act by mimicking natural oestrogens, either enhancing (agonistic) or blocking (antagonistic) their effects. It is thought that human sperm production has been lowered by xenoestrogens ingested by mothers which then influence the development of their offspring. The male foetal reproductive tract would then be affected while still *in utero*, with lifetime consequences. The hypothesis that oestrogen-mimicking substances affect human sperm will be referred to in this chapter as the Xenoestrogen Hypothesis. The unspecified implication of the Danish Study is that a continued decline in human sperm counts will cause widespread infertility and, ultimately, the potential extinction of our species.

Given these concerns, this chapter will review the evidence for a decline in human sperm counts focusing primarily on the data provided by the Danish Study and follow-up reports. It will first cover various xenobiotic pollutants, and the evidence provided by wildlife and laboratory studies for their effects on reproductive function. There will also be a brief description of naturally occurring plant oestrogens, known as phytoestrogens, that also act as environmental xenoestrogens. The next section outlines what is known about the effects of xenobiotics on human health. A major section reviews the Danish Study, the numerous responses to it, and the follow-up studies of sperm counts in human and animal populations. This chapter also reviews the data for increases in other signs of adverse male reproductive development such as cryptorchidism (undescended testicles) and hypospadias (urethral openings occurring on the underside of the penis or perineum), as well as testicular cancer, suggested by the Danish Study to be increasing in parallel with a decline in human sperm counts. Indications of an increase in adverse female reproductive development are likewise covered.

The chapter concludes that the evidence for a worldwide decline in human sperm counts is inconclusive, while the Xenoestrogen Hypothesis relies on circumstantial data. This is not to imply that continued caution in the use of xenobiotic substances is unwarranted; indeed, the potential threat to human health and fertility by environmental pollutants remains ever-present and menacing. Given this threat, there is even more urgent need for careful studies that rely on sound evidence and carefully supported hypotheses.

## Xenobiotics

What substances qualify as xenobiotics and how do they affect reproductive function? Table 4.1 lists some of the more commonly associated chemicals that are known or suspected to act as hormone mimics, followed by a more detailed discussion of them.

All of the xenobiotics listed in Table 4.1 have recognized effects as either oestrogen or androgen agonists and/or antagonists. In

Table 4.1. *Xenobiotic substances that act as endocrine disruptors*

| Xenobiotic | |
|---|---|
| Persistent organochlorines: | Phenolic compounds: |
| *Dichlorodiphenyls:* | |
| Dichlorodiphenyl trichloroethane (DDT) | Alkylphenol (APE) |
| Dichlorodiphenyl dichloriethene (DDE) | Alkylphenol polyethoxylate (APEO) |
| | Nonylphenol (NP) |
| Chlordecone (Kepone) | Octylphenol (OP) |
| Metoxychlor | Nonylphenoxycarboxylic acid |
| Dicofol | (NP1EC) |
| Perthane | Nonylphenoldiethoxylate (NP2EO) |
| *Hexachlorocyclohexanes (HCH):* | *Phthalates:* |
| α-hexachlorocyclohexane | Butylbenzyl phthalate (BBP) |
| β-hexachlorocyclohexane | Di-*n*-butyl phthalate (DBP) |
| γ-hexachlorobenzene (HCB) | Di-(2-ethylhexyl) phthalate (DEHP) |
| | Mono-(2-ethyhexyl) phthalate (MEHP) |
| *Polychlorinated Cyclodienes:* | *Bisphenol A – BPA* |
| Heptachlor | (4,4′-isopropylidenediphenol) |
| Heptachlor epoxide | |
| Chlordane | |
| Oxychlordane | |
| *Trans*-nonachlor | |
| Aldrin | |
| Dieldrin | |
| *Polychlorinated biphenyls (PCBs)* | |
| Aroclor | |
| Tetrachlorobiphenyl (Kanechlor 400) | |

comparison to the effects of endogenous steroids, the xenoestrogenic and xenoandrogenic effects of any of the chemicals under discussion here are relatively weak, although there is some debate about whether chemical cocktails have the ability to act synergistically with more devastating consequences (Arnold *et al.*, 1996; Ashby *et al*, 1997, Ramamoorthy *et al*, 1997). Not all xenobiotic effects are harmful. Some endocrine antagonists are beneficial since they block hormone receptors and thereby reduce levels of steroid hormones implicated in certain cancers. For example, in areas contaminated with a type of polychlorinated biphenyl known as 2,3,7,8-tetrachlorodibenzo-*p*-dioxin (TCDD), rates of breast and endometrial cancer have been reduced, while laboratory studies have shown that TCDD and related compounds inhibit tumor growth *in vitro* (Safe, 1995). Safe also points out that humans are probably exposed to equal amounts of oestrogenic antagonists and agonists, including many phytoestrogens (discussed below), the effects of which would cancel each other out.

Most evidence for the hormone-disrupting effects of xenobiotics *in vivo* comes from laboratory and wildlife studies. Some scholars dispute the validity of extrapolating findings from laboratory animal studies to humans, arguing that doses given in such studies frequently exceed those that would be normally found in human populations, while the same developmental stages at which animals are dosed may not be comparable between different studies (Kimbrough, 1991). Some animal species are much more sensitive to toxic effects from certain chemicals. For example, hamsters are relatively insensitive to dioxins and polychlorinated biphenyls (PCBs), guinea-pigs are very sensitive to these substances (Gray and Gangolli, 1986; Kimbrough, 1991; Sauer *et al.*, 1994), while mice are more sensitive than humans to diethylstilbestrol (DES) (Wilcox *et al.*, 1995). We should therefore be extremely cautious in applying these animal models to human populations.

Most wildlife studies involve acute exposures to extremely high levels of xenobiotics caused by accidents such as industrial spills, or have been conducted among wildlife populations living close to sources of industrial effluents. In some cases, we are also able to evaluate the acute toxic effects of some xenobiotics among human populations where disastrous accidents have resulted in mass poisonings. What is lacking, however, are *prospective* studies measuring the effects of chronic exposure to low doses of the relevant chemicals (Robison *et al.*, 1985; White *et al.*, 1994). Thus the effects (reproductive or otherwise) of long-term exposure of human populations to xenobiotics with endocrine effects can only be conjectured at present.

## *Persistent organochlorines*

One of the major classes of chemicals that have come under scrutiny for their effects on human reproduction is the so-called persistent organochlorines (Table 4.1). These are industrially produced chemicals containing chlorine, such as dichlorodiphenyl trichloroethane (DDT), and one of its major metabolites dichlorodiphenyl dichloriethene (DDE), and PCBs. DDT was first developed in the 1930s as a highly effective insecticide. It was used extensively in both developed and developing countries, particularly in malarial regions where human habitations and clothing were sprayed directly with this chemical. PCBs were produced industrially in large quantities beginning in the 1930s. Because they were chemically stable and resistant to heat and electricity they were widely used in electrical products such as transformers and switches, as well as for electrical and fire insulation and fire retardants. Dioxins and furans are the waste byproducts of organochlorines and are released into the environment when plastics and paper containing bleaching agents are burned. Some are also released naturally from forest fires and volcanic eruptions.

In mammals, organochlorine chemicals are efficiently absorbed through the skin, lungs and gastrointestinal tract. DDT and PCBs are both lipophilic (that is they tend to concentrate in the fat of living organisms) and therefore bioaccumulate and magnify in higher trophic level animals. This results in humans having among the highest exposure of any mammalian species. Over 90% of both DDT and PCBs are absorbed from fatty foods, with lower absorption thresholds for congeners with higher chlorinations (Jensen and Slorach, 1991*b*). Because of their chemical stability, neither DDTs nor PCBs degrade easily in the environment, particularly the latter – DDT has a half-life of over 60 years (Walker and Peterson, 1992). There is also a biomagnification effect for the organochlorines since they migrate from warmer to colder latitudes by sea and air. The higher latitudes now have pollution levels that are much higher than would otherwise be warranted by virtue of their comparative isolation from industrial sites (Loganathan and Kannan, 1994). Populations living at these high latitudes therefore face the highest risks of lifetime accumulation. Inuits in the Canadian Arctic, for example, can accumulate up to 100 times more organochlorines in their blood during their lifespan than humans in southern Canada. This is partly due to their latitude, but also to their dietary reliance on seals and beluga whales that harbour large amounts of organochlorines in their blubber (Anonymous, 1998; DeWailly *et al*, 1989).

Production of PCBs and DDT was gradually phased out in developed countries during the 1970s when their persistence and toxicity were recognized. As a result of this industrial ban, there has certainly been a decrease in DDT levels in Western areas (Solé *et al.*, 1994). However, many developing countries particularly in the tropical regions and southern hemisphere continue to use DDT as a pesticide to help control disease vectors for malaria, typhus, typhoid and cholera, and levels there remain high. In contrast, because PCBs were incorporated into many products that are still in use today, PCB levels have not declined as quickly as when they were first monitored (Robinson *et al.*, 1990), and in some places levels have remained almost unchanged (Loganathan *et al.*, 1993; Loganathan and Kannan, 1994; Somogyi and Beck, 1993; van Hove Haldrinet *et al.*, 1977).

While the toxicity and carcinogenicity of the organochlorines has long been known, their effects as endocrine disrupters were first recognized in the 1970s. Structurally, the organochlorines are dissimilar from natural oestrogens which has made it difficult to predict any xenobiotic effects from their molecular structure alone. (Natural oestrogens contain a phenolic ring A, and even synthetic oestrogens, such as DES, have two phenolic rings.) Instead, the oestrogenic activity of organochlorines may depend on structural alterations (aromatic phenolic substitution) during metabolic conversion (Bitman and Cecil, 1970). For example, it is the major metabolite of DDT – DDE – that is a highly effective androgen antagonist *in vivo* and *in vitro*. Through competitive binding to the androgen receptor, it effectively inhibits normal transcriptional activity at the cellular level. Other congeners, such as *p,p'*-DDT and *p,p'*-dichlorodiphenyl dichloroethane (*p,p'*-DDD), are also xeno-androgens but their effects are much weaker (Kelce *et al.*, 1995; Turner and Sharpe, 1997). Laboratory experiments have confirmed these effects. Male weanling rats treated with $p,p'$-DDE experienced significantly delayed puberty in comparison to controls, while older male rats (120 days) treated similarly had significantly reduced ventral prostate and seminal vesicle weights, despite having high testosterone levels (Kelce *et al.*, 1995).

In contrast, the congeners chlordecone (Kepone) and $o,p'$-DDT both act as weak xenoestrogens *in vitro* and *in vivo* (Gray, 1992; Kelce *et al.*, 1995), with the latter having a stronger effect. In earlier laboratory studies, administration of $o,p'$-DDT to female rats increased uterine and ovarian weights, and hastened the onset of puberty (Gellert *et al.*, 1972). However, Safe (1995) has argued that levels of $o,p'$-DDT are low to nondetectable in most environmental samples. Other organochlorines such as endosulfan, toxaphene and dieldrin have oestrogenic effects *in vitro* (Soto *et al.*, 1994), and cause proliferation of MCF-7 human breast cancer cells (Safe, 1995), a class of cells routinely used in the laboratory to assess the carcinogenicity of various substances.

Laboratory studies have confirmed the adverse effects of PCB exposure on reproduction. Pregnant rats exposed to high doses of two PCB congeners (169 and 77) had prolonged gestational periods, and delivered fewer offspring with lower birth weights. The offspring followed through to adulthood had fewer pregnancies (Sauer *et al*, 1994). In a different study, mothers of neonatal male rats were given varying doses of a PCB mixture (Aroclor 1254) and the offspring were allowed to suckle normally. These males were later mated with normal females when they reached adulthood (120 days). All but the males exposed to the lowest dose (8 µg/g) of PCB via their mother's milk had reduced fertility. Despite having sperm counts, sperm morphology and testosterone levels that appeared normal, sperm from these exposed males either did not reach the oviducts or ova of their mates in about 50% of cases or failed to fertilize the eggs. Of those eggs that fertilized, significantly fewer developed normally compared to a control group (Sager *et al*, 1991).

Perinatal exposure to the dioxin TCDD in male rats resulted in dose-related, lower foetal and neonatal levels of testosterone, delayed testicular descent, and a decrease in spermatogenesis and seminiferous tubule diameter (Peterson *et al.*, 1992). Although these males exhibited abnormal mating behaviour with lower numbers of mounts and intromissions, there was no apparent effect on sperm motility, morphology, or male fertility.

## *Alkylphenols*

Alkylphenols (APEs) are primarily the byproducts of microbial breakdown during sewage treatment of a group of industrial surfactants, the alkylphenol polyethoxylates (APEOs). APEOs are the second largest group of nonionic surfactants in commercial production, and were introduced in the 1940s. They are used as antioxidants in the production of most plastics such as polyvinyl chloride (PVC) and polystyrene, as industrial surfactants for detergents, paints, herbicides, cosmetics, as petrol additives, in tanning and textile processing, and as spermicides in condoms. Their ubiquity means that they are probably present in most plastic items in use today. Production of APEs in the U.S.A. alone was almost one million tonnes in 1988, of which approximately 60% have ended up in the aquatic environment after sewage treatment (Clark *et al.*, 1992; Jobling *et al.*, 1996; Soto *et al.*, 1991; Turner and Sharpe, 1997; White *et al.*, 1994).

Like organochlorines, APEs are highly lipophilic and are easily absorbed into the body. However, levels of these compounds in humans have not, as yet, been monitored by any agency, nor have any standards been established for 'safe' levels of exposure to these chemicals. Levels of APEs in domestic sewage have been reported to range from <5 to >100 µg/l, while industrial effluents such as those originating from pulp mills and textile companies can contain significantly higher concentrations. Clark *et al.* (1992) have detected over 20 alkylphenol compounds in the drinking water of New Jersey State in the U.S.A.

Laboratory studies have illustrated the oestrogenic effects of APEs. A major effect of oestrogen exposure on teleost fish is the stimulation and secretion of a protein called vitellogenin by the liver, its major function being to stimulate oocyte growth in the females prior to ovulation. Although vitellogenin is generally associated with females, males will also produce this protein if exposed to oestrogen, making it a sensitive biomarker of the presence of this hormone. All of the APE compounds are oestrogenic and cause significant increases in vitellogenin concentrations measured in the plasma of exposed fish (Jobling *et al.*, 1996; White *et al.*, 1994). Jobling *et al.* (1996) exposed male rainbow trout to measured concentrations of different APE compounds to see how this might affect testicular growth. These fish were compared to another group exposed to the synthetic potent oestrogen, 17α-ethinyloestradiol (EE2). Although all the fish survived and grew, there were significant increases in vitellogenin concentrations in the male trout as well as significant decreases in rates of testicular growth. Octylphenol (OP) had similar effects to EE2, although at a 10,000-fold greater concentration, and halved the rate of testicular growth, while other APEs had somewhat lesser effects. These effects were not observable in fully mature adult males exposed to similar doses of APEs.

The APEs appear to be able to mimic the effects of endogenous oestradiol by binding to the oestrogen receptor and stimulating transcription, with OP being the most potent, and 4-nonylphenol-diethoxylate (NP2EO) having no effect. The oestrogenicity of the APEOs depends on their chain length – APEOs with more than three ethoxylate groups have little if any oestrogenic activity. APEs also have carcinogenic effects and can stimulate the growth of MCF-7 breast cancer cells *in vitro* (White *et al.*, 1994). Again OP has the most potent effects but nonylphenol, NP2EO and 4-nonylphenoxycarboxylic acid (NP1EC) are also active. There is no direct evidence at present for adverse effects from these chemicals in any species observed in the wild, but the demonstrated xenoestrogenic properties of APEs, their widespread use in the environment and their persistence provide cause for concern (White *et al.*, 1994).

### *Phthalates*

Phthalates are one of largest groups of industrial chemicals used in the plastics industry to impart flexibility. They are used in the manufacture of food-packaging plastics, vinyls including PVC, cellulosics, and certain types of elastomers. Phthalates leach from these materials into water, soil or food, and have been detected in oceans, rivers, waste materials, drinking waters, marine organisms and marine sediments. Significant quantities of phthalates are thought to leach from landfill sites into groundwater (Giam *et al.*, 1978; Jobling *et al.*, 1995; Mayer *et al.*, 1972). Clark *et al.* (1992) detected several phthalate plasticizers in the drinking water of New Jersey, U.S.A. Phthalates are known to be xenoestrogenic, have been found to concentrate in the cellular fraction of sperm, and can act as testicular toxicants at high concentrations (Jobling *et al.*, 1995).

In laboratory studies, male rat offspring exposed to di-(2-ethyl-hexyl) phthalate (DEHP) *in utero* developed smaller testes, had a significantly higher occurrence of cryptorchidism and had lower sperm counts as adults when compared to control groups (Imajima *et al.*, 1997; Tandon *et al.*, 1991). Administration of DEHP to four- and ten-week-old male rats resulted in lower testes, seminal vesicle and prostate weights with greater effects on the younger rats, and no effect on older rats exposed to similar doses at 15 weeks (Gray and Gangolli, 1986). The main site of action of DEHP was the seminiferous tubules which showed abnormalities just hours after doses of DEHP were given. Adult female rats exposed to DEHP suffered from hypoestrogenic anovulatory cycles (Davis *et al.*, 1994*a*). These effects were apparently caused by DEHP's metabolite, mono-(2-ethylhexyl) phthalate which suppresses aromatose conversion of testosterone to oestradiol (Davis *et al.*, 1994*b*).

Jobling *et al.* (1995) examined the effects *in vitro* of two phthalate esters, butylbenzyl phthalate (BBP) and di-*n*-butylphthalate (DBP), as well as a food antioxidant, butylated hydroxyanisole (BHA). All three compounds inhibited binding of tritiated oestradiol to the fish oestrogen receptor, although the exact mechanism of this inhibition was not fully known. Jobling *et al.* (1995) suggested that the effects of these phthalates were agonistic since they stimulated transcriptional activity of the oestrogen receptor. All three substances also had mitogenic effects on cell growth, but growth responses to these chemicals were all lower than the maximal responses shown by oestradiol.

Many more studies of phthalates are required to assess their effects *in vivo*, particularly the effects of chronic exposure. Little is known at present about the absorption and metabolism of phthalates from the body (Jobling *et al.*, 1995). Resolution of this issue is particularly urgent given the recent findings of phthalates in baby milk formulas and the resulting panic that ensued in the U.K. (Bradbury, 1996; Jenkins and Nuttall, 1996).

## Bisphenol A

Bisphenol A – 4,4′-isopropylidenediphenol (BPA) – is a monomer used in the manufacture of polycarbonates and a wide variety of plastic and other products, such as acrylic resins, false teeth, and in lacquer coatings on food cans. It is also used in photocopying production and in some fungicides. Current producers in the U.S.A. were calculated to produce over a billion pounds of BPA (Krishnan *et al.*, 1993). Bisphenols have been shown to be oestrogenic *in vitro* and *in vivo*.

Krishnan *et al.* (1993) found that small amounts of BPA were leached from polycarbonate tubes during autoclaving of distilled water in polycarbonate flasks during laboratory experiments (2.5–3.5 µg/l water). The oestrogenic activity of BPA, deduced from its capacity to encourage proliferation of MCF-7 cancer cells, was found by accident in experiments searching for a yeast oestrogenic substance. Brotons *et al.* (1995) have found somewhat higher quantities of BPA in lacquer-coated cans after extraction (0–33 µg/can) implying that BPA leaches from the coatings and may enter can contents prior to ingestion. Receptor displacement data indicate that the oestrogenic activity of BPA is oestrogen-receptor mediated.

## The effects of xenobiotics: wildlife studies

### Effects of DDT

Prior to the 1970s various populations of seagulls in Southern California (Western Gulls) and the Great Lakes area (Herring

Gulls) were exposed to high levels of industrial effluents and particularly DDT. During the 1960s and 70s, several anomalies were observed among these populations: females were nesting together, there were more eggs than usual in gull nests, there were higher rates of embryo and chick mortality, chick deformities, and growth retardation (Fox, 1992; Fry and Toone, 1981). In the laboratory, Fry and Toone (1981) attempted to replicate the possible effects of acute DDT and DDE exposure on gull eggs. On hatching they found male chicks suffered from varying degrees of feminization in reproductive development with some maturing as hermaphrodites. They speculated that this phenomenon in the wild had caused a reduction in the number of available mates for female gulls, resulting in the female–female nest pairs observed in California and the Great Lakes.

Lake Apopka in Florida has been exposed to various agricultural and municipal contaminants and suffered from major pesticide spills (dicofol and DDT with its metabolites DDE and DDD), and a sulphuric acid spill from the Tower Chemical Company in 1980. Guillette *et al.* (1996) found numerous developmental abnormalities in male alligators hatched from eggs laid by female alligators resident in the Lake in comparison with hatchlings from an unpolluted control lake nearby. These anomalies included significantly lower plasma testosterone levels comparable to normal female levels, a reduction in penis size, and abnormal cell structure in the seminiferous tubules. The effects are most compatible with an anti-androgenic action probably caused by $p,p'$-DDE.

Kelce *et al.* (1995) have found that the concentration of $p,p'$-DDE required to inhibit androgen receptor transcriptional activity in cell culture (63.6 parts per billion–ppb) is much less than that measured in affected eggs from Lake Apopka (5800 ppb), and even that found in human serum in areas where DDT contamination still exists, or where DDT use continues. For example, median DDT/DDE levels were 140 ppb in serum taken from individuals living in DDT-treated dwellings for malaria control in South Africa. In laboratory experiments, levels of serum DDT/DDE in pregnant rats ingesting 25–200 mg DDT/kg per day throughout the gestational period ranged from 700 to 1700 ppb while levels in their newborn rat pups were 2100 ppb. In the 1960s, when DDT was still in use in the U.S.A., high concentrations of $p,p'$-DDE were measured in tissues taken from stillborn infants in Georgia (650 ppb in the brain to 3570 ppb in the kidney). These reports confirm that $p,p'$-DDE can cross the placenta and reach levels known to inhibit human androgen receptor transcriptional activation *in vitro*, and induce anti-androgenic effects in rats *in vivo*.

Other wildlife studies suggest adverse effects on reproductive hormones from exposure to DDT and its derivatives. For example, Subramanian *et al.* (1987) found a significant negative correlation ($p < 0.05$) between testosterone and DDE levels in blubber samples taken from 12 male Dall's porpoises (*Phocoenoides dalli*) from the northwestern North Pacific.

### PCBs

In the western most part of the Wadden Sea, in The Netherlands, population levels of the common seal (*Phoca vitulina*) declined dramatically from the 1950s through the 1970s, dropping from 3000 in 1950 to < 500 in 1975 (Reijnders, 1986). This area was known to be polluted with PCBs primarily from the river Rhine draining into the Wadden. As a consequence of this observed population decline, Reijnders (1986) experimented with feeding seals polluted fish from the western Wadden Sea and comparing health parameters with those of control seals fed fish from the north-east Atlantic where pollution levels were much lower. There were no significant differences in progesterone or oestradiol levels between the two groups, but reproductive success was significantly lower among seals fed with fish from the polluted Wadden Sea. Although the exact causes of reproductive failure could not be explained, reproductive losses occurred around the time of implantation.

Fish may be affected by PCBs during early development, and early fry mortality increased by deposition of these lipophilic chemicals from maternal tissues to the oocytes during vitellogenesis. PCBs have been detected in eggs of lake trout, Chinook Salmon, and Coho Salmon in the Great Lakes of mid-Western U.S.A., starry flounder in San Francisco Bay, Atlantic Salmon, Baltic

Herring, Baltic Flounder in the Baltic Sea, whiting in the North Sea and Arctic Char in Lake Geneva (Walker and Peterson, 1992).

## Phytoestrogens

In addition to chemical products, a number of plants, fungi and moulds contain oestrogen-mimicking compounds – referred to as phytoestrogens – and are thus capable of acting as endocrine disrupters (Whitten and Naftolin, 1992; Whitten *et al.*, 1992). Development of these phytoestrogens is presumably adaptive in that potential plant predators may suffer from reduced fertility as a result of ingesting sufficient quantities of the plant in question (Hughes, 1988; Shutt, 1976). Since this chapter will incorporate some discussion of these substances for comparative purposes, they are listed in Table 4.2.

Phytoestrogens are considerably more oestrogenically potent than any of the manufactured xenobiotics mentioned above and are present in normally consumed products such as soya beans, coffee, grains, many vegetables and fruit. The oestrogenic components are found in differing amounts in all parts of plants including seeds, flowers, leaves, roots and fruits (Kaldas and Hughes, 1989). The potential effects of plant oestrogens in the modern world were first realized in 1946 when ewes grazing on subterranean clover in Western Australia between 1941 and 1944 experienced a progressive and inexplicable decline in their fertility, with a 30% decline in production of lambs (Shutt, 1976). The source of their problem was eventually traced to the large quantities of clover they consumed in pastures that contained quantities of phytoestrogens known as isoflavones (Table 4.2).

Although the contraceptive effects of plant preparations on humans were for a long time derided by modern scholars and clinicians, there is little question now that the contraceptive effects of certain plants were recognized and readily exploited in the ancient world (Riddle, 1992). One plant, known as silphium, a kind of fennel belonging to the genus *Ferula*, was so efficacious that its demand led to soaring prices in ancient Greece and Rome where it was mainly used between the seventh century B.C. and third century A.D.

Table 4.2. *Phytoestrogenic plants*

| Family | Common name | Phytoestrogens |
|--------|-------------|----------------|
| Chenopodiaceae | Beet | |
| Compositae | Sunflower | Coumestans |
| Cruciferae | Rape | |
| Euphorbiaceae | Castor oil plant | |
| Graminae | Barley | Isoflavonoids, coumestans and |
| | Oats | resorcylic acid lactones |
| | Rye | |
| | Ryegrass | |
| | Rice | |
| | Wheat | |
| | Bluegrass | |
| | Orchard grass | |
| Labitae | Sage | |
| Leguminosae | Alfalfa | Isoflavonoids and coumestans |
| | Clovers | |
| | Soybean | |
| Liliaceae | Garlic | |
| Malvaceae | Hollyhock | |
| Palmaceae | Date palm | |
| Polygonaceae | Rhubarb | |
| Rosaceae | Apple | |
| | Cherry | |
| | Plum | |
| Rubiceae | Coffee | |
| Salicaceae | Willow | |
| Solanaceae | Potato | |
| Umbelliferae | Parsley | |

(Riddle *et al.*, 1994). Silphium was also depicted on coins from the ancient city of Cyrene the major source of its distribution. Silphium's limited range along the coast of North Africa and its high demand eventually led to its extinction.

Despite the potentially disruptive effect on fertility of some plants, there is general agreement that normal dietary ingestion of phytoestrogenic plants is, in fact, beneficial for humans in lowering hormone levels that are related to cancer, and particularly breast cancer (Cassidy *et al*, 1994; Henderson *et al.*, 1988). The heavy dietary reliance of Asian women on soya, a plant rich in isoflavones, is a major factor explaining their reduced risk of breast cancer (Cassidy *et al*, 1994). The commercial development of the phytoestrogenic drug paclitaxel (Taxol) from the yew tree, and its use to treat breast cancer is an excellent clinical example of this consensus. What is not currently clear are the long-term, developmental implications of feeding soya-based formulas to infants who are lactose intolerant or otherwise allergic to milk-based products.

## The effects of xenobiotics: observations on humans

There is no question that acute exposure to large amounts of organochlorines is deleterious to human health. There have been a few well-documented cases of the toxic effects of exposure to PCBs. In 1968, a serious mass intoxication occurred in Japan when a leak from a heat-transfer installation contaminated a batch of rice-bran oil with the organochlorine tetrachlorobiphenyl (Kanechlor 400). The resulting illness was referred to as 'Yusho Disease' and mainly involved severe dermatological abnormalities including chloracne (Higuchi, 1976). More than 1700 people became ill and over 20 died. In female victims, over 60% reported abnormal menstrual function following ingestion of the contaminated oil. Studies of these women suggested luteal phase deficiencies and possible anovulation in many cases (Hirayama, 1976).

In 1979 in Taiwan, there was a similar mass poisoning called 'Yu-Cheng' (oil-disease) involving cooking oil that was contaminated with PCBs, polychlorinated dibenzo-furans (PCDFs) and polychlorinated quaterphenyls (Kuratsune and Shapiro, 1984). There were over 2000 victims in this accident. Studies of the children of women exposed during their pregnancies showed that they were shorter and lighter compared to nonexposed controls. They also showed a higher incidence of gingival, dermal, dental and bronchial abnormalities, as well as behavioural and other developmental abnormalities (Rogan *et al.*, 1988). Approximately 11% of exposed women complained of menstrual dysfunction (Lü and Wong, 1984).

In another Japanese study, Takamatsu *et al.* (1984) examined industrial workers who had been chronically exposed to PCBs in the workplace, many of whom showed plasma levels of PCBs that were higher than those of the victims of the Yusho poisoning. In contrast, almost none of these workers had symptoms that were analogous to those of the Yusho patients.

In the mid1970s, a 33-year-old man living in Virginia, U.S.A. complained to his physician of headaches, tremors and irritability (Guzelian, 1982). After several tests, it was discovered that the patient and a number of other workers in a plant producing chlordecone (Kepone) had toxic levels of this organochlorine in their blood. The surrounding environment had also been contaminated by industrial discharge of this pollutant into the nearby James River. The clinical manifestations of this 'Kepone Episode' were neurological, hepatological and gonadal in nature. Many of the victims exhibited temporary sterility, with oligospermia and azoospermia. Testicular function returned to normal following metabolic clearance of Kepone.

One of the most significant routes of exposure to organochlorine pesticides for juveniles of any mammalian species is through lactation (Jensen and Slorach, 1991*a*). Since breastfeeding represents the most efficient process of elimination of these compounds in females, a suckling offspring is necessarily the repository of large amounts of potentially toxic contaminants. In the late 1950s about 500 people died and 4000 became ill after eating bread baked from wheat treated with the fungicide hexachlorobenzene (HCB). In some villages almost all the children below the age of two who were still being breastfed died in this incident (Jensen, 1991).

In humans, the amounts of contaminant transferred decrease with total nursing time, parity, and among women who have been vegetarians for extended periods of time prior to breastfeeding (Jensen and Slorach, 1991*b*). Unfortunately, despite a number of studies on levels of organochlorines in human milk (e.g. Jensen and Slorach, 1991*a*; Somogyi and Beck, 1993), the long-term effect of chronic exposure on the health and reproductive function of suckling offspring is still uncertain, although the general conclusion is that, for most populations, there is no reason at present to be concerned (Jensen and Slorach, 1991*a*; Somogyi and Beck, 1993). One exception may be Inuit women living in the Canadian Arctic who have among the highest recorded levels of PCBs in their breast milk compared to other populations (111.3 µg/l) compared to 28.4 µg/l for Caucasian women living in southern regions of Canada (DeWailly *et al*, 1989). It has been estimated that the average PCB dose for Inuit infants is 120 ml/kg per day and these high levels are suggested to be associated with lower immunity among Inuit children (DeWailly *et al*, 1989). In contrast, exposure to organochlorines in baby formula appears to be almost negligible (but see above about phthalates in milk formulas).

There are also some studies examining the effects of organochlorine exposure *in utero* as well as via lactation on children in North America. Children born to mothers with higher tissue levels of PCBs and DDT had lower psychomotor test scores, but normal mental indices as measured using Bayley Scales of Infant Development (Gladen *et al.*, 1988). Similarly, Fein *et al.* (1984) studied 242 children born in the mid-West U.S.A. to mothers who consumed either moderate amounts of PCB-contaminated fish from the Great Lakes or to controls who did not. Children born to contaminated-fish-eating mothers were lighter and had smaller than expected head circumferences given their body size. There did not appear to be any evident difference in reproductive tract anomalies in these cohorts.

A major supporting component of the Xenoestrogen Hypothesis is the disastrous experience with the synthetic oestrogen DES in the U.S.A. in the mid-part of the twentieth century. This drug was prescribed to about two to three million American women between the late 1940s and early 1970s by doctors who believed (at the time) that taking exogenous oestrogen would reduce the risk of early miscarriages as well as reduce toxaemia, premature deliveries and stillbirths. Unfortunately, when clinical trials were undertaken to assess the efficacy of DES, results showed that the drug in fact increased these risks. During the 1970s, it was also realized that administration of the drug during the first trimester of pregnancy had in most cases resulted in adverse effects on the developing reproductive tract of the foetus *in utero*.

Problems were first realized when a number of adolescent girls who turned out to be offspring of mothers dosed with DES were diagnosed with an extremely rare form of vaginal cancer called clear cell adenocarcinoma (Stillman, 1982). Since then, the number of reproductive tract anomalies diagnosed in both male and female DES offspring has increased. In women, in addition to clear cell adenocarcinoma, such anomalies include structural defects of the cervix, vagina, uterus and fallopian tubes, menstrual dysfunction, increased rates of spontaneous abortion, ectopic pregnancies, premature deliveries and perinatal deaths as well as infertility. In males, problems include microphallus, cryptorchidism, testicular hypoplasia and abnormal spermatogenesis (Stillman, 1982). It is the latter problems, evident in male offspring of DES-exposed mothers, that provide significant support for the proponents of the Xenoestrogen Hypothesis.

## Decreasing sperm counts in humans

Aside from the studies outlined above, there is little *direct* evidence at present for detrimental effects on human fertility from environmental xenoestrogens. In fact most of the concern and publicity for a purported decline in human fertility since 1992 originates from a paper published in the *British Medical Journal*. This was written by a Danish team of researchers (the Danish Study) headed by Niels Skakkebaek, with first author Elisabeth Carlsen (Carlsen *et al.*, 1992). This meta-analysis purported to show an approximate 50% worldwide decline in sperm counts during the previous 50 or so years, and linked this decline to environmental xenoestrogens. The Danish Study examined 61 papers reporting sperm concentrations and semen volume published between 1938 and 1991, with a total number of 14,947 subjects.

The authors found a significant decrease in mean sperm counts from $113 \times 10^6$/ml in 1940 to $66 \times 10^6$/ml in 1990 ($p < 0.0001$), and a significant decrease in mean seminal volume from 3.40 ml to 2.75 ml ($p = 0.03$). The study used a linear regression of mean sperm densities and mean seminal volume against the year of publication of these means weighted by the number of subjects in each study. The Danish Study concluded that there had been a 'genuine' and 'world-wide' decline in sperm quantity. Furthermore, the article went on to blame this decline, as well as increasing rates of reproductive cancers and male developmental abnormalities such as cryptorchidism and hypospadias, specifically on xenoestrogens.

The appearance of this paper prompted widespread publicity in the popular press, such that many lay people who would not otherwise read such academic articles became aware of the debate (e.g. Begley and Glick, 1994; Cadbury, 1997; Colborn *et al.*, 1996; Hileman, 1994; Hunt, 1997; Raloff, 1994*a*, *b*; Rocco, 1999). A surge of studies that either support or refute the claims for a decline in sperm counts followed, and continue to appear even now in various journals and magazines. Some have discussed the controversy generated by the Danish Study, and criticized or supported its results; others comprise independent studies of sperm counts published since 1992. This section of the chapter then will specifically focus on a variety of statistical and methodological problems attributed to the Danish Study. In addition, it covers 17 follow-up studies on sperm counts from different geographical regions in Europe, the Mediterranean, and the U.S.A. that either support or negate a decline in sperm density, and two studies of sperm counts in farm animals that contradict the findings of the Danish Study.

Both positive and negative outcomes have emerged from the publicity over declining sperm counts. First, a large number of critiques have called into question the original conclusions of the Danish Study, although the mass media still tend to support the worst-case scenarios. Second, the Danish Study has stimulated many other projects investigating the potential health hazards from environmental xenoestrogens. Third, and perhaps most important, is the attention drawn to the issue of regional variability in sperm counts that exists in humans and probably other mammals as well. This feature of our biology, and its relationship to male fecundity, deserves further study, especially since a convincing explanation for such variability is currently lacking.

Before turning to a further discussion of the Danish Study, a brief definition of sperm counts is presented to clarify use of this term.

Sperm counts, in fact, usually refer to sperm *density* or *concentration* rather than total numbers of sperm in an ejaculate. Sperm counts are usually reported as millions of sperm per millilitre of semen (the fluid containing both sperm and essential nutrients to keep the sperm alive).

### Criticisms of the Danish Study

The major criticisms of the Danish Study are gathered here into sections concerned with statistical design, and sampling bias.

#### Statistical criticisms

The most consistent statistical criticism of the Danish Study is that linear regression represents an unsophisticated choice of analytical techniques. To illustrate this problem, Younglai *et al.* (1998) ran a number of different analyses of 51,101 sperm counts collected from 11 infertility centres in Canada between 1975 and 1996. These included linear regression of all sperm counts, mean sperm counts by centre, and multiple regressions controlling for centre. The results obtained differed according to the unit of analysis. For example, linear regressions of all sperm counts showed no significant trends through time ($F = 0.72$, $p = 0.4$), but when divided into two separate periods (1975–83 and 1984–96) showed a significant decline for the latter ($F = 220.8$, $p < 0.0001$). When this period was reanalysed using linear regression of mean sperm counts by centre, this significant downward trend was lost ($F = 1.42$, $p = 0.24$). Younglai *et al.* concluded that results were highly dependent both on the choice of statistic and the way the data were manipulated.

Olsen *et al.* (1995) fit three alternative models – a quadratic, spline and stairstep – to the same data set used in the Danish Study. The stairstep model provided the best fit but, given the uneven distribution of data, still left about 50% of the variance unexplained. Both the quadratic and spline fits showed a decline in sperm counts up to about 1980 followed by a slight increase. Bahadur *et al.* (1996) were able to replicate these results adding to their analysis more recently published studies of sperm counts (specifically, Auger *et al.*, 1995; Bujan *et al.*, 1996; Irvine *et al.*, 1996). Their quadratic model also showed a gradual and significant rise in sperm counts since 1975 ($r^2 = 0.48$, $p<0.0001$). This observed rise in sperm counts during the later periods has been replicated by other critics of the Danish Study (Brake and Krause, 1992; cf. Keiding and Skakkebaek, 1996), while others found no significant decline in sperm counts for the same late period (Bahadur *et al.*, 1996; Becker and Berhane, 1997; Paulsen *et al.*, 1996).

Swan *et al.* (1997) reanalysed 56 of the original 61 articles used by the Danish Study using multivariate analyses. These analyses included mean (or median) sperm density, year of publication, location of the study, subjects' ages, goal of the study, the percentage of men with proven fertility, method of semen collection and period of abstinence. Variables were also added to indicate the degree of missing data. The analyses also controlled for sperm counting method, source of population (e.g. sperm donors, volunteers), year of sample collection (as opposed to publication year), and criteria used for proving fertility, as well as some other variables not listed. A multiple linear regression including all covariates gave a much improved fit ($r^2 = 0.80$) compared to the original linear model of the Danish Study ($r^2 = 0.36$), and the models used by Olsen *et al.* (1995) outlined above. Swan *et al.*'s model revealed an even greater decline in sperm counts in the U.S.A. (1938–1988) and in Europe (1971–1990) compared with the Danish Study, but no decline in nonWestern countries. Swan *et al.* also considered other confounding factors and concluded that these were insufficient to explain the general decline. This paper provides the most support for the Danish Study, but did not consider any of the more recent studies conducted since 1992. The important role of intra- and inter-regional differences in sperm quality, also discussed by Swan *et al.*, is considered further below (p. 122).

*Sampling bias*

Many authors have suggested that the Danish Study is subject to sampling bias from several possible sources, although it might also be the case that such effects, aggregated over many subjects and a variety of studies utilizing different data collection protocols, would cancel each other out, and hence not influence the major result. However, for purposes of this review they are mentioned here.

A. BIAS INTRODUCED THROUGH DISPROPORTIONATE SAMPLING. The Danish Study may show a decline in sperm counts from 1938 to 1991 due to disproportionate sampling, both numerical and chronological (Farrow, 1994; Fisch and Goluboff, 1996; Olsen et al., 1995). Only 20 of the 61 papers in the Danish Study had sample sizes greater than 100 men, and these papers accounted for > 90% of all subjects. Most of the studies also cluster during the final 20-year period representing 79% of all studies and 88% of all subjects (Olsen et al., 1995). Of the total 14,947 subjects in the Danish Study, only 596 (4%) represent the pre1950 period, 1184 (8%) represent the period 1950–1970, and 13,167 (88%) since 1970. Between 1950 and 1970, 40% of the time period is represented by <10% of the data, making any analysis of the total period highly imbalanced. Farrow (1994) also pointed out that no allowance was made for differences between the date of the study and date of publication even when there were substantial discrepancies. The largest study with a sample size of > 4000 was based on data collected between 11 and 5 years prior to publication.

B. BIAS THROUGH FAILURE TO COLLECT MULTIPLE SEMEN SAMPLES FROM INDIVIDUAL MEN. A single semen sample collected from the same man could yield a sperm count of from $50 \times 10^6$ to $230 \times 10^6$/ml depending on his age (Haidl et al., 1996; Johnson, 1986; Schwartz et al., 1983), time since last ejaculation (Matilsky et al., 1993; Schwartz et al., 1979), health status, exercise regime, diet, ambient temperature and season of the year (Levine et al., 1990; Snyder, 1990; Tjoa et al., 1982; Vierula et al., 1996), among other factors. Essentially, sperm counts as well as sperm volume and total number of sperm show very high intra-subject variability, with standard deviations almost as high as the means (Mallidis et al., 1991; Schwartz et al., 1979). Most sperm samples tend to cluster at the low end of the distribution. Therefore, in attempting to assess sperm counts accurately, several sperm samples should be collected and averaged from any one individual. Few of the original 61 articles examined in the Danish Study are likely to have followed this procedure. This aspect alone could bias averaged figures for sperm counts.

C. BIAS INTRODUCED THROUGH FAILURE TO ACCOUNT FOR VARIA-
BILITY IN SPERM COLLECTION METHODS. The period of abstinence prior to sperm donation was only available for 32 (53%) of the original papers consulted by the Danish Study, and it is not clear how these 32 papers were distributed through time. Differences in abstinence periods could contribute significantly to variation in reported sperm counts. MacLeod and Gold (1951) found that an abstinence period of ten days instead of the more standard three that is generally required in semen donor programmes could double sperm counts in the same individual. Periods of abstinence and age are also likely to be confounded together, as pointed out by Swan *et al.* (1997); older men tend to have longer periods of abstinence, thus paradoxically increasing their sperm counts. In addition, a standardized period of abstinence was not rigorously controlled for in the largest of the 61 studies used in the Danish Study because the subjects in this paper were prevasectomy donors who questioned why a semen analysis was required (Tjoa *et al.*, 1982). This latter study contributed 30% (4435 subjects) of the total number of subjects covered by the Danish Study (Olsen *et al.*, 1995). [Bahadur *et al* (1996), however, reanalysed the data from the Danish Study excluding this very large study, but found it made no significant difference to the final results.]

Semen collection methods can also bias sperm counts. For example, collection during intercourse results in higher sperm counts compared to semen collected by masturbation (Zavos and Goodpasture, 1989). Most of the articles used in the Danish Study reported masturbation as the collection method, but some used other methods or did not specify how semen was collected (Swan *et al.*, 1997). The alternative methods tended to be used in earlier studies, thus possibly confounding results of the meta-analysis.

D. BIAS INTRODUCED THROUGH FAILURE TO ACCOUNT FOR INTER-
AND INTRA-LABORATORY ERRORS. Sperm counting is itself subject

to many methodological errors ranging from errors in pipetting, dilution, poorly calibrated counting chambers, and intra-observer error in visual cell counting (Comhaire, 1993). Although the Danish Study eliminated from its meta-analysis studies that used flow cytometry or computer-assisted systems of counting, considerable inter-study errors may have introduced bias. Forti and Serio (1993) point out that standardized methods for semen analysis were lacking until 1980 when the World Health Organization recommended unified procedures (World Health Organization, 1980, 1992).

Two external quality control studies of sperm density report high coefficients of variation in measurements between different laboratories, as well as for sperm morphology (Matson, 1995; Neuwinger et al., 1990). In contrast, Jørgensen et al. (1997) compared the results of semen analyses in four different laboratories using semen samples from 26 men. (It should be noted that the participating laboratories had all published data supporting a decline in sperm density.) Although the authors of this paper claim that sperm density and semen volume can be reliably compared between laboratories due to the finding of 'remarkable consistency', analysis of variance of both sperm density ($F = 4.47$, $p = 0.0061$) and semen volume ($F = 10.16$, $p = 0.0002$) showed significant differences between these laboratories.

E. AGE BIASES INTRODUCED BY UNEVEN SAMPLING ACROSS ALL AGE RANGES. Information on subjects' ages was available in only 42 of the papers used by the Danish Study, but ranged from 17 to 64 years; older men are sampled more frequently in later publications (Swan et al., 1997). Age is known to affect sperm quality and quantity, as well as observed periods of abstinence which would alter sperm density (Bujan et al., 1996; Haidl et al., 1996; Johnson, 1986; Schwartz et al., 1983; Swan et al., 1997). In a study of 64 men who observed a period of sexual abstinence of three to five days (Haidl et al., 1996), sperm density and motility were significantly different among younger men ($< 35$ years, mean $= 32$) compared to older ones ($> 45$ years, mean $= 50$). In the younger group, sperm density was $115 \times 10^6$/ml ($p = 0.01$) while motility was 30%

$(p = 0.04)$. Among the older men, sperm density was $67 \times 10^6/\text{ml}$ and motility 23%. Bujan *et al.* (1996) found that sperm counts increased with increasing age of the subjects in their study, which is probably related to differential periods of abstinence as discussed above.

F. SAMPLING BIAS DUE TO SPECIAL CHARACTERISTICS OF DONOR POPULATIONS. Articles purporting to show a decrease in sperm counts using data drawn from the same clinic may in fact reflect changes in the characteristics of sperm donors or in methods used to recruit such donors (Fisch *et al.*, 1996). For example, Cook and Golombok (1995) report that the majority of sperm donors in the U.K. are unmarried students in their early twenties whose prime motivation is financial. How this age-bias might affect sperm quality was not explored by Cook and Golombok, who focused on the attitudes and motivations of semen donors. But other studies have suggested that younger donors are more likely to smoke and consume alcohol, factors known to affect sperm quality as outlined below.

Handelsman (1997) also recently confirmed that sperm donors are a select group unlikely to be representative of the general population. To prove this point, he published data from a group of 509 sperm donors from a hospital in Sydney, Australia, and 180 volunteers taking part in five consecutive male contraception studies. There were significant differences between the median sperm density of men in the first two of these contraception studies compared to the final three, and between the median sperm density of the former and the 509 sperm donors.

G. SAMPLING BIAS FROM CHANGES IN THRESHOLDS FOR SPERM COUNTS. The cutoff point for sperm below which men are considered infertile decreased threefold in 1951 as the result of newer studies on male infertility (Bromwich *et al.*, 1994). A study of 294 men in 1929 chosen without reference to their fertility status reported that men with sperm densities $< 60 \times 10^6/\text{ml}$ were rarely fertile (Macomber and Sanders, 1929). This figure became the accepted threshold for fertility until 1951, when MacLeod and

Gold published a large study suggesting a lower figure of $20 \times 10^6$/ml was a more accurate threshold (Lipshultz, 1996). Both studies were concentrated in the northeastern U.S.A., obviating problems associated with regional differences. As a result of this change in fertility thresholds, papers used by the Danish Study that were published before 1951 might well have excluded men with sperm densities $< 60 \times 10^6$/ml. The Danish Study openly acknowledged this major shift. Such an omission would automatically bias upwards the reported mean sperm counts from earlier articles, thus explaining the apparent recent decline. Bromwich *et al.* (1994) demonstrated how an artificial decline of this sort could occur statistically. Lerchl and Nieschlag (1996) also suggest that the choice of supposedly 'normal' men might specifically have been affected during the 1980s by the official adoption of $40 \times 10^6$/ml as a threshold by the World Health Organization, followed by a revision to $20 \times 10^6$/ml in 1987. That this threshold should decline further is now advocated by several researchers (e.g. Chia *et al.*, 1998; Lemcke *et al.*, 1997).

H. SAMPLING BIAS CAUSED BY FAILURE TO CONTROL FOR BIO-RHYTHMS IN SPERM COUNTS. A number of studies have shown a seasonal effect on sperm counts, which tend to be lower in the summer (Levine *et al.*, 1992; Snyder, 1990; Tjoa *et al.*, 1982; Vierula *et al.*, 1996; Zerah *et al.*, 1997). A recent article has also shown an unanticipated diurnal effect with higher sperm counts in the afternoon (Cagnacci *et al.*, 1999). Information about the season of sperm collection or the time of sample collection is unlikely to have been included in most of the original articles in the Danish Study.

I. SAMPLING BIAS CAUSED BY FAILURE TO CONTROL FOR OTHER FACTORS THAT AFFECT SPERM QUANTITY SUCH AS SMOKING AND ALCOHOL CONSUMPTION. A number of articles point out that smoking and alcohol intake result in decreased sperm quality and quantity (Baird and Wilcox, 1986; Feichtinger, 1991; Rubes *et al.*, 1998; Vine, 1996; Vine *et al.*, 1994). Information on these factors was not included in the Danish Study, and is unlikely to be indicated in the original articles.

*Other criticisms*

Olsen *et al.* (1995) point out a substantial inconsistency between the findings of the Danish Study and those of MacLeod and colleagues who presented data on sperm counts from the same laboratory over an extended period of time and failed to find any significant difference. In 1951, MacLeod and Gold examined a sample of 1000 fertile men with a mean sperm density of $107 \times 10^6$ sperm/ml. A comparative sample of 1000 men from infertile partnerships (where either the male or female might have a fertility problem) gave a mean sperm density of $90 \times 10^6$/ml. Twenty-eight years later, MacLeod and Wang (1979) published a second study of sperm counts from the same laboratory with a much larger sample size ($n = 14,476$), nearly equal to the total sample size of the Danish Study ($n = 14,947$). Nine thousand of this sample were men comparable to 1000 of the subjects in the 1951 study, that is men from infertile marriages of unknown aetiology. Mean sperm count for these 9000 men ($96 \times 10^6$/ml) was comparable to the previous findings. The Danish Study included the 1951 paper by MacLeod and Gold in its meta-analysis. In fact, the high values for sperm counts in this article were largely responsible for the high historical values in their linear model. However, it did not include the later study from 1979 by MacLeod and Wang.

*Summary*

Many criticisms have been levelled against the Danish Study calling into question the validity of their conclusions that there has been a 'worldwide' decline in human sperm counts, although there may indeed have been local declines during certain periods. Further light on this issue may be shed by the number of follow-up papers stimulated by the Danish Study that have examined sperm density in a number of different human populations. These are detailed below.

## Comparative studies of sperm density

There are at least 17 studies of which I am aware (and very likely more) relating to sperm parameters from men in different areas that have been published since 1992. Nine of these report a decrease in sperm counts, while eight report no change, a slight increase, or ambivalent results. These are reviewed below including comments on potential problems associated with each study.

*Studies reporting a decrease in sperm density*

1. Ginsburg *et al.* (1994) looked at sperm characteristics among 260 men who were partners of infertile women being treated with hormone therapy, and living in the London area from 1978–83 to 1984–89. Although the figures given for all subjects show a slight decrease in sperm density ($101 \times 10^6$/ml to $96 \times 10^6$/ml), as well as sperm morphology and motility, the decrease is not reported to be statistically significant. When analysed by water supply area, the authors found a significant decrease in sperm density ($105 \times 10^6$/ml to $96 \times 10^6$/ml, $p < 0.05$) for those men living in the Thames Water Authority region. The authors link these findings to possible water pollution.

2. Auger *et al.* (1995) report semen quality parameters in 1351 healthy, fertile men who donated semen between 1973 and 1992 at a sperm bank in Paris. Data were analysed as a function of year of donation, age of the donor, the donor's date of birth, and the duration of sexual abstinence before donation. The authors found a decrease in mean sperm density by 2.1%/year from $89 \times 10^6$/ml in 1973 to $60 \times 10^6$/ml in 1992 ($p < 0.001$), but no change in mean semen volume (3.8 ml). The proportion of motile and normal sperm also decreased during this time by 0.6% for motility and 0.5% for morphology ($p < 0.001$). Each calendar year of birth accounted for 2.6% of the observed yearly decline in sperm density, and for 0.3% and 0.7% respectively for the annual declines in the proportion of motile and morphologically normal sperm.

3. Adamopoulos *et al.* (1996) report a significant decline in sperm density (from $46 \times 10^6$/ml between 1977 and 1985, to $38 \times 10^6$/ml between 1986 and 1993), for 2385 men from the Greater Athens area. Semen volume also declined from 3.97 ml from 1977–85, to 3.73 ml from 1986–93 ($r^2 = 0.34$, $p < 0.05$). The men represented a random sample (10%) of male partners

attending a subfertility clinic with their wives. The fertility status of these subjects is, therefore, unknown (either they or their wives, or both, might have had infertility problems) and the proportion of males with such problems could have increased in the sample during the 15 years of study.

4. de Mouzon *et al.* (1996) used a large database from the French National Register which has recorded sperm counts since 1989 from men participating in *in vitro* fertilization (IVF) programmes, as well as details for 90% of all IVF cycles. The authors of this paper analysed 19,848 sperm samples from 7714 subjects with a sperm density $> 20 \times 10^6$/ml, total motility of $> 40\%$ and normal morphology of $> 40\%$. Subjects were in partnerships with women suffering from tubal infertility. They found a decline in sperm density for men born between 1950 and 1975, from $84 \times 10^6$/ml in men born before 1939, to $77 \times 10^6$/ml in men born from 1965 onwards. In looking at sperm density by year of data collection (1989–94), there was only a decline in 1991–92. Problems associated with this dataset include lack of knowledge of the age and characteristics of the sperm donors.

5. Irvine *et al.* (1996) looked at sperm counts from 577 Scottish men born between 1951 and 1973. The semen samples were collected in a single laboratory over an 11-year period. Subjects were volunteer donors who offered to provide semen samples for a programme in gamete biology research. The researchers examined a number of indicators of sperm quality and quantity, including semen volume, sperm density, sperm motility, the total number of sperm in the ejaculate and the total number of motile sperm. They found that a later year of birth was associated with a lower median sperm density (from $98 \times 10^6$/ml among donors born before 1959, to $78 \times 10^6$/ml among donors born after 1970, $p = 0.002$), a lower total number of sperm in the ejaculate (from $301 \times 10^6$/ml to $214 \times 10^6$/ml, $p = 0.0005$), and a lower number of motile sperm (from $170 \times 10^6$/ml to $129 \times 10^6$/ml, $p = 0.0065$). This study, however, mixed different types of cohorts – one composed of older men with proven fertility, and the other comprising

younger undergraduates of unproven fertility. It is possible that the latter group might well have had lower sperm counts as a result of their age, higher rates of alcohol consumption and possibly higher rates of smoking (Eccersley, 1996; Farrow, 1996; Raab, 1996).

6.  Van Waeleghem *et al.* (1996) studied sperm characteristics in 416 healthy young men in Ghent, Belgium, who provided semen samples over a 19-year period from 1977 to 1995. Subjects comprised mostly students and unmarried para-medical personnel aged between 20 and 40; 90% were aged 20–30. Sperm counts decreased between 1977 and 1980, from $71 \times 10^6$/ml to $59 \times 10^6$/ml ($p = 0.04$) but since sperm volume also increased slightly between these periods from 2.9 to 3.29 ml ($p = 0.07$), there was no significant change in sperm count per ejaculate (this relationship does not appear to have been taken into account in many other studies). The proportion of sperm with normal morphology decreased from 39% in 1977–80 to 27% in 1990–95, while motility decreased from 53% to 32% between these two periods. The authors concluded that sperm quality declined among young men, but did not provide any specific information about the characteristics of the donor population that might have changed with time.

7.  Menchini-Fabris *et al.* (1996) looked at data from 4518 men who were referred to the University of Pisa, Department of Andrology for fertility analyses. These men were divided into three time-based cohorts spanning 1975 to 1994. There was a trend towards lower sperm counts from $(72 \pm 16) \times 10^6$/ml in 1975–79, to $(65 \pm 19) \times 10^6$/ml in 1991–94, and a more dramatic decline in sperm motility. However, we are not told if these declines are statistically significant and few data are given on subjects characteristics.

8.  Zheng *et al.* (1997) examined sperm counts, seminal volume and percentage of morphologically normal sperm in 8608 men who, together with their partners, were undergoing infertility consultations at four Danish hospitals. Methodology for semen analyses varied slightly between the four hospitals. A subset of these men were followed up with a questionnaire to ascertain

various lifestyle parameters that might shed further light on results from the semen analyses. Linear regression was used to examine the relationship between year of birth of the subjects and semen characteristics. Multiple regression was used to measure interaction terms between birth-year and centre, and birth-year and calendar-year of semen analysis. Zheng *et al.* found that sperm counts decreased significantly for men born in 1950 up to 1970 by $1.6 \times 10^6$/ml each year after controlling for duration of sexual abstinence, sampling season and effects of calendar time. In addition, mean sperm counts declined by year from $61 \times 10^6$/ml in 1968–74 to $47 \times 10^6$/ml in 1985–89.

9.  Pajarinen *et al.* (1997) report an increase in abnormal spermatogenesis in two necropsy series in Finland from 1981 and 1991, totalling 528 men aged 35–69 years at the time of death. They found that the ratio of normal spermatogenesis declined from 56% in 1981, to 27% in 1991. In addition, testicular weight decreased, the amount of fibrotic tissue in the testes increased, and the size of the seminiferous tubules decreased. These changes were not associated with the body mass index, or with smoking, alcohol or drug intake as determined from interviews with close relatives.

Given that this paper involved autopsies, the data are not directly comparable with those of other studies. Moreover, the findings contradict other reports that Finnish sperm counts are among the highest in the world and have remained unchanged in the past 30 years (Suominen and Vierula, 1993). Pajarinen *et al.* (1997) stress that their subjects were older compared to men in other studies, and came from more densely populated, industrialized (and thereby possibly more polluted) parts of Finland, near Helsinki. In contrast, Suominen and Vierula (1993) point out that the highest sperm counts came from Finnish men who live in the most rural (and presumably less polluted) areas.

*Studies reporting no significant changes in sperm density or a slight increase*

1.  Wittmaack and Shapiro (1992) examined the semen quality of 159 potential sperm donors who applied to the semen donation

programme at the University of Wisconsin between 1978 and 1987. Donors were healthy men of unproven fertility drawn from the university population who followed a three-day period of abstinence. There were no significant changes in sperm density (range $56 \times 10^6$/ml to $106 \times 10^6$/ml), sperm motility (range 50% to 62%) or sperm morphology.

2. Suominen and Vierula (1993) looked at six studies of Finnish men published between 1958 and 1992. They found a mean sperm count of $114 \times 10^6$/ml (range $96 \times 10^6$ to $145 \times 10^6$/ml), with no significant decrease during the three decades under scrutiny. Like many other studies showing a decline in sperm density, characteristics of subjects contributing to this analysis varied considerably, and included normal men of either known or unknown fertility, vasectomy patients and semen donors. This study confirms the regionally high sperm counts of Finnish men which are approximately twice as high as in other areas in the world.

3. In a later publication, Vierula *et al.* (1996) examined sperm counts in 238 normal Finnish men between 1984 and 1986, and 5481 semen samples from men attending a clinic for couple infertility between 1967 and 1994. The mean age of the latter group increased significantly from 28 to 33 years during the period of study. Both groups followed a recommended abstinence period of three to five days. Controlling for age of the subjects, season of year and duration of sexual abstinence, results show no significant change in sperm counts (from $82 \times 10^6$ to $85 \times 10^6$/ml) or total number of sperm ($345 \times 10^6$ to $325 \times 10^6$/ml), but a significant decrease in semen volume (from 4.5 to 4.1 ml). Mean sperm counts among the normal men in this study were $134 \times 10^6$/ml.

4. Bujan *et al.* (1996) examined the sperm density from 302 healthy fertile men aged 20–45 who contributed semen between 1977 and 1992 at a sperm bank in Toulouse, France, after a three- to five-day abstinence. The mean sperm count was $83 \times 10^6$/ml and this did not decline with time.

5. Paulsen *et al.* (1996) studied 510 healthy sperm donors from the greater Seattle area, U.S.A., who donated multiple semen

samples as participants in clinical studies between 1972 and 1993. Mean sperm density in 1972 was $47 \times 10^6$/ml compared to a mean of $52 \times 10^6$/ml in 1992–93 ($p = 0.01$). This statistically significant increase was dismissed as clinically unimportant by the authors. There was also a slight increase in semen volume, total number of sperm per ejaculate and percentage of normal sperm morphology.

6. Benshushan *et al.* (1997) looked at sperm samples from 188 healthy, young medical students from Israel aged 20–30 who donated sperm to a university sperm bank between 1980 and 1995, after an abstinence period of three to four days. Using linear regression, a decline in sperm density (from $68 \times 10^6$/ml to $65 \times 10^6$/ml, $p = 0.71$) and sperm motility (by 0.27%) was observed, but these results were not statistically significant. In contrast, mean semen volume increased significantly from 1.95 ml in 1982 to 3.3 ml in 1995 ($p < 0.001$), and the total number of motile sperm increased significantly from $75 \times 10^6$/ml to $120 \times 10^6$/ml ($p < 0.0001$). Percentage normal sperm morphology decreased by 1.04% per year from 93 to 76% ($p < 0.0001$).

7. Younglai *et al.* (1998) analysed sperm density from 51,101 semen samples collected between 1975 and 1996 from 11 university infertility clinics in Canada. Subjects included healthy men who were referred with their infertile female partners as well as presumably infertile men who were either outpatient referrals or attending the clinics for infertility analyses preparatory to assisted reproductive technologies. Semen samples from all these men were collected by masturbation following a minimal three-day abstinence period; only data for sperm density were presented. Linear regression of all 51,101 sperm densities showed no significant trend, but when the samples were plotted by two separate time periods characterized by different sample sizes (1975–83, with 2133 samples, and 1984–96 with 48,968 samples), there was a significant downward trend in the latter ($F = 220.8$, $p < 0.0001$). This decline amounted to 1.44% for each year, but contributed only 0.4% to the overall variability. A multiple regression, controlling

for infertility centre, also showed a significant decline ($p < 0.0001$), but again only accounted for 3.1% of the variability in sperm counts.

Younglai *et al.* then analysed the data for 1984–96 and 1975–96 using linear regression of mean sperm counts by infertility centre (essentially duplicating the type of analysis represented in the Danish Study). For the former period, no significant decline was observed ($F = 1.42$, $p = 0.24$); there was a significant interaction among the group means (analysis of variance, ANOVA, $p < 0.0001$). For the latter period, 1975–96, linear regression of mean sperm counts through time by centre showed a significant increase ($F = 4.26$, $p = 0.04$). Linear regression of the data by individual centre showed a decrease in sperm counts for some centres and an increase in others. In fact, although most of the infertility centres showed no significant change in mean sperm counts during the 21-year period, three centres showed a twofold decrease. The authors stressed that the population they analysed was probably unrepresentative of the normal population, and more than likely included mixed ethnic groups because of large numbers of immigrants to Canada. The significant decrease in sperm counts for the period 1984–86 was acknowledged but dismissed as clinically unimportant.

8.  Andolz *et al.* (1999) retrospectively examined the semen parameters of 20,411 men referred to their laboratory for infertility problems between 1960 and 1996 who lived in both urban and rural areas around Barcelona in Spain. These authors found no statistically significant decline in sperm counts during the 36-year period of study, a significant (but clinically unimportant) decline in semen volume, a statistically significant increase in the percentage of motile sperm, and a significant decline in the percentage of normal spermatozoa. The conclusion drawn from this study was that there was no evidence from these data for a recent decline in sperm quality.

*Additional studies*

A few other related studies of interest are worth mentioning here. Abell *et al.* (1994) reported significantly higher sperm densities

among members of a Danish organic farmers' association compared to blue-collar workers (printers/electricians and metal
workers), after adjustment for periods of abstinence (farmers had
shorter periods of abstinence). No conclusive explanation was
offered for this finding, but it was suggested that organic farmers
would be less exposed to chemical pesticides and fertilizers thus
supporting the idea that environmental pollutants affect sperm
function.

Farrow (1994) and Olsen *et al.* (1995) both suggested that the
veterinary literature should be checked for data on sperm counts
among farm animals since presumably they would also be affected
by exposure to organochlorines and other xenobiotics, and would
provide a link in the food chain to potential human tissue
accumulation of xenobiotics. Van Os *et al.* (1997) and Setchell
(1997) have obligingly provided two such analyses. Van Os *et al.*
examined 75,238 sperm samples from 2314 bulls used in artificial
insemination programmes in The Netherlands and found no long-
term decline in sperm counts between 1977 and 1996 after
adjusting for several possible confounding variables. A comparison
of these data with earlier records from dairy bulls published
between 1962 and 1977 yielded the same result.

Setchell undertook a meta-analysis of published reports on sperm
counts in farm animals used in artificial insemination programs:
bulls ($n = 137$ studies), boars ($n = 76$) and rams ($n = 130$), the
references having been obtained from *Animal Breeding Abstracts*.
Sample sizes were not always available from the references but
included a minimum of 153,893 semen samples from at least 4113
bulls, 57,465 samples from 2000 boars and 30,194 semen samples
from 2121 rams. Like the Danish Study, samples have a worldwide
distribution. Results showed that there has been no significant
change in sperm counts in bulls or boars, and a significant increase
in sperm counts among rams over the past 60 years.

The results from these two studies of farm animals are reassuring
that no general trend towards decreasing sperm counts exists
among other mammalian species that are readily accessible for
analyses in a manner comparable to humans. Setchell concludes
that, 'if the fall in sperm concentrations in humans is real, it must

be due to something specific to this species (e.g. lifestyle factors), or to some environmental factor(s) to which the farm animals were not exposed or were not susceptible' (p. 211).

*Summary*

The additional studies summarized here illustrate that the data on human sperm counts are neither concordant nor consistent. Furthermore, two studies of sperm counts in farm animals, species that might reasonably be supposed to have been exposed to the same environmental hazards as our own, fail to support a decline in sperm counts. Rather, the variability shown by the papers on human males support the notion of a wide inter-regional difference in sperm density that is probably one of the major confounding factors in the Danish Study. This topic is covered further below.

## Regional variation in sperm density

The probability of regional variation was not considered by the Danish Study when analysing their data (Fisch and Goluboff, 1996). In the U.S.A. alone, for example, men in New York (for unknown reasons) have among the highest sperm counts $(134 \times 10^6/\text{ml})$, while men from Texas and Iowa have among the lowest (as low as $48 \times 10^6/\text{ml}$). Men from industrialized nations tend to have higher sperm counts in general; Finnish men have much higher sperm counts compared to men almost anywhere (Suominen and Vierula, 1993; Vierula *et al.*, 1996), and possibly higher fertility (Joffe, 1996), while Danish men have comparatively low sperm counts (Bostofte *et al.*, 1983).

Why such geographical variation in sperm counts exists is not totally understood, but it could be related to nutritional, genetic, socioeconomic, or other environmental aspects that require further study. That there is such variation should not be particularly surprising. Many other aspects of human reproduction are known to exhibit normal biological variation – for example levels of reproductive hormones such as progesterone, oestrogen and testosterone are known to differ greatly within and between populations, but are not thought to affect human fertility (Bentley *et al*, 1998; Ellison *et al*., 1993; Vitzthum *et al*., 1998).

To control for such regional variability in sperm counts, Fisch *et al*. (1996) analysed data collected in three different sperm banks in Minnesota, New York and California between 1970 and 1994 to assess whether sperm counts had declined significantly in the U.S.A. Their total sample comprised 1283 men who banked sperm prior to vasectomy. These were men collected from the general population without regard to proven fertility. Contrary to the Danish Study, they found a slight increase in sperm counts for the entire sample, and within Minnesota and New York when analysed separately. Using linear regression, this study found a significant increase in sperm density over the 25-year period from a mean of $77 \times 10^6$/ml in 1970, to $89 \times 10^6$/ml in 1994 ($r = 0.06$, $p = 0.04$), an increase of 0.65% per year. There was a significant increase in sperm density in New York ($r = 0.15$, $p = 0.002$) and Minnesota ($r = 0.11$, $p = 0.006$), but not in California where the sample size was smaller ($r = 0.03$, $p = 0.06$). There were also significant differences in sperm counts and motility between the three regions. Linear regression similarly showed no significant change in sperm motility over the 25-year period, but a significant decrease in semen volume ($p = 0.001$). Mean age at sperm donation increased significantly over the 25 years from 30 to 38 ($r = 0.32$, $p < 0.001$). A multiple regression controlling for age, period of abstinence and year of donation still showed a significant increase in sperm density ($p = 0.004$) over the three different areas.

In the Danish Study, most of the pre1970 papers reporting the highest sperm counts were from the U.S.A. (11 out of 13) and clustered in New York, while the later studies included regions characterized by lower sperm counts (15 nonWestern countries, 16 European countries and 17 from the U.S.A.). Thus mere geographical variation could explain the results that the Danish Study reported, as well as results found in other earlier publications (Lipshultz, 1996). For example, Nelson and Bunge (1974) had also suggested that there was a general decline in sperm counts, but their later and lower figures originated from men requesting vasectomies in Iowa where sperm counts are lower, while the earlier, higher sperm counts to which the Iowan ones were compared were from the study by MacLeod and Gold (1951) in New York where sperm counts are higher.

Bahadur *et al.* (1996), and Becker and Berhane (1997) confirm that a major factor accounting for a decline in sperm counts in the Danish Study, particularly between 1938 and 1974, was a bias towards U.S. subjects. Bahadur *et al.* (1996) separated out the U.S. studies from Europe/Australia and all other regions (Asia/Africa/South America). Using linear regression, they found a significant decline only for the U.S. studies, but not for the European, or other area studies. These findings were replicated by Becker and Berhane using multiple linear regression (1997) and Olsen *et al.* (1995). Given the findings of regional variation, Bahadur *et al.* (1996) suggested factors such as diet and pollution might be important on a local basis.

One of the most comprehensive models used to explore the effect of regional variation on sperm density is provided by Swan *et al.* (1997), also reviewed above on p. 107. In addition to the multiple linear regression used on their data, these authors fit four different kinds of models to the data – a linear, quadratic, spline and step – with the data separated into three regions: U.S.A., Europe and Australia, and nonWestern countries. Unlike Bahadur *et al.* (1996) and Becker and Berhane (1997), the U.S. and European data in the linear model showed a significant decline in sperm density, while the nonWestern countries showed a significant increase. The spline model showed a significant decrease in sperm counts in the U.S. only prior to 1970, but a significant decline in Europe (data from 1971 onwards), and a nonsignificant increase for the nonWestern data. Furthermore, Swan *et al.* (1997) admit that their study did not rule out important *intra*-regional differences that might shed further light on their finding of a general decline in sperm counts.

### Summary

This is not the first time that a debate on declining sperm counts has appeared in the medical literature, as pointed out by Farrow (1994). In fact, several earlier studies reported this phenomenon (e.g. Leto and Frensilli, 1981; Murature *et al.*, 1987; Nelson and Bunge, 1974), as well as making a link to environmental pollutants as potential factors involved in sperm declines (Bendvold, 1989; Bendvold *et al.*, 1991; Murature *et al.*, 1987 Nelson and Bunge, 1974). One of the earliest such studies, published more than 20 years ago (Nelson and Bunge, 1974), was successfully refuted five years later by a much larger study that showed no decline in sperm density (MacLeod and Wang, 1979). What differs in the most recent debate is the level of attention drawn to the issue of male fertility and environmental health by the media (e.g. Begley and Glick, 1994; Hileman, 1994; Raloff, 1994*a, b*) and the publication of two recent books on this topic for the popular press (Cadbury, 1997; Colborn *et al.*, 1996). A more recent publication also examines the sociocultural context that has encouraged acceptance of the Xenoestrogen Hypothesis (Krimsky, 1999). It is thus much more likely that the general public is aware of clinical concerns about sperm quality and the future fertility of humankind, thus further fuelling debate on this topic.

This review of the available evidence for a decline in human sperm counts should be reassuring. The Danish Study by Carlsen *et al.* (1992) which initiated the recent polemical debate has been subject to so many criticisms that its claim for a worldwide, temporal trend in sperm counts is in question. Follow-up studies of sperm counts in other areas by independent researchers are contradictory in their results, making it more difficult to reach a conclusion that there is a worldwide, general decline in sperm quality. Instead, these additional studies reinforce the notion that regional variation is an important characteristic of human sperm quality, a topic that deserves further study in its own right. Whether or not areas of higher pollution (from xenoestrogens or other sources) might influence regionally low sperm counts remains unknown, but is certainly possible. Recognition of regional variation and its underlying causes should, therefore, form an explicit part of future studies aimed at assessing any long-term trends in human semen quality.

Proponents of the Danish Study have also pointed to a number of other reproductive health areas that they claim are influenced by environmental xenoestrogens, such as abnormal male genital development *in utero*, and increases in rates of testicular and breast cancers. These topics are now reviewed below.

## Other male reproductive health problems

The Xenoestrogen Hypothesis relies not just on the Danish Study for support of increasing problems with male reproductive health but also on the evidence for increasing rates of cryptorchidism (undescended testicles), hypospadias (where the urethral opening in males is abnormally positioned on the penis, e.g. on the underside) and testicular cancer. In a discussion then of the potential role of xenobiotics in human fertility, it is necessary to examine the evidence for these conditions as well. Many scholars have pointed out that interpretation of rates for hypospadias and cryptorchidism are fraught with difficulties due to differing registration systems, changes in these systems, differing diagnoses of hypospadias and cryptorchidism (e.g. boys with retractile testes are often mistakenly included in this group). These conditions are not always independent; boys born with hypospadias often have cryptorchid testes, while cryptorchidism itself significantly increases the risk of low sperm count, infertility and testicular cancer (Gill and Kogan, 1997).

### *Cryptorchidism*

There are several risk factors for neonatal cryptorchidism including toxaemia during gestation, low birth weight, prematurity, season of birth, congenital subluxation of the hip, hypospadias, a breech birth, a high maternal body mass index, and elevated maternal oestrogen levels whether endogenous or exogenously administered (Bernstein *et al.*, 1988; Depue, 1984; Gill and Kogan, 1997; Jackson and the John Radcliffe Hospital Cryptorchidism Research Group, 1988; Scorer, 1964). All these factors may differ from population to population, making it difficult to interpret possible causes of this birth defect.

The methodological standard for assessing cryptorchidism was set in the late 1950s (Scorer, 1964), and Scorer included warnings of the potential pitfalls in misdiagnosing this condition. Scorer found that 2.7% of 3312 full-term boys in the U.K. were diagnosed with cryptorchidism with a higher rate of 21% for 300 preterm, low-weight ($\leq 2500$g) babies. Two other studies have more recently attempted to replicate the methods and standards established by Scorer. Berkowitz *et al.* (1993) examined 6935 infants born at the Mount Sinai Hospital in New York City. Of these, 6360 infants were ($\geq 2500$g in birth weight with a 2.2% prevalence rate for cryptorchidism. There were 575 infants weighing $< 2500$g with a prevalence rate of 20%. These figures are analogous to Scorer's findings. In contrast, the John Radcliffe Hospital Cryptorchidism Study Group (1992) found an elevated rate of 3.8% for 7032 boys with birth weights $\geq 2500$g born primarily at the John Radcliffe Hospital, Oxford, U.K., and a 25% rate for 338 infants with birth weights below the 2500g threshold. This represents an increase in cryptorchidism of 40% for full-term infants, and a 2% increase for low birth weight babies.

There is no agreement, however, in the literature that rates of cryptorchidism are generally increasing. One of the main references used in the Danish Study, and by proponents of the Xenoestrogen Hypothesis, to support claims of rising cryptorchidism rates was Chilvers *et al.* (1984). In fact, this article reports orchiopexy rates (the surgical procedure to correct cryptorchidism) as opposed to paediatric diagnosis of undescended testicles. Rates for orchiopexy increased from 1.4% among boys less than 15 years of age in 1952, to 2.9% in 1977. This increase may, however, represent a general move towards earlier ages for performing this operation as well as the possibility that boys with retractile, as opposed to cryptorchid, testes may have been operated on, thus inflating figures for this condition (Anonymous, 1989; Gill and Kogan, 1997; The John Radcliffe Hospital Cryptorchidism Study Group, 1992). In addition, few studies of cryptorchidism are methodologically comparable, particularly when comparing earlier with more recent papers (Berkowitz *et al.*, 1993).

A very recent review of trends in the occurrence of cryptorchidism using data from the International Clearinghouse for Birth Defects Monitoring Systems (ICBDMS) concluded that there has been no general increase in rates from the mid1960s through to the late 1990s, although there are fewer data available for this kind of defect compared to hypospadias (Paulozzi, 1999).

## *Hypospadias*

Risk factors for hypospadias include subfertility (Källén and Winberg, 1982; Siffel and Czeizel, 1997; Sweet *et al.*, 1974), a family history of hypospadias or other genital anomaly (Källén and Winberg, 1982), prematurity (Källén and Winberg, 1982; Sweet *et al.*, 1974), low birth weight (Källén and Winberg, 1982), threatened abortion during pregnancy (Källén and Winberg, 1982), and presumably exposure to xenoestrogens *in utero*. Again, little is known about potential regional or populational variation in risk factors for this condition.

There are few longitudinal studies on hypospadias. Figure 4.1 plots data from those articles most frequently cited to support increasing rates of this genital anomaly, as well as more recent data from the Office of Population Censuses and Surveys, and Office for National Statistics, Congenital Anomaly Statistics Notifications, U.K. While rates do appear to increase during the 1960s and early 1970s, in many areas these level off during the 1970s (Sweden from 1974 onwards, Hungary from 1979) and even decrease (England and Wales from 1983 onwards, and Atlanta, U.S.A. from 1990 onwards). There is no general agreement in the literature about whether rates are generally increasing or not.

Paulozzi *et al.* (1997) drew on two registration systems: (1) the Metropolitan Atlanta Congenital Defects Program (MACDP) which uses active case assessments from 22 hospitals in the Atlanta, Georgia (U.S.A.) area dating from 1968; and (2) the Birth Defects Monitoring Program (BDMP), based on discharge data that were first collected in 1970 from a U.S. nationwide sample of hospitals. The problem with comparing these data is that they appear to reflect rates for total hypospadias rather than isolated ones, that is hypospadias that occur in conjunction with other abnormalities for

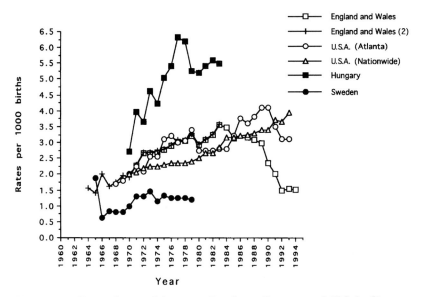

Figure 4.1. Rates for total hypospadias from Europe and U.S.A. Data are extracted from the Office of Population Censuses and Surveys, and Office for National Statistics, Congenital Anomaly Statistics Notifications, U.K.

which the risk factor may be much greater. Using these figures, hypospadias rates nearly doubled between 1968 and 1993 for the MACDP, while the BDMP rates nearly doubled from 1970 until 1993, from 20.2 to 39.7 per 10,000 births. Both sets of figures were statistically significant.

Källén and Winberg (1982) report data from the Register of Congenital Malformations in Sweden. From 1970 onwards, there was a 60% increase in registered rates for hypospadias, from about 0.8 per 1000 births to 1.3/1000. Czeizel *et al.* (1986) have also published data from Hungarian records that support an increase in hypospadias rates. Between 1970 and 1983 the rate for simple hypospadias in male live births increased from 1.08% to 4.28%. Czeizel *et al.* admit that changes in diagnosis and notification could explain some of this rise, but primarily link it to a change in the ratio of fertile to infertile couples giving birth in Hungary. Siffel and Czeizel (1977) found much higher rates of hypospadias in male offspring born to subfertile couples.

Czeizel *et al.* (1986) point out that the proportion of children born to subfertile couples would have been low in developed countries some decades ago because of the relatively high reproductive rate of fertile couples. However, in more recent years fertile couples are increasingly using effective contraceptives, while subfertile couples are able to seek increasingly effective fertility treatments. This has probably increased the proportion of children born to subfertile couples, thus altering the risk factors for hypospadias in newborn males. This hypothesis does not appear to have been applied to data from other countries, but Paulozzi (1999) does not believe that the risks associated with infertile couples could explain the magnitude of increase in hypospadias rates in some countries.

In contrast, drawing on records from the British Columbia Health Surveillance Registry, Leung *et al.* (1985) found the incidence of isolated hypospadias in British Columbia, Canada, was 3.55 per 1000 male live births, while the total incidence was 4.44 per 1000 births from 1966 to 1981. No significant increase was observed throughout this period.

Again, in a very recent review, Paulozzi (1999) reviews trends in the occurrence of hypospadias using data from the ICBDMS. These data show a large increase in some industrialized countries during the 1970s and 1980s, but with a later reversal of this trend in many cases as well. Paulozzi concluded that, given the variation in reporting methods and other factors, the rates are probably not directly comparable, and that many apparent increases in hypospadias may be due to artefacts such as better monitoring of such conditions by physicians.

Finally, some interesting data on the link between hypospadias, cryptorchidism and organochlorines has been published by Kristensen *et al.* (1997). They examined the risk for birth defects among offspring born to Norwegian farming families that used pesticides between 1967 and 1991. Although there were a higher number of males born with hypospadias and cryptorchidism among farming families compared to nonfarming families, the risk of cryptorchidism did not increase in the earlier years when organochlorine pesticides were used, and the risk of hypospadias was highest among grain farmers where the use of xenoestrogenic pesticides was low.

*Summary*

The data for both cryptorchidism rates and hypospadias are not sufficiently uniform to warrant the conclusion that a general increase in these developmental defects has occurred. In addition, there are no data that directly link the occurrence of these abnormalities to environmental pollutants.

## *Testicular cancer*

There is little doubt that rates of testicular cancer have increased dramatically in developed parts of the world in recent decades (Adami *et al.*, 1994; Forman and Moller, 1994; Gilliland and Key, 1995; Hatton *et al.*, 1995; Liu *et al.*, 1999; McCredie *et al.*, 1995; Stone *et al.*, 1991; Weir *et al.*, 1999). But, is this increase due to the increase in environmental xenoestrogens and reproductive abnormalities as has been suggested in several publications (Giwercman *et al.*, 1993; Jensen *et al.*, 1995; Kelce and Wilson, 1997; Sharpe, 1993; Sharpe and Skakkebaek, 1993; Skakkebaek *et al.*, 1998; Toppari *et al.*, 1996)? Other factors are implicated in this rise, such as an increasingly early age at puberty which may expose males to endogenous reproductive hormones for longer periods, prenatal exposure to smoking, and lack of exercise (Bergstrom *et al.*, 1996; Clemmesen, 1997; United Kingdom Testicular Cancer Study Group, 1994; Weir *et al.*, 1998).

I have found only one published study that attempts to relate the incidence of testicular cancer to the occurrence of environmental xenoestrogens such as the organochlorines. Cocco and Benichou (1998) studied the relationship between adipose concentrations of $p,p'$-DDE in various parts of the U.S.A. and mortality rates from testicular and prostate cancer. There was no positive association for either. Furthermore, rates for testicular cancer among circumpolar Inuit are much lower than in Western countries. The Inuit have been exposed to much higher levels of organochlorines than populations in more southerly latitudes (Prener *et al.*, 1996). These statistics reinforce the idea that male cancers of the reproductive tract are more likely to be associated with factors other than environmental xenoestrogens. Similarly, evidence for any increase in testicular cancer among DES-exposed sons remains controversial (Giusti *et al.*, 1995; Hatch *et al.*, 1998), although laboratory studies of DES-exposed male mice showed that 5% of the exposed population developed a rare form of testicular cancer – rete testis carcinoma (McLachlan *et al.*, 1998).

## Xenoestrogens and female reproductive health

Aside from the weight of criticisms levelled against the Danish Study, a fundamental problem with the Xenoestrogen Hypothesis is the almost exclusive association with male reproductive problems (Sharpe and Skakkebaek, 1993; see also Giwercman *et al.*, 1993; Jensen *et al.*, 1995; Sharpe, 1993). This is especially problematic given the reliance for this Hypothesis on the results of DES exposure, since the latter has had far greater effects on the female reproductive system and was first noticed in women (Stillman, 1982). There is also conclusive evidence for a decrease in female fertility among DES-exposed daughters in comparison to un-exposed women, but no similar data for a decrease in fertility (or libido) among DES-exposed sons (Senekjian *et al.*, 1988; Wilcox *et al.*, 1995). This is in spite of the fact that significantly more men who had been exposed to DES *in utero* reported genital abnormal-ities compared to a nonexposed control group. Studies of male and female mice exposed to DES *in utero* also show stronger effects on female rather than male reproductive function (McClachlan, 1977). We would have to expect then that any reproductive problems in women resulting from xenobiotics would be reported at least coincident with male problems if not much earlier. So far, this does not appear to be the case. In fact, the notification rate for abnormalities of the vagina and external genitalia in females declined from 2.14 per 10,000 births in 1969, to 1.53 per 10,000 births in 1983 (Matlai and Beral, 1985), the same period of time for which increasing cases of cryptorchidism and hypospadias are apparently reported (Figure 4.2).

The proponents of the Xenoestrogen Hypothesis do cite the

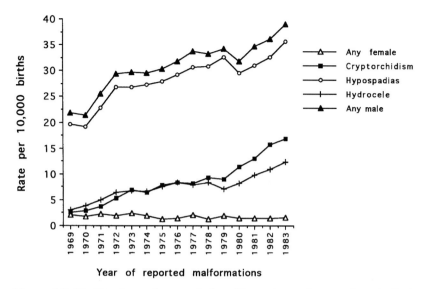

Figure 4.2. Notifications of congenital malformations of external genitalia in England and Wales, 1969–83. Data are from Matlai and Beral, 1985.

rising incidence of breast cancer as one marker of proof for female problems, but there does not seem to be much reason to blame xenobiotics for these statistics. There are a number of generally accepted reasons for the increases in breast cancer rates in developed countries, including heredity, modern dietary changes with a higher lipid and lower fibre intake, obesity, lower rates of exercise, higher exposures to endogenous reproductive steroids caused by earlier menarche, lower and later fertility, and shorter periods of lactation (Adlercreutz *et al.*, 1989; Armstrong *et al.*, 1981; Bagga *et al.*, 1995; Bernstein *et al.*, 1987; Casagrande *et al.*, 1979; Henderson *et al.*, 1985; Hill *et al.*, 1977; Kirschner *et al.*, 1982; La Vecchia *et al.*, 1985; MacMahon *et al.*, 1982; Sherman *et al.*, 1982; Toniolo, 1997; Toniolo *et al.*, 1995; Trichopoulos *et al.*, 1984).

In addition, while earlier studies were conflicting about whether exposure to organochlorines increased the risk of breast cancer, the majority of recent studies (with larger sample sizes) show no association between exposure to organochlorines and the risk of breast cancer (Adami *et al.*, 1995; Krieger *et al.*, 1994; van't-Veer, 1997; Zheng *et al.*, 1999), even in countries that still routinely use

DDT as a pesticide (Lopez-Carrillo, 1997; Schecter *et al.*, 1997). Some studies even show a reduced risk among women with a higher exposure which may relate to the anti-oestrogenic activity of some of the organochlorines (Helzlsouer *et al.*, 1999; Hunter *et al.*, 1997; Safe and Zacharewski, 1997). Furthermore, a recent analysis of cancer rates among DES-exposed ($n = 4536$) and nonexposed ($n = 544$) daughters showed no increase in the risk for breast or other cancers except for clear-cell adenocarcinoma among the former (Hatch *et al.*, 1998). As noted, a major limitation of this study was the comparatively young age of the women, most of whom were still under 50 years. It, therefore, remains uncertain whether risks of breast and other cancers will dramatically increase at older ages among DES-exposed daughters. This problem is especially relevant since DES-exposed mothers have an increased risk of breast cancer (Giusti *et al.*, 1995).

In general, the lack of any reported increase in female reproductive dysfunction or breast cancers reinforces the impression that environmental xenoestrogens are not currently causing problems for human reproductive health.

## Human fertility

Finally, it should be stressed that the link between sperm counts alone and fertility is unclear (Bartoov *et al.*, 1993; Forti and Serio, 1993; MacLeod and Gold, 1951). The currently accepted fertility threshold of $20 \times 10^6$/ml does not allow the prediction of individual fertility but is merely a useful guideline (Hargreave and Elton, 1983; Polansky and Lamb, 1988). Similarly useful guidelines have been published for sperm morphology (Kruger *et al.*, 1986, 1988). In 1951, MacLeod and Gold stated that, '*on the basis of sperm count alone* a semen specimen with a count of 140 million/cc ($140 \times 10^6$/ml) does not have a higher fertility potential than one of 40 million/cc' (pp. 442–3, original emphasis). In other words, there is no linear relationship between sperm counts and fertility. Bartoov *et al* (1993:69) in their study of the relationship between various semen parameters and fertility concluded that:

male fertility potential is a multifactorial phenomenon dependent upon various semen properties? Therefore, evaluation of fertility potential by the deviation of a single 'major' semen characteristic from normal, or that of a set of semen characteristics assessed on an equal basis, will not detect the maximum expression of fertility and will not allow differentiation of males of known fertility and suspected infertility.

Perhaps, then, the most telling evidence for a detrimental effect of environmental pollutants on human reproduction would be if there was any recent evidence (particularly during the past 50 years) for a decrease in human fertility. Judging by the other chapters in this volume (summarized in the Introduction) rates for infertility vary widely depending on the population under review. Such rates are also difficult to interpret given the changing prevalence of sexually transmitted diseases (STDs), and an increasing public awareness of infertility and the new technologies that are available that may lead to an increase in the reporting of infertility. Recent data from the U.S. National Center for Health Statistics indicates that self-reported rates for female infertility remained stable during the 1980s, with a slight increase documented in the 1995 dataset from 8 to 10% (Stephen and Chandra, 1998). This increase has been attributed to the larger numbers of women from the baby-boom cohort who delayed childbearing until their less fecund years (Chandra and Stephen, 1998).

## Conclusion

The application of the Xenoestrogen Hypothesis to humans is primarily one from analogy, either with wildlife studies, or from *in vitro* and *in vivo* laboratory experiments. As mentioned above, most of these studies involve acute exposures to high levels of xenobiotics rather chronic exposures to low doses. Moreover, some studies show that the effects of xenobiotics may be beneficial due to specific effects of the substances involved. The anti-oestrogenic effect of some of the organochlorines is a case in point and has led to the reduction of the incidence of breast cancer in some areas. In addition, our exposure to naturally occurring xenoestrogens, such as phytoestrogens, is likely both now and historically to be higher than exposure to industrially produced xenoestrogens.

The evidence for detrimental effects from xenoestrogens specifically on human reproductive health remains questionable. There is no consensus that sperm counts are declining on a worldwide basis although there are regions where a decline has certainly been documented. On the other hand, there are regions where an increase is also documented. Whether such changes represent ongoing trends is unclear and will require further monitoring. As for other indications of male reproductive function, there are no consistent data showing an increase in the incidence of hypospadias and cryptorchidism, nor are there any studies that relate these conditions specifically to exposure to xenoestrogens. Relying on this form of evidence, therefore, to support the Xenoestrogen Hypothesis is untenable. Nor is there good evidence to associate the increase in rates of testicular cancer with environmental xenoestrogens.

A major omission in the Xenoestrogen Hypothesis is the failure to deal adequately with female reproductive health. There are no data to support an increase in female reproductive health problems, including breast cancer, that could be associated with xenoestrogens, other than through clinical exposure to DES. Finally, as we pass the six billion threshold for human individuals on this planet, there are no data to support a general increase in human infertility that might be associated with xenobiotics.

Richard Sharpe – one of the most vocal advocates for the detrimental effects of xenoestrogens – has suggested in recent years that it is 'equally possible that such compounds pose no significant risk to humans' (Turner and Sharpe, 1997). The risk from xenobiotics has no doubt been exaggerated, partly due to the public attention this issue has received and continues to receive in the popular press. This review paper should reassure us that a real decline in sperm counts is unlikely in human populations. We should, however, continue to be concerned about the potential health effects of all environmental pollutants. Such concern should translate into efforts to continue monitoring the levels and effects of such substances, particularly for their teratogenic effect on unborn children.

# Acknowledgements

Thanks are due to Robert Aunger who made valuable criticisms of early versions of this chapter. This work was supported by the Royal Society.

# References

Abell, A., Ernst, E., Bonde, J. P. (1994) High sperm density among members of organic farmers' association. *The Lancet* **343**:1498.

Adami, H., Bergström, R., Möhner, M., Zatonsk, W., Storm, H., Ekbom, A., Tretli, S., Teppo, L., Ziegler, H., Rahu, M., Gurevicius, R., Stengrvics, A. (1994) Testicular cancer in nine northern European countries. *International Journal of Cancer* **59**:33–8.

Adami, H., Lipworth, L., Titus-Ernstoff, L., Hsieh, C., Hanberg, A., Ahlborg, U., Baron, J., Trichopoulos, D. (1995) Organochlorine compounds and estrogen – related cancers in women. *Cancer Causes and Control* **6**:551–66.

Adamopoulos, D. A., Pappa, A., Nicopoulou, S., Andreou, E., Karamertzanis, M., Michopoulos, J., Deligianni, V., Simou, M. (1996) Seminal volume and total sperm number trends in men attending subfertility clinics in the Greater Athens area during the period 1977–1993. *Human Reproduction* **11**:1936–41.

Adlercreutz, H., Fotsis, T., Höckerstedt, K., Hämäläinen, E., Bannwart, C., Bloigu, S., Valtonen, A., Ollus, A. (1989) Diet and urinary estrogen profile in premenopausal omnivorous and vegetarian women and in premenopausal women with breast cancer. *Journal of Steroid Biochemistry* **34**:1–6.

Andolz, P., Bielsa, M., Vila, J. (1999) Evolution of semen quality in Northeastern Spain: a study in 22 759 infertile men over a 36 year period. *Human Reproduction* **14**:731–5.

Anonymous (1989) Testicular descent revisited. *The Lancet* February **18**:360–1.

Anonymous (1998) Poisoned lives. *New Scientist* August **28**:19.

Armstrong, B. K., Brown, J. B., Clarke, H. T., Hahnel, R., Masarei, J. R., Ratajczak, T. (1981) Diet and reproductive hormones: a study of vegetarian and nonvegetarian postmenopausal women. *Journal of the National Cancer Institute* **67**:761–7.

Arnold, S., Klotz, D., Collins, B., Vonier, P., Guillette, L. J., McLachlan, J. (1996) Synergistic activation of estrogen receptor with combinations of environmental chemicals. *Science* **272**:1489–92.

Ashby, J., Lefevre, P., Odum, J., Harris, C., Routledge, E., Sumpter, J. (1997) Synergy between synthetic oestrogens. *Nature* **385**:494.

Auger, J., Kunstmann, J. M., Czyglik, F., Jouannet, P. (1995) Decline in semen quality among fertile men in Paris during past 20 years. *New England Journal of Medicine* **332**:281–5.

Bagga, D., Ashley, J., Geffrey, S., Wang, H., Barnard, R. J., Korenman, S., Heber, D. (1995) Effects of a very low fat, high fiber diet on serum hormones and menstrual function: implications for breast cancer prevention. *Cancer* **76**:2491–6.

Bahadur, G., Ling, K., Katz, M. (1996) Statistical modelling reveals demography and time are the main contributing factors in global sperm count changes between 1938 and 1996. *Human Reproduction* **11**:2635–9.

Baird, D. D., Wilcox, A. J. (1986) Future fertility after prenatal exposure to cigarette smoke. *Fertility and Sterility* **46**:368–72.

Bartoov, B., Sites, F., Pansky, M., Lederman, H., Caspi, E., Soffer, Y. (1993) Estimating fertility potential via semen analysis data. *Human Reproduction* **8**:65–70.

Becker, S., Berhane, K. (1997) A meta-analysis of 61 sperm count studies revisited. *Fertility and Sterility* **67**:1103–8.

Begley, S., Glick, D. (1994) The estrogen complex. *Newsweek* **123**:44–5.

Bendvold, E. (1989) Semen quality in Norwegian men over a twenty year period. *International Journal of Fertility* **34**:401–4.

Bendvold, E., Golttlieb, C., Bygdeman, M., Eneroth, P. (1991) Depressed semen quality in Swedish men from barren couples: a study over three decades. *Archives of Andrology* **26**:189–94.

Benshushan, A., Shoshani, O., Paltiel, O., Schenker, J. G., Lewin, A. (1997) Is there really a decrease in sperm parameters among healthy young men? A survey of sperm donations during 15 years. *Journal of Assisted Reproduction and Genetics* **14**:347–53.

Bentley, G., Vitzthum, V., Caceres, E., Spielvogel, H., Crone, K., May, L., Chatterton, R. (1998) Reproduction and ecology in Provincia Aroma, Bolivia: fecundity of women with low levels of salivary progesterone. *American Journal of Physical Anthropology Supplement* **26**:110.

Bergstrom, R., Adami, H., Mohner, M., Zatonski, W., Storm, H., Ekbom, A., Tretli, S., Teppo, L., Akre, O., Hakulinen, T. (1996) Increase in testicular cancer incidence in six European countries: a birth cohort phenomenon. *Journal of the National Cancer Institute* **88**:727–33.

Berkowitz, G. S., Lapinski, R. H., Dolgin, S. E., Gazella, J. G., Bodian, C. A., Holzman, I. R. (1993) Prevalence and natural history of cryptorchidism. *Pediatrics* **92**:44–9.

Bernstein, L., Ross, R., Lobo, R., Hanisch, R., Krailo, M., Henderson, B. (1987) The effects of moderate physical activity on menstrual-cycle patterns in adolescence: implications for breast cancer prevention. *British Journal of Cancer* **55**:681–5.

Bernstein, L., Pike, M., Depue, R., Ross, R., Moore, J., Henderson, B. (1988)

Maternal hormone levels in early gestation of cryptorchid males: a case – control study. *British Journal of Cancer* **58**:379–81.

Bitman, J., Cecil, H. (1970) Estrogenic activity of DDT analogs and polychlorinated biphenyls. *Journal of Agriculture and Food Chemicals* **18**:1108–12.

Bostofte, E., Serup, J., Rebbe, H. (1983) Has the fertility of Danish men declined through the years in terms of semen quality? A comparison of semen qualities between 1952 and 1972. *International Journal of Fertility* **28**:91–5.

Bradbury, J. (1996) UK panics over phthalates in babymilk formulae. *The Lancet* **347**:1541.

Brake, A., Krause, W. (1992) Decreasing quality of semen. *British Medical Journal* **305**:1498.

Bromwich, P., Cohen, J., Stewart, I., Walker, A. (1994) Decline in sperm counts: an artifact of changed reference range of 'normal'? *British Medical Journal* **309**:19–22.

Brotons, J. A., Olea-Serrano, M. F., Villalobos, M., Pedraza, V., Olea, N. (1995) Xenoestrogens released from lacquer coatings in food cans. *Environmental Health Perspectives* **103**:608–12.

Bujan, L., Mansat, A., Pontonnier, F., Mieusset, R. (1996) Time series analysis of sperm concentration in fertile men in Toulouse, France between 1977 and 1992. *British Medical Journal* **312**:471–2.

Cadbury, D. (1997) *The feminization of nature: our future at risk*. London: Hamish Hamilton.

Cagnacci, A., Maxia, N., Volpe, A. (1999) Diurnal variation of semen quality in human males. *Human Reproduction* **14**:106–9.

Carlsen, E., Giwercman, A., Keiding, N., Skakkebaek (1992) Evidence for decreasing quality of semen during past 50 years. *British Medical Journal* **305**:609–13.

Carson, R. (1962) *Silent spring*. Boston, MA: Houghton Mifflin.

Casagrande, J. T., Louie, E. W., Pike, M. C., Roy, S., Ross, R. K., Henderson, B. E. (1979) 'Incessant ovulation' and ovarian cancer. *The Lancet* Vol. 2(July):170–2.

Cassidy, A., Bingham, S., Setchell, K. (1994) Biological effects of soy protein rich in isoflavones on the menstrual cycle of premenopausal women. *American Journal of Clinical Nutrition* **60**:333–40.

Chandra, A., Stephen, E. (1998) Impaired fecundity in the United States: 1982–1995. *Family Planning Perspectives* **30**:34–42.

Chia, S., Tay, S., Lim, S. (1998) What constitutes a normal seminal analysis? Semen parameters of 243 fertile men. *Human Reproduction* **13**:3394–8.

Chilvers, C., Pike, M., Forman, D., Fogelman, K., Wadsworth, M. (1984) Apparent doubling of frequency of undescended testis in England and Wales in 1962–81. *The Lancet* Vol.2, No.8398:330–2.

Clark, L. B., Rosen, R. T., Hartman, T. G., Louis, J. B., Suffet, I. H., Lippincott, R. L., Rosen, J. D. (1992) Determination of alkylphenol ethoxylates and their acetic acid derivatives in drinking water by particle beam liquid chromatography/mass spectrometry. *International Journal of Environmental and Analytical Chemistry* **47**:167–80.

Clemmesen, J. (1997) Is smoking during pregnancy a cause of testicular cancer? *Ugeskrift for Laeger* **159**:6815–19.

Cocco, P., Benichou, J. (1998) Mortality from cancer of the male reproductive tract and environmental exposure to the anti-androgen *p,p'*– dichlorodiphe-nyldichloroethylene in the United States. *Oncology* **55**:334–9.

Colborn, T., Peterson Myers, J., Dumanoski, D. (1996) *Our stolen future: how man-made chemicals are threatening our fertility intelligence and survival*. Boston, MA: Little, Brown and Co.

Comhaire, F. H. (1993) Methods to evaluate reproductive health of the human male. *Reproductive Toxicology* **7**:39–46.

Cook, R., Golombok, S. (1995) A survey of semen donation: Phase II – the view of the donors. *Human Reproduction* **10**:951–9.

Czeizel, A., Toth, J., Czcvenits, E. (1986) Increased birth prevalence of isolated hypospadias in Hungary. *Acta Paediatrica Hungarica* **27**:329–37.

Davis, B., Maronpot, R., Heindel, J. (1994*a*) Di-(2-ethylhexyl) phthalate suppresses estradiol and ovulation in cycling rats. *Toxicology and Applied Pharmacology* **128**:216–23.

Davis, B., Weaver, R., Gaines, L., Heindel, J. (1994*b*) Mono-(2-ethylhexyl) phthalate suppresses estradiol production independent of FSH-cAMP stimu-lation in rat granulosa cells. *Toxicology and Applied Pharmacology* **128**:224–8.

de Mouzon, J., Thonneau, P., Spira, A., Multigner, L. (1996) Declining sperm count: semen quality has declined among men born in France since 1950. *British Medical Journal* **313**:43.

Depue, R. H. (1984) Maternal and gestational factors affecting the risk of cryptorchidism and inguinal hernia. *International Journal of Epidemiology* **13**:311–18.

DeWailly, E., Nantel, A., Weber, J. P., Meyer, F. (1989) High levels of PCBs in breast milk of Inuit women from Arctic Quebec. *Bulletin of Environmental Contamination and Toxicology* **43**:641–6.

Eccersley, A. (1996) Declining sperm count: data from two groups should not have been combined in analysis. *British Medical Journal* **313**:49.

Ellison, P., Lipson, S., O'Rourke, M., Bentley, G., Harrigan, A., Panter-Brick, C., Vitzthum, V. (1993) Population variation in ovarian function. *The Lancet* **342**: No.8868, August 14th 433–4.

Farrow, S. (1994) Falling sperm quality: Fact or fiction. *British Medical Journal* **309**:1–2.

Farrow, S. (1996) Results cannot be generalized. *British Medical Journal* **313**:43–4.

Feichtinger, W. (1991) Environmental factors and fertility. *Human Reproduction* **6**:1170–5.

Fein, G. G., Jacobson, J. L., Jacobson, S. W., Schwartz, P. M., Dowler, J. K. (1984) Prenatal exposure to polychlorinated biphenyls: effects on birth size and gestational age. *Journal of Pediatrics* **105**:316–20.

Fisch, H., Goluboff, E. T. (1996) Geographic variations in sperm counts: a potential cause of bias in studies of semen quality. *Fertility and Sterility* **65**:1044–6.

Fisch, H., Goluboff, E. T., Olson, J. H. (1996) Semen analysis in 1,283 men from the United States over a 25-year period: no decline in quality. *Fertility and Sterility* **65**:1009–14.

Forman, D., Moller, H. (1994) Testicular cancer. *Cancer Surveys* **19–20**:323–41.

Forti, G., Serio, M. (1993) Male infertility: is its rising incidence due to better methods of detection or an increasing frequency. *Human Reproduction* **8**:1153–4.

Fox, G. A. (1992) Epidemiological and pathobiological evidence of contaminant-induced alterations in sexual development in free-living wildlife. In: Colborn, T., Clement, C. (eds.) *Chemical-induced alterations of sexual differentiation: a review of effects in humans and rodents* (pp. 147–58). Princeton, NJ: Princeton University Press.

Fry, D. M., Toone, C. K. (1981) DDT-induced feminization of gull embryos. *Science* **213**:922–4.

Gellert, R., Heinrichs, W., Swedloff, R. (1972) DDT homologues: estrogen-like effects on the vagina, uterus and pituitary of the rat. *Endocrinology* **91**:1095–100.

Giam, C., Chan, H., Neff, G., Atlas, E. (1978) Phthalate ester plasticizers: a new class of marine pollutant. *Science* **199**:419–21.

Gill, B., Kogan, S. (1997) Cryptorchidism: current concepts. *Pediatric Clinics of North America* **44**:1211–27.

Gilliland, F., Key, C. (1995) Male genital cancers. *Cancer* **75**:295–315.

Ginsburg, J., Okolo, S., Prelevic, G., Hardiman, P. (1994) Residence in the London area and sperm density. *The Lancet* **343**:230.

Giusti, R., Iwamoto, K., Hatch, E. (1995) Diethylstilbestrol revisited: a review of the long-term health effects. *Annals of Internal Medicine* **122**:778–88.

Giwercman, A., Carlsen, E., Keiding, N., Skakkebaek, N. E. (1993) Evidence for increasing incidence of abnormalities of the human testis: a review. *Environmental Health Perspectives* **101**:65–71.

Gladen, B. C., Rogan, W. J., Hardy, P., Thullen, J., Tingelstad, J., Tully, M. (1988) Development after exposure to polychlorinated biphenyls and dichlorodiphenyl dichloroethene transplacentally and through human milk. *Journal of Pediatrics* **113**:991–5.

Gray, J. L. E. (1992) Chemical-induced alterations of sexual differentiation: a review of effects in humans and rodents. In: Colborn, T., Clement, C. (eds.) *Chemically induced alterations in sexual and functional development: the wildlife/human connection* (pp. 203–30). Princeton, NJ: Princeton Scientific Publishing Co. Inc.

Gray, T. J., Gangolli, S. D. (1986) Aspects of the testicular toxicity of phthalate esters. *Environmental Health Perspectives* **65**:229–35.

Guillette, L. J., Pickford, D., Crain, D., Rooney, A., Percival, H. (1996) Reduction in penis size and plasma testosterone concentrations in juvenile alligators living in a contaminated environment. *General and Comparative Endocrinology* **101**:32–42.

Guzelian, P. S. (1982) Comparative toxicology of chlordecone (Kepone) in humans and experimental animals. *Annual Review of Pharmacology and Toxicology* **22**:89–113.

Haidl, G., Jung, A., Schill, W. (1996) Ageing and sperm function. *Human Reproduction* **11**:558–60.

Handelsman, D. J. (1997) Sperm output of healthy men in Australia: magnitude of bias due to self-selected volunteers. *Human Reproduction* **12**:2701–5.

Hargreave, T., Elton, R. (1983) Is conventional sperm analysis of any use? *British Journal of Urology* **55**:774–9.

Hatch, E., Palmer, J. R., Titus-Ernstoff, L., Noller, K. L., Kaufman, R. H., Mittendorf, R., Robboy, S., Hyer, M., Cowan, C. M., Adam, E., Colton, T., Hartge, P., Hoover, R. N. (1998) Cancer risk in women exposed to diethylstilbestrol *in utero*. *Journal of the American Medical Association* **280**:630–4.

Hatton, M., Paul, J., Harding, M., MacFarlane, G., Robertson, A., Kaye, S. (1995) Changes in the incidence and mortality of testicular cancer in Scotland with particular reference to the outcome of older patients treated for nonseminomatous germ cell tumours. *European Journal of Cancer* **31A**:1487–91.

Helzlsouer, K., Alberg, A., Huang, H., Hoffman, S., Strickland, P., Brock, J., Burse, V., Needhamn, L., Bell, D., Lavigne, J., Yager, J., Comstock, G. (1999) Serum concentrations of organochlorine compounds and the subsequent development of breast cancer. *Cancer Epidemiology Biomarkers and Prevention* **8**:525–32.

Henderson, B. E., Ross, R. K., Judd, H. L., Krailo, M. D., Pike, M. C. (1985) Do regular ovulatory cycles increase breast cancer risk? *Cancer* **56**:1206–8.

Henderson, B. E., Ross, R., Bernstein, L. (1988) Estrogens as a cause of human cancer: the Richard and Hinda Rosenthal Foundation Award Lecture. *Cancer Research* **48**:246–53.

Higuchi, K. E. (1976) *PCB poisoning and pollution*. New York: Academic Press.

Hileman, B. (1994) Environmental estrogens linked to reproductive abnormalities, cancer. *Chemical and Engineering News* **72**:19–23.

Hill, P., Chan, P., Cohen. L., Wynder, E., Kuno, K. (1977) Diet and endocrine-related cancer. *Cancer* **39**:1820–6.

Hirayama, C. (1976) Clinical aspects of PCB poisoning. In: Higuchi, K. (ed.) *PCB poisoning and pollution* (pp. 87–104). New York: Academic Press.

Hughes C. L. Jr. (1988) Phytochemical mimicry of reproductive hormones and modulation of herbivore fertility by phytoestrogens. *Environmental Health Perspectives* **78**:171–5.

Hunt, L. (1997) Why today's man is losing his virility. *The Independent*, 6 January.

Hunter, D., Hankinson, S., Laden, F., Colditz, G., Manson, J., Willett, W., Speizer, F. E., Wolff, M. (1997) Plasma organochlorine levels and the risk of breast cancer. *New England Journal of Medicine* **337**:1253–8.

Imajima, T., Shono, T., Zakaria, O., Suita, S. (1997) Prenatal phthalate causes cryptorchidism postnatally by induced transabdominal ascent of the testis in fetal rats. *Journal of Pediatric Surgery* **32**:18–21.

Irvine, S., Cawood, E., Richardson, D., MacDonald, E., Aitken, J. (1996) Evidence of deteriorating semen quality in the United Kingdom: birth cohort study in 577 men in Scotland over 11 years. *British Medical Journal* **312**:467–70.

Jackson, M. and the John Radcliffe Hospital Cryptorchidism Research Group (1988) The epidemiology of cryptorchidism. *Hormone Research* **30**:153–6.

Jenkins, R., Nuttall, N. (1996) Concern grows over suspect baby milk. *The Times*, 28 May.

Jensen, A. A. (1991) Levels and trends of environmental chemicals in human milk. In: Jensen, A. A., Slorach, S. A. (eds.) *Chemical contaminants in human milk* (pp. 45–198). Boca Raton, FL: CRC Press.

Jensen, A. A., Slorach, S. A. (eds.) (1991*a*) *Chemical contaminants in human milk.* Boca Raton, FL: CRC Press.

Jensen, A. A., Slorach, S. A. (1991*b*) Factors affecting the levels of residues in human milk. In: Jensen, A. A., Slorach, S. A. (eds.) *Chemical contaminants in human milk* (pp. 199–208). Boca Raton, FL: CRC Press.

Jensen, T. K., Toppari, J., Keiding, N., Skkabaek, N. E. (1995) Do environmental estrogens contribute to the decline in male reproductive health. *Clinical Chemistry* **41**:1896–901.

Jobling, S., Reynolds, T., White, R., Parker, M. G., Sumpter, J. P. (1995) A variety of environmentally persistent chemicals including some phthalate plasticizers, are weakly estrogenic. *Environmental Health Perspectives* **103**:582–7.

Jobling, S., Sheahan, D., Osborne, J., Matthiesson, P., Sumpter, J. (1996) Inhibition of testicular growth in rainbow trout (*Oncorhynchus mykiss*) exposed to estrogenic alkylphenolic chemicals. *Environmental Toxicology and Chemistry* **15**:194–202.

Joffe, M. (1996) Decreased fertility in Britain compared with Finland. *The Lancet* **347**:1519–22.

John Radcliffe Hospital Cryptorchidism Study Group (1992) Cryptorchidism:

a prospective study of 7500 consecutive male births, 1984–8. *Archives of Disease in Childhood* **67**:892–9.

Johnson, L. (1986) Spermatogenesis and aging in the human. *Journal of Andrology* **7**:331–54.

Jørgensen, N., Auger, J., Giwercman, A., Irvine, D., Jensen, T., Jouannet, P., Keiding, N., le Bon, C., MacDonald, E., Pekuri, A., Scheike, T., Simonsen, M., Suominen, J., Skakkebaek, N. (1997) Semen analysis performed by different laboratory teams: an intervariation study. *International Journal of Andrology* **20**:201–8.

Kaldas, R., Hughes, C. J. (1989) Reproductive and general metabolic effects of phytoestrogens in mammals. *Reproductive Toxicology* **3**:81–9.

Källén, B., Winberg, J. (1982) An epidemiological study of hypospadias in Sweden. *Acta Paediatrica Scandinavica Supplement* **293**:1–21.

Keiding, N., Skakkebæk, N. (1996) Rise in semen quality between 1970 and 1990 in meta-analysis was nonsignificant. *British Medical Journal* **313**:44.

Kelce, W. R., Wilson, E. M. (1997) Environmental antiandrogens: developmental effects, molecular mechanisms, and clinical implications. *Journal of Molecular Medicine* **75**:198–207.

Kelce, W. R., Stone, C., Laws, S., Gray, L., Kemppainen, J., Wilson, E. (1995) Persistent DDT metabolite *pp'*-DDE is a potent androgen receptor antagonist. *Nature* **375**:581–5.

Kimbrough, R. D. (1991) Toxicological implications of human milk residues as indicated by toxicological and epidemiological studies. In: Jensen, A. A., Slorach, S. A. (eds.) *Chemical contaminants in human milk* (pp. 271–84). Boca Raton, FL: CRC Press.

Kirschner, M. A., Schneider, G., Ertel, N. H., Worton, E. (1982) Obesity, androgens, estrogens, and cancer risk. *Cancer Research* **42**:3281–5.

Krieger, N., Wolff, M., Hiatt, R., Rivera, M., Vogelman, J., Orentriech, N. (1994) Breast cancer and serum organochlorines: a prospective study among white, black, and Asian women. *Journal of the National Cancer Institute* **86**:589–99.

Krimsky, S. (1999) *Hormonal chaos: the scientific and social origins of the environmental endocrine hypothesis.* Baltimore, MD: Johns Hopkins University Press.

Krishnan, A. V., Stathis, P., Permuth, S.F., Tokes, L., Feldman, D. (1993) Bisphenol-A: an estrogenic substance is released from polycarbonate flasks during autoclaving. *Endocrinology* **132**:2279–86.

Kristensen, P., Irgens, L. M., Andersen, A., Snellingen Bye, A., Sundheim, L. (1997) Birth defects among offspring of Norwegian farmers, 1967–1991. *Epidemiology* **8**:537–44.

Kruger, T. F., Menkveld, R., Stander, F. S., Lombard, C. J., Van der Merwe, J. P., van Zyle, J. A., Smith, K. (1986) Sperm morphologic features as a prognostic factor in *in vitro* fertilization. *Fertility and Sterility* **46**:1118–23.

Kruger, T. F., Acosta, A. A., Simmons, K. F., Swanson, R. J., Matta, J. F.,

Oehninger, S. (1988) Predictive value of abnormal sperm morphology in *in vitro* fertilization. *Fertility and Sterility* **49**:112–17.

Kuratsune, M., Shapiro, R. E. E. (1984) *PCB poisoning in Japan and Taiwan.* New York: Alan R. Liss.

La Vecchia, D. A., Di Pietro, S., Franceschi, S., Negri, E., Parazzini, F. (1985) Menstrual cycle patterns and the risk of breast disease. *European Journal of Cancer and Clinical Oncology* **21**:417–22.

Lemcke, B., Behre, H., Nieschlag, E. (1997) Frequently subnormal semen profiles of normal volunteers recruited over 17 years. *International Journal of Andrology* **20**:144–52.

Lerchl, A., Nieschlag, E. (1996) Decreasing sperm counts? A critical (re)view. *Experimental and Clinical Endocrinology and Diabetes* **104**:301–7.

Leto, S., Frensilli, F. J. (1981) Changing parameters of donor semen. *Fertility and Sterility* **36**:766.

Leung, T., Baird, P., McGillivray, B. (1985) Hypospadias in British Columbia. *American Journal of Medical Genetics* **21**:39–48.

Levine, R., Mathew, R., Chenault, C., Brown, M., Hurtt, M., Bentley, K., Mohr, K. L., Working, P. K. (1990) Differences in the quality of semen in outdoor workers during summer and winter. *New England Journal of Medicine* **323**:12–16.

Levine, R. J., Brown, M. H., Bell, M., Shue, F., Greenberg, G. N., Bordson, B. L. (1992) Air-conditioned environments do not prevent deterioration of human semen quality during the summer. *Fertility and Sterility* **57**:1075–83.

Lipshultz, L. I. (1996) 'The debate continues' – the continuing debate over the possible decline in sperm quantity. *Fertility and Sterility* **65**:909–11.

Liu, S., Wen, S., Mao, Y., Mery, L., Rouleau, J. (1999) Birth cohort effects underlying the increasing testicular cancer incidence in Canada. *Canadian Journal of Public Health* **90**:176–80.

Loganathan, B., Tanabe, S., Hidaka, Y., Kawano, M., Hidaka, H., Tatsukawa, R. (1993) Temporal trends of persistent organochlorine residues in human adipose tissue from Japan. *Environmental Pollution* **81**:31–9.

Loganathan, B. G., Kannan, K. (1994) Global organochlorine contamination trends: an overview. *Ambio* **23**:187–91.

Lopez-Carillo, L., Blair, A., Lopez-Cervantes, M., Cebrian, M., Rueda, C., Reyes, R., Mohar, A., Bravo, J. (1997) Dichlorodiphenyltrichloroethane serum levels and breast cancer risk: a case–control study from Mexico. *Cancer Research* **57**:3728–32.

Lü, Y., Wong, P. (1984) Dermatological, medical and, laboratory findings of patients in Taiwan and their treatments. In: Kuratsune, M., Shapiro, R. E. (eds.) *PCB poisoning in Japan and Taiwan* (pp. 81–115). New York: Alan R. Liss.

MacLeod, J., Gold, R. Z. (1951) The male factor in fertility and infertility. II. Spermatozoon counts in 1000 cases of infertile marriage. *Journal of Urology* **66**:436–49.

MacLeod, J., Wang, Y. (1979) Male fertility potential in terms of semen quality: a review of the past, a study of the present. *Fertility and Sterility* **31**:103–16.

MacMahon, B., Trichopoulos, D., Brown, J., Anderson, A. P., Aoki, K., Cole, P., DeWaard, F., Kauraniemi, T., Morgan, R. W., Purde, M., Ravnihar, B., Stormby, N., Westlund, K., Woo, N. (1982) Age at menarche, probability of ovulation and breast cancer risk. *International Journal of Cancer* **29**:13–16.

Macomber, D., Sanders M (1929) The spermatozoa count: its value in the diagnosis, prognosis, and treatment of sterility. *New England Journal of Medicine* **200**:981–4.

Mallidis, C., Howard, E., Baker, H. (1991) Variation of semen quality in normal men. *International Journal of Andrology* **14**:99–107.

Matilsky, M., Battino, S., Ben-Ami, M., Geslevich, Y., Eyali, V., Shalev, E. (1993) The effect of ejaculatory frequency on semen characteristics of normozoospermic and oligospermic men from an infertile population. *Human Reproduction* **8**:71–3.

Matlai, P., Beral, V. (1985) Trends in congenital malformations of external genitalia. *The Lancet*, Vol.1, No.8420:108

Matson, P. (1995) External quality assessment for semen analysis and sperm antibody detection: results of a pilot scheme. *Human Reproduction* **10**:620–5.

Mayer, F. L., Stalling, D. L., Johnson, J. L. (1972) Phthalate esters as environmental contaminants. *Nature* **238**:411–13.

McClachlan, J. (1977) Prenatal exposure to diethylstilbestrol in mice: toxicological studies. *Journal of Toxicology and Environmental Health* **2**:527–37.

McCredie, M., Coates, M., Day, P., Bell, J. (1995) Changes in cancer incidence and mortality in New South Wales. *Medical Journal of Australia* **163**:520–3.

McLachlan, J., Newbold, R., Li, S., Negishi, M. (1998) Are estrogens carcinogenic during development of the testes? *Acta Pathologica Microbiologica et Immunologica Scandinavica* **106**:240–4.

Menchini-Fabris, F., Rossi, P., Palego, P., Simis, S., Turchi, P. (1996) Declining sperm counts in Italy during the past 20 years. *Andrologia* **28**:304.

Murature, D. A., Tang, S., Steinhardt, G., Dougherty, R. C. (1987) Phthalate esters and semen quality parameters. *Biomedical and Environmental Mass Spectrometry* **14**:473–7.

Nelson, C., Bunge, R. (1974) Semen analysis: evidence of changing parameters of male fertility potential. *Fertility and Sterility* **25**:503–7.

Neuwinger, J., Behre, H., Nieschlag, E. (1990) External quality control in the andrology laboratory: an experimental multicenter trial. *Fertility and Sterility* **54**:308–14.

Olsen, G. W., Ross, C. E., Bodner, K. M., Lipshultz, L. I., Ramlow, J. M. (1995) Have sperm counts been reduced 50 percent in 50 years? A statistical model revisited. *Fertility and Sterility* **63**:887–93.

Pajarinen, J., Laippala, P., Penttila, A., Karhunen, P. J. (1997) Incidence of disorders of spermatogenesis in middle aged Finnish men, 1981–91: two necropsy series. *British Medical Journal* **314**:13–18.

Paulozzi, L. J. (1999) International trends in rates of hypospadias and cryptorchidism. *Environmental Health Perspectives* **107**:297–302.

Paulozzi, L. J., Erickson, J. D., Jackson, R. J. (1997) Hypospadias trends in two US surveillance systems. *Pediatrics* **100**:831–4.

Paulsen, C. A., Berman, N. G., Wang, C. (1996) Data from men in greater Seattle area reveals no downward trend in semen quality: further evidence that deterioration of semen quality is not geographically uniform. *Fertility and Sterility* **65**:1015–20.

Peterson, R. E., Moore, R. W., Mably, T. A., Bjerke, D. L., Goy, R. W. (1992) Male reproductive system ontogeny: effects of perinatal exposure to 2,3,7,8-tetrachlorodibenzo-*p*-dioxin. In: Colborn, T., Clement, C. (eds.) *Chemically induced alterations in sexual and functional development: the wildlife/human connection* (pp. 175–93). Princeton, NJ: Princeton Scientific Publishing Co.

Polansky, F., Lamb, E. (1988) Do the results of semen analysis predict future fertility? A survival analysis study? *Fertility and Sterility* **49**:1059–65.

Prener, A., Storm, H., Nielsen, N. (1996) Cancer of the male genital tract in Circumpolar Inuit. *Acta Oncologica* **35**:589–93.

Raab, G. (1996) Results of Scottish study may be due to confounding with age. *British Medical Journal* **313**:44.

Raloff, J. (1994*a*) The gender benders. *Science News* **145**:24–7.

Raloff, J. (1994*b*) That feminine touch. *Science News* **145**:56–9.

Ramamoorthy, K., Wang, F., Chen, I., Safe, S., Norris, J., McDonnell, D., Gaido, K., Bocchinfuso, W., Korach, K. (1997) Potency of combined estrogenic pesticides. *Science* **275**:405–6.

Reijnders, P. J. (1986) Reproductive failure in common seals feeding on fish from polluted coastal waters. *Nature* **324**:456–7.

Riddle, J. M. (1992) *Contraception and abortion from the Ancient World to the Renaissance*. Cambridge, MA: Harvard University Press.

Riddle, J. M., Estes, J. W., Russell, J. C. (1994) Ever since Eve? Birth control in the Ancient World. *Archaeology* **47**:29–35.

Robinson, P. E., Mack, G. A., Remmers, J., Levy, R., Mohadjer, L. (1990) Trends of PCB, hexachlorobenzene, and β-benzene hexachloride levels in the adipose tissue of the U.S. population. *Environmental Research* **53**:175–92.

Robison, A. K., Mukku, V. R., Stancel, G. M. (1985) Analysis and characterization of estrogenic xenobiotics and natural products. In: McLachlan, J. A. (eds.) *Estrogens in the environment. II. Influences on development* (107–15). New York: Elsevier.

Rocco, F. (1999) Out for the count. *Telegraph Magazine* 23 January, pp. 46–52.

Rogan, W. J., Gladen, B.C., Hung, K., Koong, S., Shih, L., Taylor, J. S., Wu, Y., Yang, D., Ragan, N. B., Hsu, C. (1988) Congenital poisoning by polychlorinated biphenyls and their contaminants in Taiwan. *Science* **241**:334–6.

Rubes, J. L., Moore, D. I., Perreault, S., Slott, V., Evenson, D., Selevan, S. G., Wyrobek, A. J. (1998) Smoking cigarettes is associated with increased sperm disomy in teenage men. *Fertility and Sterility* **70**:715–23.

Safe, S. H. (1995) Environmental and dietary estrogens and human health: is there a problem? *Environmental Health Perspectives* **103**:346–51.

Safe, S. H., Zacharewski, T. (1997) Organochlorine exposure and risk for breast cancer. *Progress in Clinical and Biological Research* **396**:133–45.

Sager, D., Girard, D., Nelson, D. (1991) Early postnatal exposure to PCBs: sperm function in rats. *Experimental Toxicology and Chemistry* **10**:737–46.

Sauer, P., Huisman, M., Koopman-Esseboom, C., Morse, D., Smits-van Prooije, A., van de Berg, K., Tuinstra, L. T., van der Paauw, C., Boersma, E., Weisglas-Kuperus, N., Lammers, J., Kulig, B., Brouwer, A. (1994) Effects of polychlorinated biphenyls (PCBs) and dioxins on growth and development. *Human and Experimental Toxicology* **13**:900–6.

Schecter, A., Toniolo, D., Dai, L., Thuy, L., Wolff, M. (1997) Blood levels of DDT and breast cancer risk among women living in the north of Vietnam. *Archives of Environmental Contamination and Toxicology* **33**:453–6.

Schwartz, D., Laplanche, A., Jouannet, P., David, G. (1979) Within-subject variability of human semen in regard to sperm count, volume, total number of spermatozoa and length of abstinence. *Journal of Reproduction and Fertility* **57**:391–5.

Schwartz, D., Mayaux, M., Spira, A., Moscato, M., Jouannet, P., Czyzglik, F., David, G. (1983) Semen characteristics as a function of age in 833 fertile men. *Fertility and Sterility* **39**:530–5.

Scorer, C. (1964) The descent of the testis. *Archives of Disease in Childhood* **39**:605–9.

Senekjian, E., Potkul, R., Frey, K., Herbst, A. (1988) Infertility among daughters either exposed or not exposed to diethylstilbestrol. *American Journal of Obstetrics and Gynecology* **158**:493–8.

Setchell, B. (1997) Sperm counts in semen of farm animals, 1932–1995. *International Journal of Andrology* **20**:209–14.

Sharpe, R. M. (1993) Declining sperm counts in men – is there an endocrine cause? *Journal of Endocrinology* **136**:357–60.

Sharpe, R. M., Skakkebaek, N. E. (1993) Are oestrogens involved in falling sperm counts and disorders of the male reproductive tract? *The Lancet* **341**:1392–5.

Sherman, B. M., Wallace, R. B., Bean, J. A. (1982) Cyclic ovarian function and breast cancer. *Cancer Research* **42**:3286–3288.

Shutt, D. A. (1976) The effects of plant oestrogens on animal reproduction. *Endeavour* **35**:110–13.

Siffel, C., Czeizel, A. E. (1997) Using the Hungarian Birth Defects Registry for surveillance, research and intervention. *Central European Journal of Public Health* **5**:79–81.

Skakkebaek, N. E., Rajpert-de Meyts, E., Jørgensen, N., Carlsen, E., Meidahl Peterson, P., Giwercman, A., Andersen, A., Jensen, T. K., Andersson, A., Müller, J. (1998) Germ cell cancers and disorders of spermatogenesis: an environmental connection? *Acta Pathologica Microbiologica et Immunologica Scandinavica* **106**:3–12.

Snyder, P. J. (1990) Fewer sperm in the summer. It's not the heat, it's? *The New England Journal of Medicine* **323**:54–6.

Solé, M., Porte, C., Pastor, D., Albaigés, J. (1994) Long-term trends of polychlorinated biphenyls and organochlorinated pesticides in mussels from the western Mediterranean coast. *Chemosphere* **28**:897–903.

Somogyi, A., Beck, H. (1993) Nurturing and breast-feeding: exposure to chemicals in breast milk. *Environmental Health Perspectives* **101** [Suppl. 2]:45–52.

Soto, A. M., Justicia, H., Wray, J.W., Sonnenschein, C. (1991) *p*-Nonylphenol: an estrogenic xenobiotic released from 'modified' polystyrene. *Environmental Health Perspectives* **92**:167–73.

Soto, A. M., Chung, K. L., Sonnenschein, C. (1994) The pesticides endosulfan, toxaphene, and dieldrin have estrogenic effects on human estrogen-sensitive cells. *Environmental Health Perspectives* **102**:380–3.

Stephen, E. H., Chandra, A. (1998) Updated projections of infertility in the United States:1995–2025. *Fertility and Sterility* **70**:30–4.

Stillman, R. J. (1982) *In utero* exposure to diethylstilbestrol: adverse effects on the reproductive tract and reproductive performance in male and female offspring. *American Journal of Obstetrics and Gynecology* **142**:905–20.

Stone, J., Cruikshank, D., Sandeman, T., Matthews, J. (1991) Trebling of the incidence of testicular cancer in Victoria, Australia (1950–1985) *Cancer* **68**:211–19.

Subramanian, A., Tanabe, S., Tatsukawa, R., Saito, S., Miyazaki, N. (1987) Reduction in the testosterone levels by PCBs and DDE in Dall's porpoises of northwestern north Pacific. *Marine Pollution Bulletin* **18**:643–6.

Suominen, J., Vierula, M. (1993) Semen quality of Finnish men. *British Medical Journal* **306**:1579.

Swan, S. H., Elkin, E. P., Fenster, L. (1997) Have sperm densities declined? A reanalysis of global trend data. *Environmental Health Perspectives* **105**:1228–32.

Sweet, R. A., Schrott, H. G., Kurland, R., Culp, O. S. (1974) Study of the incidence of hypospadias in Rochester, Minnesota, 1940–1970, and a case-control comparison of possible etiologic factors. *Mayo Clinic Proceedings* **49**:52–8.

Takamatsu, M., Oki, M., Maeda, K., Inoue, Y. H., Yoshizuka, K. (1984) PCBs in blood of workers exposed to PCBs and their health status. *American Journal of Industrial Medicine* **5**:59–68.

Tandon, R., Seth, P., Srivastava, S. (1991) Effect of *in utero* exposure to di(2-ethylhexyl)phthalate on rat testes. *Indian Journal of Experimental Biology* **29**:1044–6.

Tjoa, W. S., Smolensky, M. H., Hsi, B. P., Steinberger, E., Smith, K.D. (1982) Circannual rhythm in human sperm count revealed by serially independent sampling. *Fertility and Sterility* **38**:454–9.

Toniolo, P. (1997) Endogenous estrogens and breast cancer risk: the case for prospective cohort studies. *Environmental Health Perspectives Supplement* **105** [Suppl. 3]:587–92.

Toniolo, P. G., Levitz, M., Zeleniuch-Jacquotte, A., Banarjee, S., Koenig, K. L., Shore, S. E., Strax, P., Pasternack, B. S. (1995) A prospective study of endogenous estrogens and breast cancer in postmenopausal women. *Journal of The National Cancer Institute* **87**:190–197.

Toppari, J., Larsen, J. C., Christiansen, P., Giwercman, A., Grandjean, P., Guillette, J. L. J., Jégou, B., Jensen, T. K., Jouannet, P., Keiding, N., Leffers, H., McLachlan, J. A., Meyer, O., Müller, J., Rajpert-De Meyts, E., Scheike, T., Sharpe, R. S., Skakkebaek, N. E. (1996) Male reproductive health and environmental xenoestrogens. *Environmental Health Perspectives* **104** [Suppl. 4]:741–802.

Trichopoulos, D., Yen, S., Brown, J., Cole, P., MacMahon, B. (1984) The effect of Westernization on urine estrogens, frequency of ovulation, and breast cancer. *Cancer* **53**:187–92.

Turner, K. J., Sharpe, R. M. (1997) Environmental oestrogens – present understanding. *Reviews of Reproduction* **2**:69–73.

United Kingdom Testicular Cancer Study Group (1994) Social, behavioural and medical factors in the aetiology of testicular cancer: results from the UK study. *British Journal of Cancer* **70**:513–20.

van Hove Haldrinet, M., Braun, H., Frank, R., Stopps, G., Smout, M., McWade, J. (1977) Organochlorine residues in human adipose tissue and milk from Ontario residents, 1969–1974. *Canadian Journal of Public Health* **68**:74–80.

van Os, J. L., de Vries, M. J., den Daas, N. H., Kaal Lansbergen, L. M. (1997) Long-term trends in sperm counts of dairy bulls. *Journal of Andrology* **18**:725–31.

van Waeleghem, K., De Clercq, N., Vermeulen, L., Schoonjans, F., Comhaire, F. (1996) Deterioration of sperm quality in young healthy Belgian men. *Human Reproduction* **11**:325–9.

van't-Veer, P., Lobbezoo, I., Martin-Moreno, J., Guallar, E., Gomez-Aracena, J., Kardinaal, A., Kohlmeier, L., Martin, B., Strain, J., Thamm, M., van Zoonen, P., Baumann, B., Huttunen, J., Kok, F. (1997) DDT (diclophane) and postmenopausal breast cancer in Europe: a case–control study. *British Medical Journal* **315**:81–5.

Vierula, M., Niemi, M., Keiski, A., Saaranen, M., Saarikoski, S., Suominen, J.

(1996) High and unchanged sperm counts of Finnish men. *International Journal of Andrology* **19**:11–17.

Vine, M. F. (1996) Worldwide decline in semen quality might be due to smoking. *British Medical Journal* **312**:506.

Vine, M. F., Margolin, B. H., Morrison, H. I., Hulka, B. S. (1994) Cigarette smoking and sperm density: a meta-analysis. *Fertility and Sterility* **61**:35–43.

Vitzthum, V. J., Bentley, G. R., Spielvogel, H., Caceres, E., Heidelberg, K., Crone, K., Chatterton, R. (1998) Salivary progesterone levels at conception and during gestation in rural Bolivian women. *FASEB Journal* **12**: part 2, SS:4211.

Walker, M. K., Peterson, R. E. (1992) Toxicity of polychlorinated dibenzo-*p*-dioxins, dibenzofurans and biphenyls in early development in fish. In: Colborn, T., Clement, C. (eds.) *Chemically induced alterations in sexual and functional development: the wildlife/human connection* (pp. 195–202). Princeton, NJ: Princeton Scientific Publishing Co.

Weir, H., Kreiger, N., Marrett, L. (1998) Age at puberty and risk of testicular germ cell cancer (Ontario, Canada). *Cancer Causes Control* **9**:253–8.

Weir, H., Marrett, L., Moravan, V. (1999) Trends in the incidence of testicular germ cell cancer in Ontario by histologic subgroup, 1964–1996. *Canadian Medical Association Journal* **160**:201–5.

White, R., Jobling, S., Hoare, S., Sumpter, J., Parker, M. (1994) Environmentally persistent alkylphenolic compounds are estrogenic. *Endocrinology* **135**:175–82.

Whitten, P. L., Naftolin, F. (1992) Effects of a phytoestrogen diet on estrogen-dependent reproductive processes in immature female rats. *Steroids* **57**:56–61.

Whitten, P. L., Russell, E., Naftolin, F. (1992) Effects of a normal, human concentration, phytoestrogen diet on rat uterine growth. *Steroids* **57**:98–106.

Wilcox, A. J., Baird, D. D., Winberg, C. R., Hornsby, P. P., Herbst, A. (1995) Fertility in men exposed prenatally to diethylstilbestrol. *New England Journal of Medicine* **332**:1411–16.

Wittmaack, F. M., Shapiro, S. S. (1992) Longitudinal study of semen quality in Wisconsin men over one decade. *Wisconsin Medical Journal* **91**:477–9.

World Health Organization (1980) *WHO laboratory manual for the examination of human semen and semen cervical mucus interaction*, first edition. Singapore: Press Concern.

World Health Organization (1992) *WHO laboratory manual for the examination of human semen and semen cervical mucus interaction*, third edition. Cambridge: Cambridge University Press.

Younglai, E. V., Collins, J. A., Foster, W. G. (1998) Canadian semen quality: an analysis of sperm density among eleven academic fertility centers. *Fertility and Sterility* **70**:76–80.

Zavos, P., Goodpasture, J. (1989) Clinical improvements of specific seminal deficiencies via intercourse with a seminal collection device versus masturbation. *Fertility and Sterility* **51**:190–3.

Zerah, S., de Mouzon, J., Pfeffer, J., Taar, J. (1997) Variation saisonnières des caractéristiques du sperme. *Contraception Fertilité Sexualité* **25**:519–23.

Zheng, Y., Bonder, J. P. E., Ernst, E., Mortensen, J. T., Egense, J. (1997) Is semen quality related to the year of birth among Danish infertility clients? *International Journal of Epidemiology* **26**:1289–97.

## 5

# From STD epidemics to AIDS: a socio-demographic and epidemiological perspective on sub-Saharan Africa

J. C. CALDWELL AND P. CALDWELL

## Abstract

The formation of a global economy and society has been accompanied in developing regions of the world by an upswing in sexually transmitted diseases (STDs). This has resulted from changing patterns of living and movement and changes in sexual relations. This chapter examines why and how these changes occurred and their impact on fertility. The focus will be on sub-Saharan Africa but Asia, the Pacific and Latin America are more briefly considered. The chapter then examines the emerging evidence that human immunodeficiency virus (HIV) and acquired immune deficiency syndrome (AIDS) have both a biological and a social impact on fertility. Some attention is given to the older STDs as cofactors of AIDS and the evidence that the AIDS epidemic will lead to successful campaigns against these STDs in an effort to control HIV/AIDS. The role of cultural, social and behavioural factors is stressed.

## Introduction

Childlessness or primary sterility is still a distressing condition for nearly all married women in most of the Third World. It can endanger marriage. The reaction of the childless woman's husband, and that of his relatives and the community, can make her a second class citizen and render her life a misery. Therefore, the level of childlessness among ever-married women who have completed their reproductive span can in most developing countries be equated with the true level of biological sterility within the marriage. It cannot be assumed to be a measure of the level of sterility of the wife, for, if she has confined her sexual activity to a single husband, as is commonly the case in much of Asia, it may be the latter who is sterile. This will not prevent the wife from bearing most of the blame.

The first national estimates of childlessness for a wide range of developing countries were made from the data collected by the World Fertility Survey (WFS) in the 1970s (Vaessen, 1984; Sherris and Fox, 1983). Among women 40–49 years of age who had been continuously married for at least five years, national levels of childlessness ranged from 1.3 to 6.7%. These may be underestimates, for sterility can lead to women being less likely to be surveyed because of marriage dissolution, a determination not to be interviewed about fertility, or even premature death. Alternatively, in societies where childless women are likely to attempt impregnation by men other than their husbands, as in sub-Saharan Africa or the Caribbean, the figures may be close to representing female, rather than couple, sterility.

The WFS revealed a range of sterility in sub-Saharan Africa of 2.7–6.3%; in the Middle East of 2.2–2.9%; in mainland Asia of 1.3–2.8%; in insular Asia and the Pacific of 6.7% in Indonesia and 4.3% in Fiji; in the Caribbean (including Guyana) of 3.2–6.5%; and in mainland Latin America of 2.0–3.5%. These figures suggest that inherited physiological sterility may be as low as 2%, and that there is very little sterility arising from disease in the Middle East, mainland Asia or mainland Latin America. In contrast, sterilizing disease may play a significant role in sub-Saharan Africa, the Caribbean, Indonesia and the Pacific. As we will see later, WFS omitted certain countries in Middle Africa where sterility levels are far higher than this, probably the highest in the world, largely from the sequelae of STDs. It appears that Indonesia should likewise be treated as a region with sterility levels higher in some parts than others and highest in some eastern islands not covered in the WFS survey.

Comparison is not possible with those Western countries where some women who could conceive choose not to have children, as covered for the U.K. in Chapter 6 by F. McAllister and L. Clarke. Childlessness in the U.S.A. was, by the same measure, almost 8% in 1980 but half this proportion may have been voluntary. Other approaches must be employed in developed countries to estimate the level of biological sterility.

The WFS also attempted to measure secondary sterility, that is the proportion of women of reproductive age who, although they were once fertile, can no longer bear a child. WFS did this by measuring the percentage of noncontracepting, nonpregnant women who had been continuously married for the last five years without having borne a child over that period. In all major regions of the Third World this proportion rose from 2–3% at 20–24 years of age to over 15% by 35–39 years. In some countries, such as Lesotho, Indonesia and Guyana, it climbed to nearly 30%, evidence of the role of sterilizing disease.

Sub-Saharan Africa almost certainly has, among the world's regions, the highest levels of STDs and infertility. Without doubt, it suffers more than anywhere else from AIDS, with around two-thirds of all the world's HIV/AIDS victims among only one-tenth of the world's population. The World Health Organization (1987) concluded, after a 1979–84 study of 33 centres for the treatment of STDs in 25 countries around the world, that 'Africa had the most uniquely infectious profile of infertility . . . Our current data show that this African pattern results from cumulative insults occurring before and after the first pregnancy'. Another report (PATH, 1997) contrasted the situation elsewhere, where 8–12% of couples have difficulties in conceiving at some time, with the situation in sub-Saharan Africa where the level is probably over one-third. These assessments have not gone unchallenged: Sherris and Fox (1983) argued that the WFS had shown Africa to be not dissimilar to Asia in levels of both primary and secondary sterility, although both regions exceeded levels found in Latin America. One problem with the latter assessment is that WFS had not surveyed most of the sub-Saharan African countries with the highest levels of infertility.

## The social and historical context

Sub-Saharan Africa's situation with regard to STDs and infertility arises partly from the fact that it is the world's poorest region with inadequate health services. However, cultural, social and behavioural factors have undoubtedly played their role. Sub-Saharan Africa differs from Eurasia in that sedentary agriculture and its accompanying religions have not historically developed there. However, it contrasts with Latin America in that its indigenous population has not been largely replaced by European settlers. This has left sub-Saharan Africa with a unique set of institutions. Not all have been disadvantageous: in the past, women have enjoyed more freedom compared to their counterparts in many parts of Eurasia. But in the nineteenth and twentieth centuries this social system left them peculiarly vulnerable to attacks by STDs. The situation may have been aggravated by what was possibly the major reason for their survival from external demographic and cultural conquest, namely the severity of their insect-borne diseases such as malaria, yellow fever and sleeping sickness. These diseases are probably so virulent because the region is predominantly low-lying, hot and wet. It may well be that these unusual levels of sickness interact in some way with social factors to aggravate the transmission of STDs and the incidence of sterility.

In the past, the society has been largely characterized by communal land, shifting cultivation and inheritance of family property or communal rights down the male line. Goody (1976) has contrasted this situation with that of ancient Eurasia, where sedentary agriculture has led to private property and a jealous guarding of the inheritance rights to this property and of the social standing of the family's children. Eurasia developed social classes while sub-Saharan Africa did not. Eurasian families preserved their inheritance from adventurers by ensuring that their unmarried daughters refrained from sexual activity and gave no unsuitable suitor the opportunity to claim that a girl's pregnancy gave him a right to marriage. Female virginity and degrees of social seclusion became enshrined in the world religions that Eurasia subsequently produced.

Caldwell and Caldwell employed this framework to identify a distinct sub-Saharan Africa sexual system (Caldwell and Caldwell, 1987; Caldwell *et al.*, 1989, 1991*a*,1992*c*). This is far from being a totally permissive system, but places more emphasis on fertility than on premarital female virginity. Indeed, the punishments for pre-marital or extramarital sexual activity are more akin to those protecting property rights than to spiritual damnation and the destruction of a woman's subsequent life. The emphasis on fertility probably owes something to the very high infant and child mortality rates in this unhealthy region. Although marriage is not necessarily the gateway to sexual activity, puberty ceremonies, often associated with circumcision, at least partly fill this role and prior sexual activity brings with it occult dangers. This analysis has been contested (e.g. Leblanc *et al.*, 1991). Certainly, male control of females and of their sexual activity varies greatly, as Gluckman (1950) argued when comparing the Lozi and Zulu of southern Africa.

One aspect of sub-Saharan Africa society is polygyny, which in West Africa can still reach levels where almost half of all married women are in polygynous marriages, a situation which probably characterized most of the region until recently (Lesthaeghe *et al.*, 1989). The only way that most men can eventually marry in a system with such levels of polygyny is to marry much later than women (Goldman and Pebley, 1989). A ten-year age gap is still common at first marriage, but research in late nineteenth century Nigeria revealed that 20 years may have once characterized the society (Peel, 1983). This has important implications for sexuality and the transmission of STDs. Old men maintained the situation by their control of resources and hence of bridewealth payments. Even so, this control would probably not have been possible if the old men had demanded premarital male virginity. Instead they looked the other way. Some of the sexual partners of the unmarried men were divorced or separated women or the youngest of the polygynous wives of very old men, but much of this sexual activity was contained within the extended family by allowing single men discreet access to their married brothers' wives, their fathers' younger wives, or cousins and other more distant relatives (Caldwell *et al.*, 1991*b*). This specific institution began to collapse with colonization, because the missionaries regarded such intrafamilial relationships as incest, and because new wage-earning opportunities provided young men with money to buy commercial sex. The prostitutes had many more sexual partners than the female relatives and some of these partners patronized other prostitutes elsewhere. The overlapping sexual networks enabled an explosion of STDs.

Polygyny probably had another effect on society. Basically it was an economic system whereby the husband was provided with a number of work units, each consisting of a wife and her children (Clignet, 1970). However, for stability, it also required the justification that men are biologically programmed to need more than one woman. Research in Nigeria has shown that most men and women still believe this to be true, and this belief justifies not only polygyny but also male extramarital sexual activity (Orubuloye et al., 1997). In West Africa the polygynous system has created distinct budgetary units within the family, with husbands and wives having their own budgets. This gives wives a degree of independence, and in southwest Nigeria has given them the ability to refuse sexual relationships with a husband suffering from an untreated STD (Orubuloye et al., 1993a). The problem is that many wives do not realize that their husbands are in this condition.

Much of sub-Saharan Africa is characterized by a degree of marital instability; one cause of this is the wife being childless. Reyna's 1975 study of a population in Chad showed that divorce in these circumstances is likely but not certain; the husband may merely add more wives to the family. But the same study (pp. 68ff) shows that the average time that women spend between marriages is one year seven months, a period when they are usually neither celibate nor confined to one male partner. Nearly all African studies show that STD levels are higher among women during these periods between marriage and they are undoubtedly a mechanism for causing the spread of STDs.

More than any other culture area, sub-Saharan Africa is characterized by long female postpartum periods of sexual abstinence which may reach three years (Page and Lesthaeghe, 1981). In Ibadan city, as late as 1973, this meant that monogamously married men did not have sexual access to their wives for more than 44% of their married lives and polygynously married men for more than 69% of the time (Caldwell and Caldwell, 1977). Husbands are not expected to abstain from sex during this period. Traditionally, they often had a specific other woman as a partner, but nowadays they are more likely to have a variety of partners.

The sub-Saharan African system has probably always sustained a significant level of STDs. But it was the European-forward movement of the late nineteenth century that raised this level to epidemic proportions. This has often been explained in terms of the Europeans introducing new STDs or allowing Muslim traders, who brought such diseases with them, access to the country. It is more likely that most of the STDs were of local origin but the new economic system allowed them to become epidemic.

The new system involved more migration than had previously occurred (Caldwell, 1985). This was partly because the colonial regime allowed safe passage for people from distant ethnic groups. However, the most important reason was the new economic opportunities: ports, roads, railways and urban infrastructure were all built. In some colonies this work took the form of forced labour and in others it was necessary to pay the government-imposed poll tax. The migrant workers were overwhelmingly men, while the women and children, as had always been customary, undertook the farming back in the rural areas. Small numbers of women migrated to the work camps to sell sex, which was made possible because there were large numbers of men away from their own women and also because the men were earning, by African standards, substantial wages. There is also a suggestion that in places like the Congo Free State the absence of paternal control back in the villages led to the young experimenting with sex more often and at a younger age.

Sub-Saharan Africa has had the potential to produce considerable numbers of prostitutes. This is partly because there are widespread transactional relationships between the sexes which may include types of payment for sex and which may extend even within marriage (Orubuloye *et al.*, 1994). But the main reason has been that commercial sex is not seen as the ultimate sin and most prostitutes can later play other roles, including that of being a wife. This is helped by the fact that those selling sex often also serve food or drink, or provide other entertainment. Many young women seem to be unsure in their own minds exactly what their occupation is, and this is even more the case with their relatives and others back in their home villages. There is a particular demand for commercial sexual services in cities that have a surplus of males: in parts of East and Southern Africa where women are farmers but not traders and hence can secure little employment in the towns, and in Abidjan in West Africa where many of the migrants come from the interior Savannah characterized by societies that encourage women to stay at home. Transport routes and terminal lorry parks are also associated with higher rates of commercial sex and STDs, long-distance drivers often leading sexually high-risk lives (Orubuloye et al., 1993b).

The AIDS epidemic has encouraged the study of sexual networking. Research in Ekiti, Southwest Nigeria (Orubuloye et al., 1991, 1992) shows that, while the level of premarital and extramarital sexual activity may not be higher than in some parts of contemporary Western society, it is certainly higher than in other poor societies with inadequate provision for the treatment of diseases, such as the peasant societies of South Asia and North Africa.

One final biosocial point might be noted. Mtimavalye and Belsey (1987) showed that everywhere the female factor is more important than the male factor in sterility. This is especially so in sub-Saharan Africa because childless women have been treated so badly that very few are more afraid of being caught in adultery than of remaining childless. If a woman has failed to bear a child with her husband, she will usually try to be impregnated by another man. Once it was the duty in many societies for other men in the husband's family to do this; therefore, in this situation levels of couple sterility are probably little higher than levels of female biological sterility. On the other hand, child fostering occurs at a very high level in many African societies, and sterile women are loath to admit their condition or even to participate in a survey, with the result that survey findings may understate sterility. This is probably less so with the modern international surveys where detailed fertility histories make it more difficult for a respondent to keep up the pretence.

## Sterility

Colonial administrators long regarded African populations as fragile and likely to decline precipitously, thus exhausting the labour supply. Feldman-Savelsburg (1994) records that local rulers, missionaries and colonial bureaucrats in Cameroon have expressed these concerns for over a hundred years. Such fears are felt even more strongly by the local women, with good reason:

> Infertility and child loss put a woman at a greater risk of becoming poor and greatly attenuate her exchange and support networks. Childlessness can be the grounds for divorce . . . causing a woman to lose her access to land distributed by her husband. Even her natal family, angered at having to return her bridewealth, may give her only minimal solace. If she is able to avoid a divorce, a childless woman receives fewer gifts from her husband than her luckier co-wives. She has no children to help her cultivate her land, and no-one to support her in old age.
>
> Feldman-Savelsburg (1994)

Quite widely in Africa, barren women were suspected of having made pacts with the forces of evil, and in southwest Nigeria their bodies on death were thrown into the bush to be eaten by wild animals. One striking aspect of the Cameroon study is that these apprehensive women did not seem to link childlessness either to STDs or to the sexual networking of their partners.

As statistical systems developed in the twentieth century, it became clear that, although the region's total population was certainly growing, there were places where fertility was low even to the point of declining population numbers. François (1975) documented Gabon's decline in population between 1930 and 1950. The 1948 East African census showed that almost 40% in Zanzibar Town were childless (Blacker, 1962). Fertility was low and sterility high in Uganda among the Baganda (Griffith, 1963) and among the nomadic population of the Sudan (Henin, 1969). Africa was not unique. In the Pacific, European contact produced STD epidemics, low fertility and declining populations, a situation reversed in the first quarter of the twentieth century (Rallu, 1992). High sterility was recorded in Melanesia, in both New Ireland (Belsey, 1976) and more recently on the north coast of New Guinea (Jenkins, 1993).

The World Health Organization (WHO) world study concluded that sub-Saharan Africa is characterized by a distinct pattern of STDs and infertility (Cates *et al.*, 1985). African wives presenting themselves at infertility clinics are younger than elsewhere; secondary sterility, i.e. sterility after the birth of at least one child, is exceptionally high; African couples have unusually high levels of previous STDs and pregnancy complications; sterility among women compared with men is higher than elsewhere; African women have much higher levels of tubal occlusion and pelvic adhesions.

## The main infertility belt

The fertility and infertility patterns of sub-Saharan Africa began to emerge from the 1948 British colonial censuses, and much more clearly from demographic sample surveys carried out in French colonies during the 1950s and in the Belgian Congo in 1955–57. By the beginning of the 1960s, Romaniuk (1961) was able to show that there were parts of the Congo where almost half of the women had finished their reproductive span without bearing a child. Successive analyses (Coale and Lorimer, 1968; Frank, 1983; Page, 1975; Page and Coale, 1972) provided a more complete picture of the situation and revealed the existence of a vast belt of population in Middle Africa where infertility rates were undoubtedly the world's highest (Figure 5.1).

The maps showed high infertility in almost half of Middle Africa; an almost continuous area, where 20–50% of older women had never borne a child and where total fertility rates were under five children per woman instead of seven, stretched from southwest Sudan through eastern Central African Republic, northeastern and eastern Democratic Republic of Congo except Kivu to southeast Angola. Another, apparently separate, belt stretched from Cameroon to Gabon and presumably included Rio Muni Equatorial Guinea. The irony of this mapping of the main infertility belt is that the knowledge available by the early 1960s has increased very little since then. Much of that belt has been fairly unstable politically. As a result, the WFS and its successor

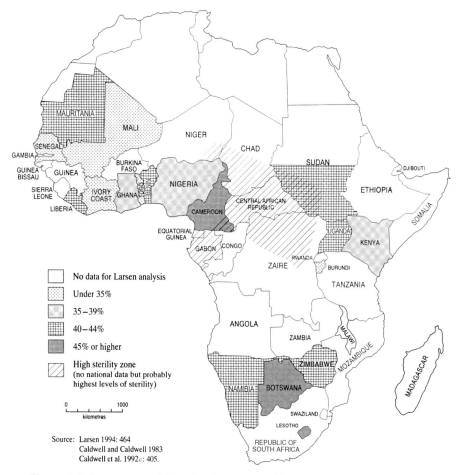

Figure 5.1 Percentage of females that are sterile, 35–39 years of age (most recent dates of national studies).

the Demographic and Health Surveys (DHS) have added new information only for Cameroon. DHS surveys have recently been conducted in the Central African Republic (1994/5), Chad (1996/7) and Congo (1997). No analysis has yet been carried out on childlessness in the first, and no data have yet been released from the last two. Ericksen and Brunette (1996) have attempted to map the data that are available from those surveys and have concluded that three countries on the southern rim of the main infertility belt have above-average infertility: Namibia, Botswana and Zimbabwe (but this conclusion is probably wrong, with the authors failing to take into account the relatively high level of contraceptive use now found in the three countries; U. Larsen, personal communication in 1999).

The main addition to knowledge was a 1974–77 demographic survey of western Congo EDOZA (Etudes démographiques de Ouest du Zaire), analysed by Tabutin (1979, 1982). Particularly important were those areas that had been included in both the 1955–57 and the 1974–77 surveys.

Employing this material, an early analysis by Romaniuk (1968) and also their own demographic study in southern Nigeria, Caldwell and Caldwell (1983) came to the following conclusions.

1. The Middle African sterility belt is characterized by massive primary sterility even when girls marry at 15 or 16 years of age, implying very early sexual contacts and subsequent infection and infertility.
2. The proportion of sterile wives reached a maximum with those married in the first half of the 1940s, after a long period of increasing primary sterility dating back to the social disruption associated with the founding of the Congo Free State in the 1880s.
3. Levels of sterility change with ethnic boundaries and hence are related to culturally determined behaviour.
4. The geographical patterns of sterility do not seem to be related to patterns of general health.
5. In much of sub-Saharan Africa secondary sterility is at higher levels than primary sterility.
6. Most secondary sterility is probably caused by infections brought into the marriage by husbands, with wives' extra-marital sexual behaviour playing a secondary role.
7. Trends of increasing primary sterility in the Congo, and probably elsewhere, reversed after the Second World War. This was almost certainly due to population-based use of penicillin in campaigns against yaws (contagious bacterial skin diseases common in tropical countries) and not by clinical treatment of STDs. These campaigns did not cure any sterile women but

    ensured that some previously infected very young women did not become sterile.

8.   The success of these campaigns in limiting new cases of sterility suggests that gonorrhoea is probably the most important sterilizing disease.

Larsen (1989) reported a decline in the proportion of young women who were sterile at marriage in Cameroon, falling from the late 1940s, and referred to a similar trend in Sudan. In a series of papers (Larsen, 1989, 1994, 1995, 1996; Larsen and Menken, 1991), she has used WFS and DHS data, despite their omission of almost all the main AIDS belt, to throw new light on sub-Saharan African sterility. More recently Ericksen and Brunette (1996) have also used these surveys.

### Primary and secondary sterility

Estimating levels of primary and secondary sterility is a matter of definition and analytical methodology. Even primary sterility or childlessness requires definition. The matter was relatively simple when looking at historical change in the kind of retrospective data that were available for the Congo. Clearly, women who had reached menopause, say 50 years old, without ever having given birth to a live child had experienced primary sterility. But other measures are needed when dealing with contemporary populations. The most common is to classify a woman beginning sexual activity as suffering from primary sterility if she has had unprotected sexual intercourse for five years without bearing a child. This should be measured from the onset of regular sexual activity, but, in the absence of information on the commencement of this period, the starting point is usually assigned to the date of marriage. Secondary sterility can be defined in terms of having previously borne at least one child but subsequently experiencing five or seven years of unprotected intercourse without further childbearing.

    It was the advent of international comparable surveys that brought the need for such demographic definitions. The definitions just discussed were originally made for the WFS (Vaessen, 1984). In recent years a sophisticated methodology has been developed for studying sterility and has been applied to sub-Saharan Africa in a series of interrelated studies (Larsen, 1994, 1995; Larsen and Menken, 1991).

There are two major difficulties in the demographic approach to measuring infertility. The first problem is the fact that the failure to conceive may be the result of the voluntary use of contraception. Until recently, this could be largely ignored in sub-Saharan Africa with the result that the region's statistics for sterility were probably the best in the world. This is no longer the case. In such countries as South Africa, Zimbabwe, Botswana and Kenya contraceptive prevalence rates exceed one-third. The other problem lies largely with the measurement of secondary sterility, because most childless African women do not practise contraception, at least when married. It might be noted that recent research in an urban area of southern Nigeria showed a steep increase in the use of contraception by unmarried childless young women in order to postpone both their first births and marriage (Caldwell *et al.*, 1992*b*). Increasingly, even African analysis will have to rely on the respondents' own statements about the period during which neither contraception nor abortion was employed.

With regard to secondary sterility, the greatest problem occurs more in sub-Saharan Africa than elsewhere. That is the level of childlessness that occurs because of the practice of terminal sexual abstinence after a woman has become a grandmother, or she has sufficient children, or her husband has turned to younger wives (Page and Lesthaeghe, 1981). One study in Ibadan City, Nigeria, showed a median age for the commencement of terminal abstinence of around 45 years (Caldwell, 1979).

Larsen (1994) showed that sterility among 20–24 year olds in sub-Saharan African countries ranges from 2 to 19% and among 40–44 year olds from 39 to 75%. The level of sterility rose ever more steeply with age. The median level was 3% for women 20–24 years of age and 30% for women 40–44 years of age. These are levels double those found among Larsen's comparative group, Hutterites in the U.S.A. The Africa medians were even higher than the Hutterite values for women aged 30–34 and 35–39 years, showing that this is the period in African women's lives when the chance of becoming sterile is unusually great.

Farley and Belsey (1988) compared African childlessness at the end of the reproductive period with that in other world regions. The range in sub-Saharan Africa was 3–32%, compared with 5–7% in the Caribbean, 2–7% in Asia and Oceania, 2–9% in Latin America, 2–4% in the Middle East, 3–11% in Europe and 6% in North America. This comparison highlights the point that primary sterility in many sub-Saharan countries is as low as anywhere else in the world, while in some countries it is very high indeed.

If there has been any recent movement in primary sterility it has been downward. Larsen (1994) examined childlessness in the six sub-Saharan African countries for which there are data from successive surveys. The three countries with very low primary sterility – 4% or less, Ghana, Kenya and Senegal – showed little movement, but the level declined in Cameroon from 12 to 5%, in Nigeria from 6 to 4% and in Sudan from 5 to 2%. In a later study, Larsen (1996) showed that between a 1973 survey and one in 1991–2, childlessness among 30- to 39-year-old women had fallen in Tanzania from 10 to 3%, and that the decline was evident in every district. In rural Ethiopia Mammo and Morgan (1986) reported during the 1980s a fertility rise of such magnitude that they felt they had to caution that it could not all be attributed to declining sterility. This may be a measure of better health services, but it is more likely to be a testimony to the easy availability of antibiotics.

## *Causes of sterility*

Most female sterility is the result of pelvic infectious disease (PID) and the subsequent spread of the infection through the reproductive tract causing tubal occlusion in the fallopian tubes. PID may be caused by a single organism or may be the result of infection by a number of different organisms. This possibility makes diagnosis difficult, and the assigning of causes of infertility problematic. Another difficulty is that the causal organisms have frequently disappeared by the time that sterility is investigated. PID is 'caused by two mechanisms: ascent of lower genital tract STDs in non-pregnant women; and nonhygienic obstetric or abortion practices in pregnant women' (Cates et al., 1985). In sub-Saharan Africa, abortion is probably the least important of the three practices. STDs are almost certainly the major cause, and this is very much the case with primary sterility, where infertility originated before the birth of any child (Wasserheit, 1989).

Blacker (1962), when reporting 38% childlessness in Zanzibar Town and 25% elsewhere in Zanzibar recorded in the 1948 census, commented that the medical authorities did not believe that sufficient people were infected with STDs to explain the phenomenon. This may have been because they were referring largely to gonorrhoea, while it is now known that chlamydia, which is often not symptomatic, is also an important cause. Bergström (1990) sums up the evidence as establishing that tubal occlusion is responsible for around two-thirds of infertility in poor societies and that the chief causes are gonorrhoea and chlamydia, probably in that order.

During the last 20 years of the twentieth century, a major research station, CIRMF International Centre for Medical Research, Franceville, was established in an area of high sterility in Gabon, probably the country most afflicted by primary sterility in the world. The national level of childlessness is probably still over one-third there, and the total fertility rate around four. Collet et al. (1988) reported on attendances at the centre's infertility clinic for 1983–84. The average woman attending was 26 years of age. She had attained menarche at 14.4 years, had her first sexual intercourse at 15.0 years and was sterile by 20.8 years. Over one-third had never been pregnant, while the rest had had their first child or abortion on average at 17.6 years of age. Tubal occlusion was the cause of infertility in 83% of all cases. Gonorrhoea and chlamydia were probably both important causes, the latter most frequently being subclinical. Others have stressed the complementary importance of vaginal trichomoniasis and bacterial vaginosis in PID (Cates et al., 1990; Grodstein et al., 1993; Wasserheit, 1989).

The WHO Task Force on Infertility (Farley and Belsey, 1988;

World Health Organization, 1987) reported that tubal factors caused a much higher proportion of infertility in sub-Saharan Africa than in any other world region. This, of course, is another way of saying that the level of infertility is very high and has been raised further above base levels of physiological infertility than anywhere else. Farley and Belsey (1988) reported that female levels of gonorrhoea were under 1% in the West but 16–20% in sub-Saharan Africa, but that chlamydia levels were not dissimilar, at around 5%.

There is some evidence that intra-uterine contraceptive devices (IUDs) can facilitate PID and subsequent tubal infection (Paavonen and Wølner-Hanssen, 1989), but their level of use in sub-Saharan Africa is still very low.

Generalizations about infertility in the region are rendered difficult by our inability to map the region in terms of levels of STDs. De Schryver and Méheus (1990) reported levels of gonorrhoea and chlamydia found in pregnant women at antenatal clinics in Gambia, Gabon, Ghana, Kenya, Nigeria, Zimbabwe and South Africa. Gonorrhoea levels ranged from 4 to 12% and chlamydia from 7 to 29%. In no country were chlamydia levels below those of gonorrhoea. Much may depend on the location of the clinics, because in South Africa the level of chlamydia recorded was 13% in urban clinics and 1% in rural ones. Piot and Tezzo (1990) estimated prevalence rates among African pregnant women to be 5–15% for gonorrhoea, 7–20% for chlamydia and 3–33% for syphilis, the latter being unimportant for female sterility.

The earlier concentration was on gonorrhoea because its presence was clearer. Griffith (1963) used the Ugandan 1959 census and 1959–61 hospital and dispensary records to show that there was a significant inverse association in the country between gonorrhoea and fertility levels. Brunham *et al.* (1992) estimated that a 20% level of active gonorrhoea among adults reduces fertility by 50%, just the reduction that has been estimated for Gabon. A similar classification is more difficult for chlamydia because most women sterilized by the disease do not have it actively present when clinically examined (Mabey *et al*, 1985). Brunham *et al.* (1993) used a mathematical model to conclude that, at a 10% prevalence of infection, gonorrhoea is predicted to reduce growth rates by 30%, whereas chlamydial infection is predicted to reduce growth rates by 10%. This difference results from the higher transmissibility and shorter duration of infectivity of gonococcal infection compared with chlamydial infection. This means that, even though the prevalence of chlamydia in sub-Saharan Africa may be one-third or more above that of gonorrhoea, the latter may still be responsible for twice the level of sterility.

There is some evidence that the progress from PID to tubal occlusion is more rapid in teenage than older women, especially if sexual activity is before or immediately after the onset of puberty (Collet et al., 1988; Reniers et al., 1989). This may explain the extraordinary level of primary sterility in the main sterility belt and the rapidity with which such sterility developed in the Congo Free State. There is also evidence that the very young are more easily infected with STDs (Ericksen and Brunette, 1996; Reniers et al., 1989).

Although most of the concentration has been on STD levels among women, more attention is warranted for levels among men. Women are infected by men and probably the majority by their husbands. Arya et al. (1973) reported on clinical treatment of males in rural Uganda, and found that men were treated without their wives coming to the clinic and that most men resumed sexual relations with their wives before they were fully treated.

### Determinants of sterility

Various studies have attempted to use WFS and DHS national data to compare sub-Saharan African countries in order to discover the determinants of infertility (Ericksen and Brunette, 1996; Larsen, 1989, 1995). In her 1989 study Larsen drew on data for Cameroon, Kenya and Sudan. In all three countries, sterility increases with age and duration of marriage because of rising secondary sterility. In all three, the district of residence was important, as demonstrated by very different levels of sterility in different parts of each country. In Kenya and Sudan, infertility is lower in monogamous than poly-gynous marriages, but this is not the case in Cameroon where overall sterility levels are higher. Differentials are not clearly shown by urban-rural residence, education, husband's education, religion, circumcision (except for Sudan where infibulation is associated with higher levels of sterility) and use of contraception. Subsequently, Larsen (1995) compared two neighbouring countries, Cameroon and Nigeria. She estimated the number of infertile years lived between 20 and 39 years of age in the early 1990s as being 6.0 years in Cameroon and 4.2 years in Nigeria, compared with 2.7 years in Togo and 1.3 years among American Hutterites. This time she found several significant determinants of sterility: early age at first sexual intercourse; marital instability; not being attended by trained health professionals when giving birth; having had abortions (Cameroon only, as the Nigeria numbers were too small for analysis); and living in urban rather than in rural areas. Socio-economic status appeared to have little importance. Ericksen and Brunette (1996) undertook a comparative analysis of 27 sub-Saharan African countries with WFS or DHS surveys. They found that those who were currently unmarried were significantly more likely to be sterile (average odds ratio around two). The characteristics significant in almost all surveys were as follows: living in an urban rather than a rural area (average odds ratio of around 2 and significant in about three-quarters of the countries), reporting more than one sex partner, and having begun sexual relations around the time of puberty.

Cates *et al.* (1993) reported not on the determinants of infertility but on risk factors for STDs, PID and tubal occlusion. They reported the following to be higher risk factors for STDs and PID: having multiple sexual partners, being a sexually active teenager, having had multiple STD infections, and having used IUDs. They found the following to be risk factors for PID leading to tubal infection: having been repeatedly infected, having had particularly severe infections and duration of time since first infection. They also reported a reduced chance of PID leading to tubal occlusion among women using copper-coated IUDs. Clearly, the risk of infertility is closely related to the risk of being infected with STDs, but is also increased by poor childbirth and abortion conditions.

The relationship with marital status is complex. A sterile woman is more likely to be divorced. In Chad, Reyna (1975) found among ever-married women that only 17% of women who had never been divorced were sterile compared with 83% of women who had experienced three or more divorces. On the other hand, divorced or separated women were more likely to have multiple sexual partners and a proportion of them became prostitutes.

Secondary sterility rises with the number of live births. This is partly a product of age but it is also a product of the number of unhygienic births the woman has endured. Romaniuk (1968) reported a statistically significant relationship, when comparing provinces in the Congo, between the level of sterility and the level of births outside marriage. The number of out-of-wedlock births was probably a measure of early teenage sex and pregnancy, but it may have also reflected multiple sexual relationships.

Perhaps the most interesting finding is the weakness or insignificance of any relationship between education and sterility. This parallels similar findings with regard to infection by HIV.

## AIDS and infertility

AIDS is an STD in that its primary method of transmission is sexual. Like syphilis, HIV can be transmitted vertically from mother to child. It differs most from other STDs in that there are no manifestations of it on the genitalia – nor does it lead to tubal occlusion. It also has two other defining characteristics. The first is a long period between infection with HIV and the symptomatic stage of AIDS, around ten years in the West before the modern 'drug cocktails' proved capable of prolonging the period. There is some evidence that the latency period is slightly shorter, perhaps eight to nine years in sub-Saharan Africa, where the immune system experiences uniquely high pressures and where only the elite have access to drugs prolonging the period. The other defining characteristic is that the disease eventually proves fatal for nearly all who are infected by it.

About two-thirds of the AIDS in the world is found in sub-Saharan Africa. Most of those infected are found among 3% of the

Figure 5.2. Main HIV/AIDS belt 1997. (Adult HIV seropositive over 9% in major city and over 5% elsewhere.)

world's population in the main AIDS belt which stretches from Southern Sudan southward to Zimbabwe, Botswana and Namibia (Figure 5.2). Among the general population of these countries, adult HIV levels may reach 15–20% outside the main cities and 30% in the cities (Health Studies Branch, 1998). Elsewhere in the world, the highest levels outside the major cities are 4% in Haiti, with 8% in its capital. Even Bangkok and Mumbai record levels of only 2–3%.

The sub-Saharan African epidemic is unique in that its primary method of transmission is almost entirely heterosexual. Thus, in this region alone as many women as men are infected, as are significant numbers of young children. This means that families are disrupted. It also means that whatever other impact the epidemic has on women, it will significantly affect the whole society.

Because of its sexual transmission, HIV has differential effects on societies, similar to other STDs. A decade of observation in the longitudinal study near Masaka in Uganda has shown that the level of infection among divorced women is 2.5 times greater than among all women (Carpenter et al, 1997). Urban levels are usually much higher than rural ones (Piot and Tezzo, 1990).

At least some of the other STDs serve as co-factors for AIDS, thus increasing the likelihood of HIV infection. The most powerful co-factor is chancroid, although all genital ulcers probably facilitate infection (Piot and Tezzo, 1990). At Masaka those who had a past record of syphilis were three times as likely to be infected (Carpenter et al, 1997), but it may be that a past record of syphilis is little more than an index of a higher-risk lifestyle.

The geographical plotting of the prevalence of sterility and that of AIDS raises a major unresolved problem. The main infertility zone lies to the west of the main AIDS belt. Indeed the main AIDS belt, especially in East Africa, has long been characterized by rather low levels of childlessness – the Baganda are an exception. When high levels of AIDS were first identified in sub-Saharan Africa, the epicentre seemed to lie in Uganda, Rwanda and Burundi. It seemed only too likely that the disease had spread from the main infertility zone, where the high levels of infertility appeared to give evidence of unusually high levels of STDs. But, with more HIV surveillance, this proved not to be the case. The only plausible explanation seems to be that different STDs play a greater role in catalysing HIV infection than they do in causing infertility. The evidence seems to be that high infertility is caused mostly by gonorrhoea and chlamydia. The former is apparently not an important co-factor for HIV infection but the latter has been suspected of playing a significant role. Possible explanations are that chlamydia is not an important co-factor for HIV, or that its role in the infertility zone has been exaggerated and that of such infections as trichomonal vaginitis and bacterial vaginosis under-estimated.

One further explanation is possible. The main AIDS belt approximates the area where cultures dictate that men should remain uncircumcised, suggesting that lack of male circumcision may also be a co-factor for AIDS (Bongaarts *et al.*, 1989; Caldwell and Caldwell, 1993, 1994; Moses *et al.*, 1990). It may also be a co-factor for chancroid, and the main AIDS belt may also be the main chancroid belt. High HIV/AIDS levels may be facilitated both by a lack of male circumcision and by the presence of chancroid.

There is increasing evidence that HIV itself reduces fertility, not by causing tubal occlusions but by biological mechanisms not yet understood. One possibility would be very early miscarriages. The first evidence was probably misunderstood. A study in the Demo-cratic Republic of the Congo (Batter *et al.*, 1994; Ryder *et al.*, 1991) followed women for three years after the birth of their first child. They were told their HIV-1 serostatus and the 238 women who were HIV-positive were urged to use family planning and were assisted in doing so. During the second year of the follow-up the seropositive women were 24% less fertile than the seronegative ones and during the third year 17% less fertile. The reduction in fertility among the seropositive group rose consistently with age, being, for the whole period of the follow-up, 23% for those under 30, rising to 60% for those over 40. The researchers believed that the lower fertility among seropositive women was probably the result of their education programme, and its exhortation to use contraception. But the contracepting levels of the seropositive group were not greatly above those of the seronegative group, especially during the first year of the follow-up. The reason is that African women, with a strong belief in lineage and descent, are often more inclined, rather than less, to bear more children if they think they are going to die. The researchers raised the possibility that the lower fertility of the seropositive women might be of biological origin.

Gregson *et al.* (1996), reporting on research in part of Zimbabwe with one of the world's highest levels of HIV infection, noted a rapid rate of fertility decline, but at first thought that it resulted from increased use of contraception both as a defence against HIV and in order to control fertility. Ntozi told a 1995 conference that his surveys in Uganda had found total fertility rates to be 17% lower in households infected with HIV than in those not infected (Ntozi *et al.*, 1997).

Various reports made to a 1997 conference of the International Union for the Scientific Study of Population (Awusabo-Asare *et al.*, 1997) made a much stronger case for HIV suppressing fertility. By 1997 Gregson *et al.* (1997) had become convinced that the fertility decline they were measuring in Zimbabwe was too steep to be explained by contraceptive use or sexual behaviour and had to have a biological component.

Carpenter *et al.* (1997) reported on the first seven annual rounds of the Masaka Longitudinal Study in Uganda carried out by the British Medical Research Council and the Ugandan Institute of Virology. They reported that the total fertility rate among seropositive women who did not know their HIV status was 27% lower than that of seronegative women. That figure was reduced to 23% when adjustment was made for age, marital status and past experience of syphilis. On the other hand, the seropositive women may have had their fertility raised disproportionately because more of them had begun sexual activity earlier and had borne a baby in their teenage years.

Gray *et al.* (1997) presented the results of a carefully controlled project in Rakai, Uganda, which had been specifically designed to examine the relationship between HIV status and fertility. This research had been set up because their 1989–92 study had shown lower fertility among seropositive women but had not measured certain factors that might have confounded the situation. Their subsequent 1994–95 research programme focused on measuring pregnancy among 4813 sexually active women, 15–49 years of age with at least one current sexual partner and who were willing to give blood for testing. Among this group, there were adequate numbers with the desired characteristics: 19.3% were pregnant; 19.8% were seropositive for HIV; and 9.3% were suffering from active syphilis. Among those with no HIV or syphilis, 21.4% were pregnant; among those with syphilis only, 20.8% were pregnant;

among those with HIV only 13.4% were pregnant; and among those with both HIV and syphilis, only 8.5% were pregnant. It should be noted with regard to controversies reported earlier in this chapter that although pregnancy was reduced among women with syphilis or gonorrhoea, it was not reduced among those with chlamydia or chancroid, but the numbers with the latter two diseases were too small for satisfactory statistical analysis. Once a range of possibly confounding factors was controlled, it was found that fertility among asymptomatic seropositive women was 51% below that of seronegative women, while fertility among symptomatic AIDS sufferers had been reduced by 77%. It might be noted that none of these women knew their HIV status although some of the symptomatic women may have surmised it.

In a country where 20% of women in their childbearing years are seropositive for HIV, we might expect a reduction in fertility of about 10%. This raises the question as to whether main AIDS belt countries with fertility declines of this order are reflecting any volitional change towards smaller family size or whether this decline is merely a reflection of the AIDS epidemic. An example of this phenomenon may well be Zambia (Caldwell, 1997). In countries where there is a proven contraceptive-induced fertility decline as well as high levels of HIV, future fertility declines may be steep indeed. Examples might include South Africa, Zimbabwe, Botswana and Lesotho. Stanecki and Way (1997) included in their most recent population projections lower future fertility levels for specific countries than in earlier projections, although it is not clear whether the full likely impact of AIDS on fertility was considered. Nevertheless, they showed by the year 2010 populations will be declining in Botswana and Zimbabwe as well as in Guyana and South America, which has only modest HIV levels but a contraceptive-induced fertility transition which has taken it to replacement-level fertility.

This also raises the question of whether surveillance is underestimating HIV/AIDS levels. Most surveillance is of pregnant women at antenatal clinics. If pregnant women have lower than average seropositive levels, then HIV/AIDS levels for all women should be higher.

## Tackling the epidemics

There is fairly hard evidence of widespread declines in infertility. There is no evidence of any rises, although there is in some areas, such as Gabon, a persistence of high sterility levels. Nevertheless, there are strong reasons why attempts should be made to reduce the levels of STDs. One is that African levels are higher than anywhere else in the world and this gives rise to pain, sickness, childlessness and premature sterility. The other reason is that some STDs act as co-factors for HIV infection.

The obvious remedy is a change in sexual behaviour away from high-risk encounters, or reducing the risk in such encounters. Urging change in sexual activity can be regarded as an unwarranted attack on a culture, a view put strongly by David and Voas (1981) with regard to STDs among the Fulani of Cameroon. The failure of behaviour to change greatly in the face of the AIDS epidemic is probably evidence that much of the population shares this view, and the failure of governments to give much leadership in this area suggests similar doubts.

The problem outlined one-third of a century ago by Griffith (1963) is still potent: there is little appreciation of the relationship between sexual behaviour and STDs and less of that between STDs and infertility. A study in Nigeria showed that gonorrhoea is widely regarded as a minor problem that has to be tolerated, and many still regard its symptoms as the inevitable characteristics of adulthood (Bakare, 1990).

If the aim is to reduce sterility, the evidence suggests that only mass antibiotic campaigns work. Such evidence comes from the mass campaigns against yaws, which followed the Second World War. It probably also comes from more recent declines in childlessness. These have not been the product of the activities of STD clinics but almost certainly of the widespread availability of antibiotics throughout the community. These are employed for a wide range of illnesses and only a small minority of use is intended to cure STDs, and practically none to fend off infertility. It is highly improbable that mass antibiotic campaigns will ever again be put into the field because of the danger of accelerating the build-up of organisms resistant to the antibiotics. It is likely that the ready availability of antibiotics without prescription will also be discouraged, although probably with little effect.

Cates *et al.* (1990) summed up the evidence on the clinical treatment of STDs, 'the failure to show that any current pelvic inflammatory disease treatment regimen has a positive effect on future fertility', concluding that prevention rather than cure should be the objective. There are, of course, other reasons for increasing the infrastructure for treating STDs. The first is the reduction of ill-health and misery. The second is that leaving STDs, especially ulcerating ones, active increases the likelihood of the AIDS epidemic spreading. These aims are especially important in urban areas because of the higher levels of both STDs and HIV/AIDS there.

The other way of limiting the epidemics is a massive increase in condom use. Mathematical modelling by Brunham *et al.* (1992) claimed to show that the gonorrhoeal chain of infection which led to a persistence of the disease in the community could be broken if 10% of the community used condoms in their sexual activities. Some of the DHS surveys give the impression that these levels are being reached, but the figures refer to ever-use while the model undoubtedly demands not only continuous use but efficient use. Many of the condoms in tropical Africa have deteriorated through long storage in a difficult climate.

Clinical treatment is also difficult because few of the persons treated are willing to bring in their spouses for parallel treatment, let alone their other sexual partners. Perhaps the most hopeful approach would be the one adopted in Thailand, and that is to insist on condom use in all commercial sex. The African situation is much more difficult than that of Thailand (P. Caldwell, 1995). There are far more gradations of commercial sex in Africa than in Thailand, and there is less likelihood of any mandatory use of condoms being successfully policed.

There is broad resistance to change in sub-Saharan Africa, as set out a decade ago (Caldwell *et al.*, 1992*a*) and little has changed since then. This resistance includes multi-causal explanations for sickness and death, which blunt beliefs in a single type of treatment.

They also include widespread beliefs in predestination which weaken efforts to achieve behavioural change.

The efforts to achieve behavioural change have been surprisingly mild in view of the magnitude of the epidemic. Some behavioural change is occurring (Konde-Lule, 1995; Pool et al., 1996), especially among younger people in Uganda. There is little evidence that this arises from the educational programmes rather than the sheer experience of death and funerals, but the two may interact.

Nevertheless, this beginning of behavioural change is probably one of the bright spots in the control of STDs and AIDS. Another is the increasing condom use. A third is the decline in childlessness, even if this results from community use of antibiotics, in a way that is not to be entirely desired.

## Acknowledgements

This work has benefited from assistance from Rebecca Kippen, Jeff Marck, Wendy Cosford and Pat Goodall.

## References

Arya, O. P., Nsanzumuhire, H., Taber, S. R. (1973) Clinical, cultural and demographic aspects of gonorrhoea in a rural community in Uganda. *Bulletin of the World Health Organization* **49**:587–95.

Awusabo-Asare, K., Boerma, J. T., Zaba, B. (eds.) (1997) *Evidence of the socio-demographic impact of AIDS in Africa.* Supplement 2 to *Health Transition Review* 7. Canberra: Australian National University.

Bakare, M. (1990) Sexual behaviour and reproductive health: a case study of urban women and men in Owo, Ondo State. MA thesis, Ondo State University, Ado-Ekiti, Nigeria.

Batter, V., Matela, B., Nsuami, M. et al. (1994) High HIV-1 incidence in young women masked by stable overall seroprevalence among childbearing women in Kinshasa, Zaire: estimating incidence from serial seroprevalence data. *AIDS* **8**:811–17.

Belsey, M. A. (1976) The epidemiology of infertility: a review with particular reference to sub-Saharan Africa. *Bulletin of the World Health Organization* **54**:319–41.

Bergström, S. (1990) Genital infections and reproductive health: infertility and morbidity of mother and child in developing countries. *Scandinavian Journal of Infectious Disease Supplement* **69**:99–105.

Blacker, J. G. C. (1962) Population growth and differential fertility in Zanzibar Protectorate. *Population Studies* **15**:258–66.

Bongaarts, J., Reining, P., Way, P., Conant, F. (1989) The relationship between male circumcision and HIV infection in African populations. *AIDS* **3**:373–77.

Brunham, R. C., Garnett, G. P., Swinton, J., Anderson, R. M. (1992) Gonococcal infection and human fertility in sub-Saharan Africa. *Proceedings of the Royal Society of London, Series B, Biological Sciences* **246**:173–77.

Brunham, R. C., Cheang, M., McMaster, J., Garnett, G., Anderson, R. (1993) *Chlamydia trachomatis*, infertility and population growth in sub-Saharan Africa. *Sexually Transmitted Diseases* **20**:168–73.

Caldwell, J. C. (1979) Variations in the incidence of sexual abstinence and the duration of postnatal abstinence among the Yoruba of Nigeria. In: Leridon, H., Menken, J. (eds.) *Natural fertility* (pp. 397–407). Liège: Ordina.

Caldwell, J. C. (1985) The social repercussions of colonial rule: demographic aspects. In: Boahen, A. A. (ed.) *Africa under colonial domination, 1880–1935*, volume 7. *UNESCO General History of Africa* (pp. 458–86). Paris: UNESCO.

Caldwell, J. C. (1997) The impact of the African AIDS epidemic. In: Awusabo-Asare, K., Boerma, J. T., Zaba, B. (eds.) *Evidence of the socio-demographic impact of AIDS in Africa*. Supplement 2 to *Health Transition Review* 7 (pp. 458–86). Canberra: Australian National University.

Caldwell, J. C., Caldwell, P. (1977) Marital sexual abstinence: a study of the Yoruba in Nigeria. *Population Studies* **31**:193–217.

Caldwell, J. C., Caldwell, P. (1983) The demographic evidence for the incidence and cause of abnormally low fertility in tropical Africa. *World Health Statistics Quarterly* **36**:2–21.

Caldwell, J. C., Caldwell, P. (1987) The cultural context of high fertility in sub-Saharan Africa. *Population and Development Review* **13**:409–37.

Caldwell, J. C., Caldwell, P. (1993) The nature and limits of the sub-Saharan African AIDS epidemic: evidence from geographic and other patterns. *Population and Development Review* **19**:817–48.

Caldwell, J. C., Caldwell, P. (1994) The neglect of an epidemiological explanation for the distribution of HIV/AIDS in sub-Saharan Africa: exploring the male circumcision hypothesis. In: Cleland, J., Way, P. (eds.) *AIDS impact and prevention in the developing world: demographic and social science perspectives*. Supplement to *Health Transition Review* 4 (pp. 23–46). Canberra: Australian National University.

Caldwell, J. C., Caldwell, P., Quiggin, P. (1989) The social context of AIDS in sub-Saharan Africa. *Population and Development Review* **15**:185–234.

Caldwell, J. C., Caldwell, P., Quiggin, P. (1991*a*) The African sexual system: reply to Le Blanc *et al. Population and Development Review* **17**:506–15.

Caldwell, J. C., Orubuloye, I. O., Caldwell, P. (1991*b*) The destabilization of the traditional Yoruba sexual system. *Population and Development Review* **17**:229–62.

Caldwell, J. C., Orubuloye, I. O., Caldwell, P. (1992*a*) Underreaction to AIDS in sub-Saharan Africa. *Social Science and Medicine* **34**:1169–82.

Caldwell, J. C., Orubuloye, I. O., Caldwell, P. (1992*b*) Fertility decline in Africa: a new type of transition?. *Population and Development Review* **18**:211–42.

Caldwell, J. C., Caldwell P., Orubuloye, I.O. (1992*c*) The family and sexual networking in sub-Saharan Africa: historical regional differences and present-day implications. *Population Studies* **46**:385–410.

Caldwell, P. (1995) Prostitution and the risk of STDs and AIDS in Nigeria and Thailand. In: Orubuloye, I. O., Caldwell, J. C., Caldwell P., Jain, S. (eds.) *The Third World AIDS epidemic.* Supplement to *Health Transition Review* 5. Canberra: Australian National University.

Carpenter, L. M., Nakiyingi, J. S., Ruberantwari, A., Malamba, S., Kamali, A., Whitworth, J. A. G. (1997) Estimates of the impact of HIV-1 infection on fertility in a rural Ugandan population cohort. In: Awusabo-Asare, K., Boerma, J. T., Zaba, B. (eds.) *Evidence of the socio-demographic impact of AIDS in Africa.* Supplement 2 to *Health Transition Review* 7 (pp. 113–26). Canberra: Australian National University.

Cates, W., Farley, T. M. M., Rowe, P. J. (1985) Worldwide patterns of infertility: is Africa different?. *Lancet* **II**:596–98; no. 8455.

Cates, W., Rolfs, R. T., Aral, S. O. (1990) Sexually transmitted diseases, pelvic inflammatory disease, and infertility: an epidemiologic update. *Epidemiologic Review* **12**:199–220.

Cates, W., Rolfs, R. T., Aral, S. O. (1993) The pathophysiology of sexually transmitted diseases in relation to pelvic inflammatory disease and infertility. In: Gray, R., Leridon, H., Spira, A. (eds.) *Biomedical and demographic determinants of reproduction* (pp. 101–25). Oxford: Clarendon.

Clignet, R. (1970) *Many wives, many powers: authority and power in polygynous families.* Evanston, IL: Northwestern University Press.

Coale, A. J., Lorimer, F. (1968) Summary of estimates of fertility and mortality. In: Brass, W., Coale, A. J., van de Walle, E. (eds.) *The demography of tropical Africa* (pp. 151–67). Princeton: Princeton University Press.

Collet, M., Reniers, J., Frost, E. *et al.* (1988) Infertility in Central Africa: infection is the cause. *International Journal of Gynecology and Obstetrics* **26**:423–8.

David, N., Voas, D. (1981) Societal causes of infertility and population decline among the settled Fulani of North Cameroon. *Man* **16**:644–64.

De Schryver, A., Méheus, A. (1990) Epidemiology of sexually transmitted diseases: the global picture. *Bulletin of the World Health Organization* **68**:639–54.

Ericksen, K., Brunette, T. (1996) Patterns and predictors of infertility among African women: a cross-national survey of twenty-seven nations. *Social Science and Medicine* **42**:209–20.

Farley, T. M. M., Belsey, E.M. (1988) The prevalence and aetiology of infertility. In: *African population conference, Dakar, 1988* (pp. 2.1.15–2.1.30). International Union for the Scientific Study of Population. Liège: Ordina.

Feldman-Savelsburg, P. (1994) Plundered kitchens and empty wombs: fear of infertility in the Cameroonian grassfields. *Social Science and Medicine* **39**:463–74.

François, M. (1975) Gabon. In: Caldwell, J. C. (ed.) *Population growth and socioeconomic change in West Africa* (pp. 630–56). New York: Columbia University Press.

Frank, O. (1983) Infertility in sub-Saharan Africa: estimates and implications. *Population and Development Review* **9**:137–44.

Gluckman, M. (1950) Kinship and marriage among the Lozi of Northern Rhodesia and the Zulu of Natal. In: Radcliffe-Brown, A., Forde, D. (eds.) *African systems of kinship and marriage* (pp. 166–206). London: Oxford University Press.

Goldman, N., Pebley, A. (1989) The demography of polygyny in sub-Saharan Africa. In: Lesthaeghe, R. J. (ed.) *Reproduction and social organization in sub-Saharan Africa* (pp. 212–37). Berkeley: University of California Press.

Goody, J. R. (1976) *Production and reproduction: a comparative study of the domestic domain.* Cambridge: Cambridge University Press.

Gray, R. H., Serwadda, D., Wawer, M.J. *et al.* (1997) Reduced fertility in women with HIV infection: a population-based study in Uganda. Paper presented to the International Union for the Scientific Study of Population conference on The Socio-demographic Impact of AIDS in Africa, Durban, 3–6 February, 1997.

Gregson, S., Zhuwau, T., Anderson, R. M., Chandiwana, S. (1996) *The early socio-demographic impact of the HIV-1 epidemic in rural Zimbabwe: summary report of findings from the Manicaland study of HIV-1 and fertility.* Harare: Blair Research Institute; and Oxford: Centre for Epidemiology of Infectious Disease, Department of Zoology, Oxford University.

Gregson, S., Zhuwau, T., Anderson, R. M., Chandiwana, S.K. (1997) HIV and fertility change in rural Zimbabwe. In: Awusabo-Asare, K., Boerma, J. T., Zaba, B. (eds.) *Evidence of the socio-demographic impact of AIDS in Africa.* Supplement 2 to *Health Transition Review* 7 (pp. 89–112). Canberra: Australian National University.

Griffith, H. B. (1963) Gonorrhoea and fertility in Uganda. *Eugenics Review* **55**:103–08.

Grodstein, F., Goldman, M. B., Cramer, D. W. (1993) Relation of tubal infertility to history of sexually transmitted diseases. *American Journal of Epidemiology* **137**:577–84.

Health Studies Branch (1998) Recent HIV seroprevalence levels by country: January 1998. Research Note 24. Washington DC: International Programs Center, Population Division, US Bureau of the Census.

Henin, R. A. (1969) The patterns and causes of fertility differentials in the Sudan. *Population Studies* **23**:171–98.

Jenkins, C. (1993) Fertility and infertility in Papua New Guinea. *American Journal of Human Biology* **5**:75–83.

Konde-Lule, J. K. (1995) The declining HIV seroprevalence in Uganda: what evidence?. In: Orubuloye, I. O., Caldwell, J. C., Caldwell P., Jain, S. (eds.) *The Third World AIDS epidemic* (pp. 27–33). Canberra: Australian National University.

Larsen, U. (1989) A comparative study of the levels and differentials of sterility in Cameroon, Kenya and Sudan. In: Lesthaeghe, R. J. (ed.) *Reproduction and social organization in sub-Saharan Africa* (pp. 167–211). Berkeley: University of California Press.

Larsen, U. (1994) Sterility in sub-Saharan Africa. *Population Studies* **48**:459–74.

Larsen, U. (1995) Differentials in infertility in Cameroon and Nigeria. *Population Studies* **49**:329–46.

Larsen, U. (1996) Childlessness, subfertility and infertility in Tanzania. *Studies in Family Planning* **27**:18–28.

Larsen, U., Menken, J. (1991) Individual level sterility: a new method of estimation with application to sub-Saharan Africa. *Demography* **28**:229–47.

Leblanc, M.-N., Meintel, D., Piché, V. (1991) The African sexual system: fact or fiction? *Population and Development Review* **17**:497–505.

Lesthaeghe, R., Kaufmann, G., Meekers, D. (1989) The nuptiality regimes in sub-Saharan Africa. In: Lesthaeghe, R. J. (ed.) *Reproduction and social organization in sub-Saharan Africa* (pp. 238–337). Berkeley: University of California Press.

Mabey, D.C.W., Ogbaselassie, G., Robertson, J. N., Heckels, J. E., Ward, M. E. (1985) Tubal infertility in the Gambia: chlamydial and gonococcal serology in women with tubal occlusion compared with pregnant controls. *Bulletin of the World Health Organization* **63**:1107–13.

Mammo, A., Morgan, S. P. (1986) Childlessness in rural Ethiopia. *Population and Development Review* **12**:533–46.

Moses, S., Bradley, J. E., Nagelkerke, N. J. D., Ronald, A. R., Ndinya-Achola, J. O., Plummer, F. A. (1990) Geographical patterns of male circumcision practices in Africa: association with HIV prevalence. *International Journal of Epidemiology* **19**:693–7.

Mtimavalye, L. A., Belsey, M. A. (1987) Infertility and sexually transmitted disease: major problems in maternal and child health and family planning.

Paper presented at International Conference on Better Health for Women and Children through Family Planning, Nairobi 5–9 October.

Ntozi, J., Nakanaabi, I., Lubaale, Y. (1997) Fertility levels and trends in the face of the AIDS epidemic in Uganda. In Ntozi, J. P. M., Anarfi, J. K., Awusabo-Asare, K., Caldwell, J. C., Jain, S. (eds.) *Vulnerability to HIV infection and effects of AIDS in Africa and Asia/India*. Supplement 1 to *Health Transition Review* 7 (pp. 145–55). Canberra: Australian National University.

Orubuloye, I. O., Caldwell, J. C., Caldwell, P. (1991) Sexual networking in the Ekiti District of Nigeria. *Studies in Family Planning* **22**:61–73.

Orubuloye, I. O., Caldwell, J. C., Caldwell, P. (1992) Diffusion and focus in sexual networking: identifying partners and partners' partners. *Studies in Family Planning* **23**:343–51.

Orubuloye, I. O., Caldwell, J. C., Caldwell, P. (1993*a*) African women's control over their sexuality in an era of AIDS: a study of the Yoruba of Nigeria. *Social Science and Medicine* **3**:859–72.

Orubuloye, I. O., Caldwell, P., Caldwell, J. C. (1993*b*) The role of high-risk occupations in the spread of AIDS: truck drivers and itinerant market women in Nigeria, *International Family Planning Perspectives* **19**:43–8.

Orubuloye, I. O., Caldwell, P., Caldwell, J. C. (1994) Commercial sex workers in Nigeria in the shadow of AIDS. In: Orubuloye, I. O., Caldwell, J. C., Caldwell, P., Santow, G. (eds.) *Sexual networking and AIDS in sub-Saharan Africa: behavioural research and the social context* (pp. 101–16). Canberra: Australian National University, Health Transition Centre.

Orubuloye, I. O., Caldwell, J. C., Caldwell, P. (1997) Perceived male sexual needs and male sexual behaviour in southwest Nigeria. *Social Science and Medicine* **44**:1195–207.

Paavonen, J., Wølner-Hanssen, P. (1989) *Chlamydia trachomatis*: a major threat to reproduction. *Human Reproduction* **4**:111–24.

Page, H. J. (1975) Fertility levels: patterns and trends. In: Caldwell, J. C. (ed.) *Population growth and socioeconomic change in West Africa* (pp. 29–57). New York: Columbia University Press.

Page, H. J., Coale, A. J. (1972) Fertility and child mortality south of the Sahara. In: Ominde, S. H., Ejiogu, C.N. (eds.) *Population growth and economic development in Africa* (pp. 51–66). London: Heinemann.

Page, H. J., Lesthaeghe, R. (eds.) (1981) *Child-spacing in tropical Africa: traditions and change*. London: Academic Press.

PATH (1997) Infertility in developing countries. *Outlook* **15**:1–6.

Peel, J. D. Y. (1983) *Ijeshas and Nigerians: the incorporation of a Yoruba Kingdom, 1890s–1970s*. Cambridge: Cambridge University Press.

Piot, P., Tezzo, R. (1990) The epidemiology of HIV and other sexually transmitted infections in the developing world. *Scandinavian Journal of Infectious Diseases, Supplement* **69**:89–97.

Pool, R., Maswe, M., Boerma, J. T., Nnko, S. (1996) The price of promiscuity:

why urban males in Tanzania are changing their sexual behaviour. *Health Transition Review* **6**:203–21.

Rallu, J.-L. (1992) From decline to recovery: the Marquesan population 1886–1945. *Health Transition Review* **2**:177–94.

Reniers, J., Collet, M., Rost, F., Leclerc, A., Ivanoff, B., Méheus, A. (1989) Chlamydial antibodies and tubal infertility. *International Journal of Epidemiology* **18**:261–3.

Reyna, S. P. (1975) Age differential, marital instability, and venereal disease: factors affecting fertility among the Northwest Barma. In: Nag, M. (ed.) *Population and social organization* (pp. 55–73). The Hague: Mouton.

Romaniuk, A. (1961) *Aspect démographique de la stérilité des femmes congolaises.* l'Université Léopoldville, Institut de Recherches Economiques et Sociales, Studia Universitatis, Lovanium.

Romaniuk, A. (1968) Infertility in tropical Africa. In: Caldwell, J. C., Okonjo, C. (eds.) *The population of tropical Africa* (pp. 214–24). London: Longmans.

Ryder, R. W., Batter, V. L., Nsuami, M., Badi, N., Mundele, L., Matela, B., Utshudi, M., Heyward, W. L. (1991) Fertility rates in 238 HIVI-seropositive women in Zaire followed for 3 years post-partum. *AIDS* **5**:1521–7.

Sherris, J. D., Fox, G. (1983) Infertility and sexually transmitted disease: a public health challenge. *Population Reports* Series L, No. 4:L113–51.

Stanecki, K. A., Way, P.O. (1997) The demographic impacts of HIV/AIDS: perspectives from the World Population Profile: 1996. IPC Staff Paper no. 86. Washington DC: International Programs Center, Population Division, US Bureau of the Census.

Tabutin, D. (1979) Fécondité et mortalité dans l'Ouest de Zaire. Working Paper no. 71. Département de démographie, Université catholique de Louvain.

Tabutin, D. (1982) Evolution régionale de la fécondité dans l'Ouest de Zaire. *Population* **37**:29–50.

Vaessen, M. (1984) *Childlessness and infecundity.* WFS Comparative Studies no. 31. Voorburg: International Statistical Institute.

Wasserheit, J. N. (1989) The significance and scope of reproductive tract infections among Third World women. *International Journal of Gynecology and Obstetrics, Supplement* **3**:145–68.

World Health Organization (1987) Infections, pregnancies and infertility: perspectives on prevention. *Fertility and Sterility* **47**:964–8.

# PART III:

# Social perspectives on infertility

# 6

## Voluntary childlessness: trends and implications

F. MCALLISTER AND L. CLARKE

## Introduction

In this chapter we look at voluntary childlessness in Britain and compare it with that in other Western countries. At first sight the topic of choosing to remain childless appears misplaced in a volume primarily concerned with infertility, yet the choice of childlessness has increasingly become a focus of research and policy interest. The low fertility regimes of the developed world have become entrenched, while concerns are periodically expressed about the relatively small number of children being born in current generations. As the average age at motherhood has increased in many Western societies, the issue of distinguishing between those who postpone parenthood and those who renounce it altogether has become of key interest. The later ages at childbirth make this distinction all the more difficult to achieve while there are still childbearing years left in any given birth cohort of women. Of course, having fewer children and/or having them later in life are not in themselves the same as deciding against having children at all. Furthermore, in a climate where postponing parenthood is more common, fertility problems may increase. This problem is dealt with more fully in Chapter 1, by Fishel, Dowell and Thornton.

If, as is the case in Britain, increasing proportions of women of reproductive age are remaining childless, and a majority delay parenthood, it is important to examine the extent to which these trends reflect a greater desire amongst adults to live without children. Demographers have focused on the connections between reduced fertility and increasing childlessness as well as widespread value shifts away from family solidarity towards more individualist concerns. Other social scientists have looked at the division of labour among couples before and after parenthood, and the changing costs and benefits of parenthood for women in an era when their roles have expanded and developed in the public sphere, especially in formal employment.

From the current state of knowledge in both demographic and sociological disciplines, it is impossible to draw absolute conclusions about trends in fertility and childlessness. The difficulties of reconstructing fertility at the population level and fertility decisions made by individuals using demographic and survey data are reviewed in the sections 'Demographic trends in childlessness in Britain' to 'Defining voluntary childlessness'. The section entitled 'Choosing childlessness: summary of the qualitative study' discusses the design and findings of an in-depth qualitative study of voluntary childlessness in Britain. This study sought to define the nature of choosing childlessness more clearly, and found that people in this category had varying perspectives on the nature and extent of their choice in this matter. It is impossible to isolate the process of choosing childlessness from the wider climate of values concerning the importance of parenthood, the status of women, and the status and treatment of infertility. In the last sections we look at the role of values in explaining fertility trends and decisions and whether these are either appropriate for, or susceptible to, policy interventions.

It might be argued that the flurry of studies that emerged in the 1970s and early 1980s concerning the choice of childlessness were borne out of an interest in childlessness as a mode of 'ultimate feminism', reflecting the shift away from seeing women as purely domestic in their interests. In the 1990s, a major impetus to find out more has been the behaviour of women themselves: with 20% of the current British cohorts predicted to remain childless, the place of choice in low-fertility regimes, and its implications for the future of social care (particularly of the elderly) have become critical issues. This chapter also explores the extent to which it is appropriate to see choosing childlessness as either a 'population problem' or a 'women problem'. Frequently we have to conclude that better data and more research are required.

# Demographic trends in childlessness in Britain

## *Lifetime experience of childlessness*

The increase in lifetime childlessness has received a great deal of attention in the past few years. There has been an increase in the proportions of women remaining childless at each age for cohorts born since 1950, as shown in Table 6.1. More than one in six women (17%) born in 1952 were childless at the end of their childbearing life (age 45), compared with only just over one in ten (11%) born a decade earlier. Current projections, based on extra-polating from the trends in each cohort and questions about family intentions from the General Household Survey (GHS), suggest that as many as 20% (one-fifth) of women born in 1975 and later will remain childless. This is double the level experienced by the 1945 cohort (10%), and one-third higher than women born in 1950 (14%) (Cooper and Shaw, 1993).

The prospect of one-fifth of women remaining childless might be viewed with alarm by some people, but it is not without precedent. Childlessness was quite common up until the early part of the twentieth century. In the past, up to one-quarter of women have remained unmarried, and of these the majority had no children (Wrigley and Schofield, 1983). Over one-fifth (21%) of women born in the 1920s remained childless. The experience of childlessness, however, reached an all-time low for women born immediately after the Second World War. Only 5% of the 1946 cohort were never married by the age of 35, and only around 9% remained childless (Kiernan, 1989). The proportion of women remaining childless has risen for every subsequent birth cohort (Table 6.1), such that 16% of women born in 1952 had not had a child by the age of 45, matching the 1922 cohort of women. Up to 23% of younger generations of women, born since the 1960s, are projected to remain childless (Ruddock *et al.*, 1998).

Table 6.1. *Percentage of childless women by age and birth cohort in England and Wales*

| Women born in: | Age (years) | | | Approx. end of child bearing |
|---|---|---|---|---|
| | 25 | 35 | 45 | |
| 1922 | 48 | 20 | 18 | 1967 |
| 1927 | 45 | 18 | 16 | 1972 |
| 1932 | 43 | 15 | 13 | 1977 |
| 1937 | 37 | 13 | 12 | 1982 |
| 1942 | 33 | 12 | 11 | 1987 |
| 1947 | 37 | 14 | 12 | 1992 |
| 1952 | 45 | 18 | 16 | 1997 |
| 1957 | 51 | 21 | 17 | 2002 |
| 1962 | 58 | 25 | 21 | 2007 |
| 1967 | 61 | 29 | 22 | 2012 |
| 1972 | 63 | 29 | 23 | 2017 |

Figures above the line represent actual events which occurred up to the end of 1997. Figures below the line incorporate projected births from 1998 onwards. Projected births are calculated using the Government Actuary's Department principal 1996-based projection.
*Source:* Ruddock *et al.* (1998).

There is some suggestion that the pattern of increasing childlessness is abating in the most recent cohorts of women (those born in the mid-1970s). While 21% of women born in 1965 and 1970 are projected to remain childless, the figure for women born in 1975 is 20%, the same as women born in 1960 (Cooper and Shaw, 1993). This is because more of the 1975 cohort had children as teenagers than those born in the mid-1960s and 1970. Only time will tell how many will remain childless at older ages. While the rate of increase in childlessness may be slowing, the phenomenon of childlessness may continue to increase for some time in spite of the shift towards later childbearing. Among young women, more than 60% of those born in both 1967 and 1972 had not had a child by the age of 25 (Table 6.1).

## Problems with demographic data

The true measure of childlessness can only be determined when women reach the end of their fertile life, but trends can be gleaned from the proportions childless by age. The problem with these statistics is that they do not reveal women's intentions or the processes involved in reaching a desired fertility level. The statistics do not distinguish between how many women are actually choosing not to have children, how many are delaying childbearing, how many are experiencing infertility problems because of their age or other problems, and how many did not intend to be childless but now have none because of unpropitious circumstances (Prioux, 1993). The issue of defining voluntary and involuntary childlessness is dealt with in the section starting on p. 201. Here we examine other problems in the interpretation of the childlessness data.

## Postponing or rejecting parenthood?

The crux of this issue is whether women are definitely rejecting parenthood, or whether the increase in childlessness reflects a postponement of parenthood. Certainly, the average age at first birth has increased for women in most Western countries (Armitage and Babb, 1996). As women face increasing fertility problems after the age of 35, delaying the decision to have children may lead to infecundity. This delay, combined with low targets for family size, may result in childlessness (Beets, 1995). The classic case of 'forgetting' to have children until it is too late has been facilitated by the advent of effective contraception, but this in itself does not create childlessness. Motivations to avoid having children may be deliberate or indirect, perhaps unwitting. The postponement of first births is part of a general trend known as the Second Demographic Transition. This includes the increased incidence of cohabitation, the postponement of marriage, lower rates of marriage, the rise in divorce, low total fertility, the increase in nonmarital births and the increased use of birth control (Van de Kaa, 1987). All of these trends in demographic behaviour are related to the increase in childlessness (Beets, 1995).

## Effects of changing behaviour

Undoubtedly, changes in behaviour have important implications for childbearing patterns. Trends such as later ages at leaving home, the increased likelihood of living alone after leaving home (especially for men) and the increasing prevalence of cohabitation – rather than marriage – as a first union, are related to later ages at first birth and increases in the proportion of births occurring outside marriage. The greater instability of cohabiting unions may also play a role in postponing first births indefinitely for some women. Women's rising age at finishing full-time education, their greater propensity to follow careers, as well as society's generally increasing aspirations for consumables must also play a role in delaying motherhood.

## Lack of data about men

Another problem with demographic data concerning fertility and childlessness lies in its emphasis on women. There is a paucity of data on male fertility behaviour that is only just beginning to be addressed (Burghes et al., 1997). Coleman (1995) noted that rates for male and female fertility and childlessness differ. He suggests that the current low fertility rates in Western countries would be even lower if they were measured using men's behaviour rather than women's. Using data from the National Survey of Health and Development (NSHD) 1946 cohort study in Britain, Coleman showed that, at age 49–50, more men than women were childless – 22% of men were childless compared with 13% of women. This was confirmed in recent analyses of men of all ages using data from the British Household Panel Study (Clarke et al., 1996, 1998) and also in Danish fertility studies (Knudsen, 1996). The results for the National Child Development Survey (NCDS) 1958 cohort, when last interviewed at age 33, fit with this result. More men (28%) than women (18%) were still childless. Age differences at partnership and first parenthood might be expected for the different genders in this study. Men tend to have children at later ages than women, certainly more men (44%) than women (26%) who did not have children said they intended to have children (McAllister and Clarke, 1998).

## Low fertility, childlessness and family intentions in an international context: childlessness in other industrialized countries

Childlessness is an important and growing component in nearly all European countries. Its prevalence is far from uniform both within and between countries, and it seems likely to generate substantial differences in fertility levels between countries (Coleman, 1993, 1998). The experience of childlessness in completed birth cohorts for a number of European countries from Eurostat is shown in Table 6.2. It can be seen that about one-fifth or more of women have remained childless in only Germany and England and Wales. This level is also projected for a number of other countries in the near future (Austria, Finland, The Netherlands and Switzerland) (Prioux, 1993). According to these earlier estimates, the U.K. would have around the fifth highest proportion of childless women in Europe for the 1955 birth cohorts, with 16% of women childless at the age of 37 in 1992. This projected figure is confirmed by the latest estimates for this cohort at the age of 40 (Office for National Statistics, 1998*b*).

These figures are similar to those of many other industrialized countries, for example Canada, Austria, and various Eastern European countries (Coleman, 1998). Such figures are difficult to obtain, however, and different sources (e.g. Eurostat, the National Family and Fertility Surveys) provide differing estimates. Projections of current trends suggest that, in many countries, from one-fifth to one-quarter of women will remain childless throughout their life-times (Morgan and Chen, 1992; Coleman 1998). While only about 5% of women are truly infertile, rates of infertility and involuntary childlessness are likely to increase with postponement of first births (Beets, 1995; Rindfuss *et al.*, 1988).

There is nothing new about childlessness in other European countries (Coleman, 1996). As many as one-fifth (20%) of women

Table 6.2. *Percentage of childless women by birth cohort in Europe, 1930–60*

| | Year of birth | | | | | | | | | |
| | | | | | | | Includes projections | | | |
| | 1930 % | 1935 % | 1940 % | 1945 % | 1950 % | 1955 % | 1956 % | 1957 % | 1958 % | 1959 % | 1960 % |
|---|---|---|---|---|---|---|---|---|---|---|---|
| Portugal | 4 | 4 | 6 | 5 | 9 | 8 | 7 | 7 | 6 | 7 | 8 |
| Finland | – | – | 14 | 14 | 16 | 18 | 18 | 18 | 18 | 18 | 18 |
| Sweden | – | – | 13 | 12 | 13 | 13 | 13 | 13 | 13 | 13 | 13 |
| E & W[1] | 13 | 11 | 11 | 10 | 14 | 17 | 18 | 18 | 19 | 21 | – |
| Norway | – | 10 | 9 | 9 | 9 | 11 | 12 | 12 | 12 | 11 | 11 |
| Belgium | – | 9 | 9 | 9 | 10 | 10 | 11 | 11 | – | – | – |
| Denmark | – | – | 10 | 8 | 10 | 13 | 13 | 13 | 13 | 13 | 12 |
| Germany | – | 9 | 11 | 13 | 15 | 22 | 23 | 24 | 25 | 26 | – |
| Spain | – | – | 8 | 6 | 10 | 10 | 11 | 10 | 10 | 12 | 11 |
| France | 12 | 10 | 8 | 7 | 7 | 8 | 8 | 8 | – | – | – |
| Ireland | – | 4 | 5 | 6 | 9 | 14 | 15 | 16 | 16 | – | – |
| Italy | – | 13 | 13 | 10 | 11 | 11 | 12 | 13 | 14 | 15 | 15 |
| Netherlands | – | 12 | 12 | 12 | 15 | 17 | 17 | 18 | 18 | 19 | 18 |

[1]   England and Wales.

*Source:* Demographic Statistics 1997, Eurostat.

and over one-tenth of men remained childless in many European countries from the sixteenth century up until the 1930s, most notably in Sweden and Ireland. Up until the late nineteenth century, however, childlessness was common because a relatively large number of people never married, or did so late in life. Childbearing outside marriage was uncommon in most European countries (seldom more than 5% of all births) but infertile marriages were at the highest level (Coleman, 1998). Voluntary childlessness in marriage was rare and birth control not generally practised. These historical features are part of what was termed the Western European marriage pattern (Hajnal, 1965). The current high levels of childlessness, while similar in magnitude, are very different from those of the past. There is the element of choice that did not exist before.

## Low fertility and childlessness

Levels of childlessness seem at odds with the relatively high annual fertility rates of England and Wales, compared with the other 15 European countries for which appropriate data are available. In fact, there appears to be no relationship between annual fertility levels and experience of childlessness (Coleman, 1998). In a comparison of 15 European countries, Coleman (1993, 1996) found no statistical correlation ($r$=0.09) between the annual 1989 Total Fertility Rate (a period measure) and the proportion of women born in 1950 who were childless in 1989 (a cohort measure). This has been confirmed by further data on 17 industrialized countries with 1994 data (Coleman, 1998). Thus, while the experience of childlessness is a common feature of these countries, national differences and trends in childbearing and family formation remain intriguing.

## Family intentions

Data about birth expectations or intentions and achieved number of children can also show interesting disparities. The most recent data on increasing childlessness among young women are at odds with their stated family intentions. There is evidence that the youngest women may be more likely to say they expect to be childless, but levels fall far short of the recent proportions experiencing childlessness at the end of their childbearing years. A comparison of the GHS birth expectations data shows that the proportion of women aged 16–22 years who stated they expected to remain childless has doubled for the 1965–69 cohort and the 1970–74 cohort, from 5% in the former to 10% in the latter. This is only half of the estimated 20% who will remain childless.

However, family-building intentions are known to change as people age (Shaw, 1989). The proportion of young women at the start of their childbearing lives who state they are likely to remain childless is much lower than that of women 10 or 20 years older, while the proportion expecting to have precisely two children is higher. The evidence concerning trends in family size, however, is that the level of childlessness is increasing for recent cohorts of women, whereas the proportion with two children is decreasing (Cooper and Shaw, 1993). It seems likely, therefore, that some women initially say they expect to have two children but, in practice, may not have children at all or only have one child. This disparity between intention and practice could result, perhaps, because some women have not considered this decision at such an early stage of their childbearing lives and are expressing some ideal family size.

The relatively low proportion of women in Britain who state they do not want to have children is also found in most other European countries (European Commission, 1990). The British figure was the joint lowest in the European Community (EC) at the end of the 1980s – 2% in 1989 – shared with Greece, Ireland and Italy. The highest figure, of 9%, was in Germany. It is interesting that the number of women preferring to have only one child at least doubled in most European countries during the 1980s, increasing from 2% to 10% in Britain (Coleman, 1993).

## Factors associated with childlessness

Childless couples are different from couples with children but not that different, while women tend to show more differences than men in the two groups (Baum, 1983; Campbell, 1985; Kiernan, 1989; Rovi, 1994; and Schneewind, 1997 cited in Coleman, 1998). Studies show that women with no children tend to be better educated, professionally or career-orientated and ambitious, are less likely to be religious or to have been married in church (Jacobson and Heaton, 1991), are individually more hedonistic, more likely to be an only child, and to be emotionally distant from their parents (Campbell, 1983) compared to the women with children. However, they are no more neurotic, immature or selfish than others (Coleman, 1998). The recent study described below shows a lack of career motivation for childlessness (McAllister and Clarke, 1998).

While childlessness has become accepted practice, it is still not a majority choice. Perhaps we should be asking why people choose to have children at all in a society that allows choice? The estimated direct (£90,000) and indirect (£250,000) costs of children suggest that an intention to have children might be considered irrational (Joshi *et al.*, 1996, Middleton *et al.*, 1998). In addition, children do not appear to bring happiness, quite the contrary in fact. Children detract sharply from marital contentment as soon as they are born, and progressively reduce it to a low point during the teenage years (Walker, 1977 cited in Coleman, 1998). Marital contentment only reappears after the last child is safely out of the house.

## *What role does education play in choosing childlessness?*

Variations in the timing of births and completed family size have been linked to women's educational level. The GHS data show that women with General Certificate of Education (GCE) Advanced (A) level, or higher, qualifications delay their childbearing and have higher than average numbers of children in their thirties compared with women with lower educational attainment. By the age of 35, the mean numbers of children were 2.22 for women with no qualifications and 1.5 for women with at least GCE A level or its equivalent. Twice as many women born in the early 1950s with higher levels of qualifications (at least GCE Ordinary (O) levels) expected to remain childless compared with women in the same cohort with no qualifications (Office for National Statistics, 1998*a*).

de Wit and Rajulton (1992) looked at the correlation between education and timing of parenthood among women in Canada. Their analysis of cohort data suggested that education was a 'primary predictor' of the timing of first birth, and they reported 'relatively large and significant rates of childlessness . . . among ever-married women with higher levels of education'. They hypothesize that in contemporary society, women with higher levels of education may tend to delay parenthood for the following reasons:

- economic costs of education;
- education equips people to make cost/benefit analyses in decision-making;

- education raises expectations which raises the investment costs of children;
- opportunity costs for careers;
- education increases knowledge of contraception; and
- encourages personal fulfillment and goals for the future (including raised parenting goals).

Jacobson and Heaton (1991) examined data from the National Survey of Families and Households in the United States (1987–8), in order to specify the relationship between voluntary childlessness and a range of social and demographic variables. Education, race, occupation, preferred working hours, age and marital status were the background factors used in multivariate modelling relating to childlessness and attitudes towards having children. Educational level was not significantly or directly related to childlessness in men, but was related to higher rates of childlessness in women: more educated women had higher rates of childlessness even when other variables were taken into account. Nevertheless, only a minority of the most educated women were childless and expected to remain so.

### Is family taking second place to work for women?

It is sometimes assumed that increasing opportunities for work outside the home has led 'automatically' to women's postponement or rejection of parenthood. However, closer examination of the trends in female employment in the U.K. suggests that the transformation of women's role in the labour market has perhaps been less dramatic. It is less than clear that fertility decisions and family life are taking second place to employment in the minds of the majority of women. It is also interesting to note that, according to the 1995 report on the British Social Attitudes Survey, nearly a quarter of women without dependent children work part-time (Thomson, 1995).

Clarke and Owen have used GHS data on women's family intentions to examine the relative importance of different characteristics of women who expect to remain childless (McAllister and

Clarke, 1998). They modelled the risks of British women expecting to be childless according to certain socio-demographic character-istics. Marital status was found to have an overwhelming influence in explaining expectations of childlessness. Women who were single were between three and four times more likely than married women to say that they would remain childless. Younger women were more likely to say they would not remain childless even when other characteristics were controlled. It was suggested, however, that the difference in the likelihood of expecting to be childless between single and married women is becoming increasingly smaller for younger cohorts. Women with no qualifications were significantly less likely to say they would remain childless than those with even minimal educational qualifications.

The lack of marriageable partners may no longer be an obstacle to childbearing, but the pursuit of other immediate goals may preclude this choice until a later stage. In determining the level of childlessness, what may matter more than a desire to avoid child-bearing are motivations that delay the decision to start a family or give it a low priority. The decision may not be faced until it is too late – women find they have 'forgotten' to have children because of other immediate priorities – or that when they do take this decision, they find they are infecund.

## Defining voluntary childlessness

Childlessness can result from intention or infertility. The distinction of the former as voluntary and the latter as involuntary, however, is misleading. It has been argued that biological infertility need not always equate with involuntary childlessness, and that voluntary childlessness does not exclude physical infertility (Condy, 1991; Rimmer, 1981). A woman who discovers an inherent fertility problem early in life may adapt positively to life without children; similarly someone who is sterilized may be functionally infertile but voluntarily so; thirdly, a woman who is positively oriented towards motherhood and considers herself to be voluntarily childless may in fact 'become' involuntarily childless through the discovery of a physical problem. This last example may be especially relevant where women are having children later in life. Some of those who have postponed childbirth may find that they are infertile or subfertile, while always having assumed that they were going to have children.

Infertility can be defined in several different ways. It is important to distinguish between:

- 'primary' infertility, which applies where a child has never been produced – i.e. there is a physical problem related to conception or bringing a pregnancy to term; and
- 'secondary' infertility, where a couple has had at least one child but then experiences problems in subsequent conception.

There is a consensus among studies from different countries that around 14% of individuals will have experience of infertility. Templeton (1992) contends that the evidence suggests that only a small proportion of infertility remains unresolved over time, to the extent that only 3–4% of couples in the population will remain involuntarily without children. This estimate of primary sterility confirms other estimates of the proportion of married couples who suffer from 'primary sterility' from the beginning of their marriage (Bongaarts and Potter, 1983; Werner, 1996). Such biological infertility is unlikely to vary between populations, at least within Europe (Coleman, 1993), although infecundity does increase with age. As the age of childbearing increases, more women who were previously fecund will find themselves sterile at a time when they want to start a family, the more so in societies where the age at first birth is delayed.Sterility in women is generally thought to reach serious levels after the age of 35, although increasing fertility problems may be faced from the age of 30 (Beets, 1995). More women are currently presenting for reproductive assistance than before, and they may 'end up as involuntarily childless' (Beets, 1995). At least one study has shown that women who declare their intention to remain childless tend to be consistent in their behaviour, but that 30% of those intending to have children remain childless after 5 years, with 10% now wishing to stay childless, notably the better educated and richer (Pol, 1983).

Noack and Ostby (1983) analysed data on involuntary and voluntary childlessness from the Norwegian Fertility Survey of 1977. The criteria for involuntary childlessness were purely physical and did not take account of women's orientation towards parenthood. Although the Norwegian data did not allow finer distinctions, they did show that the voluntary childless women (i.e. those without physical problems) were distinctive. A greater proportion of these women had a university education compared to mothers, and fewer of them were married. This study is comparatively rare in comparing women of all marital statuses, as much data pertaining to fertility trends concentrate on married women.

Noack and Ostby followed up their analysis in 1981, to see if the childless women remained so. They found that 2% of the infecund women (all of whom had been under 35 in 1977) subsequently gave birth, while 5% of the voluntarily childless (all of whom were under 40 in 1981) had had a child. They concluded, therefore, that the evidence points towards postponement and more temporary childlessness, rather than a dramatic increase in permanent childlessness. The follow-up aspect emphasizes the dynamic nature of both fertility and infertility, and shows how complex it is to measure real changes in childlessness over time.

## Screening for voluntary childlessness

Given some of the limits of our demographic knowledge of childlessness, it is easy to see why the less rigorous methods (snowballing, working through membership organizations) have often been employed to obtain a respondent group in qualitative studies.

The selection issue is especially sensitive as researchers are likely to encounter involuntary childlessness within any pool of potential respondents. There are also issues related to the age group of respondents, whether to interview individuals or couples and whether to include both sexes in studies. Each of these decisions works not only to create definitions for the research carried out, but also raises questions about the locus of choice in childlessness. If women alone are interviewed, it may imply that women are the more powerful partners in terms of fertility choices in couples, or it may reflect the nature of our knowledge base in this area: statistics regarding fertility intentions and actual births are often collected from women only. This in turn reflects the gendered nature of parenthood in most societies: it is mothers, not fathers who do most of the work involved in caring for children.

Previous studies have approached these issues in a range of ways – Nason and Poloma (1976), Marshall (1993) and Morell (1994) asked potential respondents directly if they were deliberately or intentionally childless. Other researchers drew up more specific criteria to define their respondent group. Veevers (1973, 1980) invited women to respond to a newspaper article and included those with no known fertility problems, who had been married five years or more, or were postmenopausal or sterilized. Women who had been social mothers were excluded. This meant that her study included women of a very wide age span (23–71), making any cohort effects difficult to examine. Campbell (1985) obtained her respondents in co-operation with family planning clinics, where general practitioners (GPs) carried out initial interviews of married women. Women who felt that their husbands were not in agreement about not having children were excluded. Therefore, voluntary childlessness was construed as a decision of couples rather than individuals.

In Morell's (1994) study several of the respondents had, at some time, attempted to conceive, and one reported extensive treatment for infertility. At the time of the study, all were 'permanently childless' and those who had endeavoured to conceive at an earlier stage expressed relief that it had not happened. Morell (1994) argues that childlessness was experienced by her respondents as 'a *consequence* of choosing to live their present lives', rather then being an easily defined decision point. She also contends that there are cases where the concept of postponing having children simply does not make sense and can be viewed as a pronatalist concept. For some women, repeatedly discussing the possibility of having children was a process of repeated rejection, rather than delay.

# Choosing childlessness: summary of the qualitative study

The qualitative studies cited above have tended to use 'convenience' methods of recruitment. In planning the 'Choosing childlessness' study we were committed to attempting to work from a more representative base of potential respondents.

It was important to use a sampling methodology that covered people in all socio-economic groupings, as most previous in-depth studies have concentrated on more highly educated women and professional couples. As childlessness has become more common and, as parenthood outside marriage is increasingly acceptable and frequent, it was also important to include unmarried women who had opted to remain childless as well as those currently in couple relationships.

In consultation with Social and Community Planning Research (SCPR), it was agreed that the best option available was to recruit from an existing survey population. SCPR conducts the annual British Social Attitudes Survey (BSAS), which uses a representative sample of approximately 3000 households. Data from both 1994 and 1995 surveys were combined to obtain a large enough group of childless women (176 altogether) aged 33–49 from which to recruit respondents. This gives the current study a national base which, while not strictly representative, is considerably wider in scope than previous studies of choice in childlessness. The 33–49 age group was selected to represent the latter part of the fertile lifespan – women who were likely to have had opportunities to have children but had not done so.

The 176 women identified as childless in the BSAS of 1994 and 1995 had to be screened to check that they were still childless and still within the 33–49 age range. Initial contact was established formally by a letter which carefully asked potential respondents to consider themselves eligible if they had no children and no intentions of childbearing in the future. Most of the screening took place through a short telephone interview. This screening device included questions on whether there were any children currently in the household, and whether the woman was currently planning or

Table 6.3. *Profile of the women in the study*

|  | Number of women |
|---|---|
| Marital status |  |
| Married | 15 |
| Cohabiting | 5 |
| Divorced/separated | 4 |
| Single | 10 |
| Highest qualification |  |
| A-level/HE/University | 21 |
| O-level/CSE | 10 |
| None | 3 |
| Age |  |
| 33–41 | 21 |
| 42–49 | 13 |

(*n*=34)

hoping to become pregnant in the near future. They were also asked if they had ever tried to adopt children. These questions aimed to exclude women who were involuntarily childless as well as those who were co-residential step-mothers to partners' children.

### The respondent group

The group of women for in-depth interview was purposively selected to ensure a diversity of living circumstances was represented in the study. Quotas were defined according to current marital status, highest educational qualification, and age (33–41; 42–49) and region of residence.

We eventually obtained a group of 34 women who were eligible for interview and willing to participate in the study (Table 6.3). Eleven of the interviewees had partners (either cohabiting or married) who also took part. Ten were childless men, one had children from a previous marriage, but was interviewed as his partner would otherwise have been unwilling to participate. His interview is excluded from the research analysis. The range of ages and qualifications in the pool of 176 was reflected as far as possible.

## Background to the analysis of data

The research process was informed by the 'grounded theory' perspective, whereby categories of respondents are arrived at and labelled through a detailed process of data coding and analysis. This approach emphasizes the actual words and language used by interviewees in their responses to questions. Analysis was also influenced by life history methods, whereby interview material is viewed as forming a constructed narrative of experience, reflecting social as well as personal meaning. Detailed case histories were derived, from which the key themes were distilled.

## The development of core categories

The questions that proved most appropriate in enabling us to define different types of voluntary childlessness were those asking if respondents had made a firm decision not to have children, and whether, when they were growing up, they had expected one day to be a parent. Respondents were also asked if they had ever wavered and gone through periods where they wanted to have children and whether they (or in the case of men, a partner) had ever been pregnant. In assessing the firmness of decisions, answers to questions about the influence of relatives and friends and whether respondents had regrets were also referred to. Different categories emerged – according to:

- *whether* people had a sense of making a decision;
- *how firm* that decision was (i.e. children ruled out as a future option);
- *when* they had made the decision (e.g. while growing up, since in a couple);
- *whether they had ever **wavered*** (i.e. gone through a phase of wanting/seriously contemplating having children).

Using these data, it was possible to build up a picture of the decisiveness with which respondents 'became childless' and the motivations which underlay their path to nonparenthood. The use of interviewees' own description of their route to voluntary childlessness departs somewhat from previous attempts to differentiate between groupings, which have tended to be more strictly related to reproductive behaviour or specific attitudes towards childbearing. For example, Nason and Paloma's (1976) study used sterilization as the identifier of greatest certainty with respect to remaining childfree.

On the basis of respondents' accounts, a 'continuum of childlessness' was constructed, with those who had resolved early and permanently not to have children described as *certain*. Different shades of wavering and later timing of these resolves were encapsulated in the groups named *certain now, accepting* and *ambivalent*. The category of *decision 'taken for me'* arose from the words of a small number of respondents and suggested the existence of a genuinely intermediate set of experiences 'between' voluntary and involuntary childlessness.

Categorizations were made on an individual basis, so that where we had interviewed both partners in a couple, they were categorized independently. The quotations selected here within each category are instances where interviewees have summed up the dimensions of decision-making most strikingly. To preserve confidentiality, respondents' names have been changed throughout.

### *People who are* certain *that they do not want children*

Between one-quarter and one-third of interviewees (12/44) fitted here.[1] *Certain* respondents had made a firm decision not to have children; they had usually done so as early as teenagers; they had never seriously wavered about having children. Helen Sloane's response to the question of having made a firm decision exemplifies the *certain* perspective:

> . . . sort of mid to late teens probably I would think, if not earlier, it's difficult to remember, but I think I always knew that I didn't really want them. I've always been a bit more of a tomboy and never really liked sort of girlie things. And children seem to be one of them.

---

[1] In noting the number of respondents in each category in the rest of the chapter, the intention is to portray the spread of experience in this particular study, rather than to infer distribution in the national population.

Respondents in this category had known for a long time that they did not want children. Like Helen Sloane, other *certain* respondents associated their decision with a lack of interest in traditionally feminine pursuits or an absence of 'maternal instincts'. These justifications at once emphasize the gender dimension of parenthood and its social meanings, and also remind us that even a firm decision may not have entirely rational foundations, for 'maternal instincts' are viewed as imperatives and their absence is hardly a matter of the application of reason. Men who were *certain* also invoked images of women and maternal instinct in demonstrating firm decisions. One described deciding to have children as, 'for a woman, it's an obvious choice, an obvious way of changing your life'. *Certain* respondents therefore differentiate themselves from women who put motherhood first; who behave instinctively and who create change by becoming parents.

When asked about the main factors contributing to their remaining childless, individuals in the *certain* category were more likely than others to mention negative aspects of parenthood: the responsibility and permanence of having children, the sacrifice of spontaneity and freedom, and a dislike of what was perceived as a 'parenting lifestyle' were all seen as important.

*People who are* certain *now that they do not want children*

In the second grouping, we encounter the respondents who did experience some level of wavering, but emerged still resolved not to become parents. In all the cases where people were *certain now*, partnership history appeared to have an important role in remaining childless. Three out of the five respondents in this category had been married previously, while those in first marriages indicated that their partnership was integral to their decision not to have children.

Like the *certain* respondents, Frances King alluded to a notion of broodiness or maternal instincts which *never happened*, but she had experienced some wavering over the decision more recently. Her partner's more rigid views worked to confirm her own doubts about having children.

Ben Moore, who cohabited with his partner, was the only man

who was *certain now*. In the early days of their relationship he had been more keen to have children. He was over ten years older than his partner, and reported concerns over the balance of career and parenting. However, he had not discussed his more recent certainty:

> I think we probably even up to a year ago still sort of thought well maybe one day we might have a child, even if it is late. But I think I have certainly rejected the idea now, whether Tanya has I really don't know, to be honest.

This case shows how complex it can be to identify individual- and couple-level factors clearly, an issue we will discuss further below.

Those in second partnerships who were *certain now* often said that they could imagine having had children if they had been in their current partnership earlier. They could be seen as having rejected parenthood on a more conditional basis than those in the *certain* category.

### *People who* accept *childlessness*

This grouping consisted of six women, all of whom were in their forties. The category emerged from a set of accounts in which all the women had either anticipated that they would have children from an early age, and/or had gone through a phase in their twenties or thirties when they had felt they wanted children, and later reassessed.

These women appeared to have been sensitive to the 'timetable' of marriage and parenthood – as their friends got married and had children in their twenties and thirties, they felt some unease that their own lives were not following the predictable pattern. Moving from that stage to the present was summed up by Mary Raven, a single woman in her late forties:

> . . . I think there have been times when I think 'oh I wish I was married' . . . but in my rational thinking it's not top priority and never has been . . . I've got single friends who have . . . it's been such a big issue for them and they've really longed and wanted to be married and have children, well I can't honestly say it's been that big a thing to me . . . *partly it's accepting of what you've had, as having been the best, actually for you.* [our emphasis]

These words caught the flavour of a group of women who had not made radical decisions about not having children. The early positive orientation towards childbearing indicates that attitudes formed while growing up are important but not entirely deterministic.

The accepting women had looked forward to stable marriages and having children when they were young. When this did not happen in their twenties and thirties, it was as if they confronted the possibility of becoming involuntarily childless, but resolved not to, instead accepting their lot and finding contentment – sometimes through late-formed partnerships where children were clearly ruled out.

*People who are* ambivalent *and have never taken a decision about not having or having children*

This was the second largest grouping on the continuum (11/44). Among the eight women and three men who were *ambivalent,* four felt that they had postponed having children, and in the case of three others a fertility problem was part of the story. There was a distinction between those who displayed clear evidence of postponement and those who could not identify any decision. While the former had wavered seriously and put off becoming parents, the latter never actively addressed the matter.

Nancy and Martin Hammond, married and in their late forties, expressed high levels of ambivalence. They were one of only two couples to share ambivalence. For them, the notion of making a decision simply did not apply. Early in the interview, the husband declared:

> Erm, no, I would always have liked children really . . . so if everything would have been alright and we could have guaranteed we could have had twins at 33 or something like that . . . we would have gone ahead, but . . . it just didn't work out that way.

Nonetheless, both partners were very clear that they had never tried to have children or planned them, and that there was no firm decision either way:

> Nancy: *We've never sort of said, yes, we're going to have a child or, no, we're not going to have a child.*
>
> Martin: *No, no, we never made a decision, even now if it would be biologically alright, if Nancy would be alright and the baby would be alright, I wouldn't mind one now you know.*

Emma Hill, a single woman, articulated the postponement perspective and its accompanying ambivalence most clearly, saying:

> When I was younger I didn't. I had made a decision that I didn't want to have children until a certain age and now, and I think I probably felt that if I then didn't have children because of circumstances it wouldn't worry me, I suppose. But I did see it – I wanted children, and now in the last year I have decided I don't, I feel I'm old from my own point of view. I don't think I have fully made a decision actually not to have children, no, maybe, I think probably perhaps I'd still like to.

All these individuals tell of complex uncertainties concerning their route into childlessness. Their circumstances were varied, and it is perhaps this group that most embodies the concept of childlessness as a process – and one that could still be transformed into parenthood, given the 'correct' circumstances. It may also be possible that the postponers might resolve their position later and become *accepting*, if they reject the position of involuntary childlessness at a later stage.

### People who feel that the decision not to have children was 'taken for me'

This grouping arose directly from the vocabulary of a small number of respondents, who in various ways saw their childlessness as determined by external factors, outside of their own control.

Marian Templeton had experienced problems conceiving in her late twenties. When asked if she had considered any treatments, she said:

> Not really no . . . because I didn't delve into it more deeply for myself. Erm I think if I had done I would have [pursued treatment] whereas, because at the back of my mind I wasn't that bothered whether it happened or not, then I didn't, but I think if I'd been that particularly bothered I would have done.

This clear ambivalence became firm due to her eventual hysterectomy, several years after she and her husband had first tried to have children. Her account illustrates that it is possible to be ambivalent about involuntary childlessness – through not following up signs of subfertility – as well as being ambivalent about parenthood. When asked if a decision was ever made not to have children, Marian Templeton replied, 'No, I think it was taken away from us really in the end, that decision, yeah'. There is a sense in which everyone is a 'potential parent' until physically proven otherwise – either through complications or, in women's case, the menopause. Marian Templeton had been ambivalent until the decision was taken for her.

The people who felt that the decision to remain childless had been 'taken for them' were instructive in illuminating the complexity of concepts of choice in childbearing. Physical problems may be 'decisive' in closing off options, but they are not always perceived as *the* reason for not having children. Other choices – of partner or career – have a role in keeping decisions open or postponing the day that they are made.

### People identified as not voluntarily childless

A number of cases were defined as not voluntary childless and were excluded from the main analysis. Unlike the *ambivalent* respondents, these people demonstrated a persistent intention to have a child. Unlike the *accepting* women, the older women had not turned back on their desire to have children, and they did not see themselves as having had options.

In the accounts which formed the continuum of childlessness it was clear that both marital status and the views of partners were important in choosing childlessness and we now turn to reviewing this evidence.

### Partnerships and choosing childlessness

Altogether, there were 20 co-residential partnerships in the study and in 11 of these cases both partners were interviewed. Nine women were in intact first marriages, while six were in marriages where at least one partner had been previously married. There was only one widow in the respondent group, so that first marriages had nearly always ended in divorce. A further five women were cohabiting, and four of their partners were divorced. All the men in second marriages and one of the divorced male cohabitees had to be excluded from the study because they had had children previously. Five childless male partners did not participate for a number of reasons – either logistical or they refused.

Nearly half of the women in co-residential partnerships had picked a mate who was at least five years older, and in six cases partners were more than a decade apart in age. This seems unusual when compared to the mean age difference between British spouses which has remained consistent at between two and three years (with men older) over recent decades (Werner, 1996). Relatively large differences in age may make the decision to have children more complex, as each partner may feel 'ready' at quite different times. Older men with children from previous marriages may not be inclined to have second families for reasons of age, finance, or simply the feeling that they have experienced parenthood already.

Among the previously married and single women, involvement with older men was also mentioned, and relationships with sterilized men were reported. These features raise the question of partnership choice/mate selection and its relationship to *choosing* childlessness: the two choices are intermeshed in complex ways. Psychological explanations of partnership choice clearly fall outside the scope of this study, but it could be argued that partners are chosen because they provide a scenario in which it is unlikely that ambivalence or resistance to parenthood will be challenged.

### *Partnership as the prerequisite for parenting*

Women who were currently single or divorced frequently had definite views on the necessity of partnerships for parenthood. Single women in their later forties were the most likely to be religious, which put single parenthood out of the question, but younger women living alone, like Bella Friar (in her thirties and *ambivalent*), tended to agree, 'I wouldn't be frightened to bring up a child on my own, I would do it, but I would rather not do it on my own.'

Only a small number of women living alone felt that single parenthood was preferable to being in a couple and one said that being a single mum was her 'ideal'. After a moment's consideration, she commented, 'unless . . . I think the ideal would be to have a man who would be prepared to stay at home and do the mother bit'. This view is a powerful reminder that parenthood requires decisions to be made about division of labour within relationships, decisions that nearly always result in women bearing the primary responsibility for home and children (at least for a time), while men continue to work outside the home.

## *Discussions and decision-making*

Most respondents in partnerships agreed that they had discussed the issue of children at some point, but they struggled to remember details. Answers were peppered with equivocations, 'I can't remember', 'it's not an issue', 'I'm surprised how little we have discussed it' and 'I suppose we must have'.

Probably the clearest case of discussion being integral to the decision-making process came from a married women who was *certain now*. Her account suggests that her husband was more certain than she was, and that the issue of change of lifestyle was a paramount consideration:

> . . . we've talked about it over the years and our conclusion has always been the same, that I feel very strongly that it has to be a joint thing and he feels very strongly, you know, that he would virtually carry on as normal and the responsibility would be mine. But I have to say since I was about 25 in my own mind I've been quite clear that I don't want to make this sacrifice, I don't want to make changes, I'm happy with life as it is.

This example stood out because the woman was so direct about the differences between her own and her husband's views, and the connections with the division of labour in marriage. Nonetheless, she felt that her life had gone as she wished 'by design'. Once children were ruled out, she developed a successful career and capitalized on the freedom and economic advantage of childless marriage which parenthood may have challenged. This recalls

Morrell's (1994) assertion that 'repeated rejection' of parenthood is a route to childlessness, and should not simply be subsumed under the concept of 'postponing' parenthood.

The connections between the division of labour in marriage and decision-making regarding childlessness are given additional weight through the observation that where both partners were interviewed and in different positions on the continuum men were always in categories reflecting greater certainty than their female partners. In our report, *Choosing childlessness* (McAllister and Clarke, 1998), discussions between partners are analysed further.

Where partnerships included *certain* women, domestic labour was identified as shared, and no *certain* woman reported doing house-work alone. There were only four instances where women reported being solely responsible for housework. Where partners were in the same category on the continuum, their implicit decision not to have children appeared to be associated with open negotiation con-cerning division of labour. Where partners recognized differences in their views on possible childbearing, discussions were reported more often, but it appeared that balances of division of labour were more difficult to negotiate to the satisfaction of both partners.

### Housing as commitment: a structure for childless marriage?

One of the most striking elements in the picture of commitment for childless couples was the sense that housing and the domestic environment mattered a great deal. Buying a good house and making it home appeared not simply to be an exercise in financial investment, but rather a means of consolidating relationships and sharing life together. Mike James (*certain*) summed this up when he spontaneously described housing as commitment:

> We hadn't been married very long and when we bought our first house, you know, that was the sort of commitment we made to each other and we decided we would do, so obviously we worked hard then for our first house, so eventually you know, we could have something like this.

For those who were in the *ambivalent, accepting* or *decision 'taken for me'* categories, a stable and desirable home was sometimes seen as a prerequisite for having children which had not yet been achieved. Simon Mann (*ambivalent*) talked of the importance of 'a solid place to live' and being 'rooted', to any final decision regarding children.

For women living alone (although they were less likely to own their homes) the domestic sphere was a source of satisfaction and an important part of being independent. Joanne Higham was single and planned to buy her home, *to be settled*. She contrasted other people's *huge goals* with her own ambition to own her house. Housing provided a concrete ladder of progress and the space to be oneself. In addition, for couples it came to symbolize the value of being together.

## Career versus children? Challenging myths

It is frequently assumed that women who choose not to have children are highly motivated at work, and that enhanced employment opportunities for women are associated with more women opting to remain childfree. There is no straightforward relationship between rates of female participation in the workforce and fertility trends in particular countries (European Commission, 1994). For instance, in Italy, fertility rates are among the lowest in Europe, despite relatively low rates of female employment and a culture which has historically valued children and the role of mothers very highly.

Increasingly, mothers are staying in the workplace following the birth of their children – albeit often in part-time work and low-paid industries. Such evidence suggests that 'either/or' models of women's lives, whereby they choose directly between work and family life, are overly simplistic. Men's fertility behaviour is so little studied that it is difficult to consider evidence concerning occupational and reproductive decision-making in a proper context. The evidence from our study suggests that the links between employment decisions and the decision to remain childless are by no means direct and clear. Influence in both directions is possible, and commitment to work, like commitment to childlessness, could change over time. Partnerships are a vital intervening factor in the fluctuating importance of work.

At the time of interview, 30 of the 34 woman respondents were actively employed. Three had taken early retirement in their mid-forties, while the fourth was having a break between contracts. The majority of the women (three-quarters) worked full-time. Part-time employment included working weeks ranging in length from two to four days. Only one woman worked in a skilled manual occupation, while most of the lowest earners were involved in service or personal care jobs. In the middle range, women were frequently employed as office workers, ranging from secretarial posts to managers. Teaching, healthcare and social welfare occupations were also well-represented.

### Careers and identity

A sift through the interview data identified women who saw themselves as 'career women/person/girl' or 'career-minded'. Only a minority did so, and never without provisos either of degree – 'to a certain extent', 'not to the exclusion of other things'; or of change over time – 'up until a year ago', 'in my 20s'; or of lack of design, 'only because of circumstances'. Fewer than one in six respondents agreed without qualification that they were ambitious. Half the group did not consider themselves ambitious at all. It emerged that childless men also had reservations about the extent to which careers were central to their lives. It might be anticipated that *certain* respondents would be more likely to be positively striving at work; however, half of them said that they were *not* ambitious. Of those who were ambitious, only a minority were *certain* regarding childlessness. This appears to challenge the hypothesis that childless people are inclined to prioritize work and that an orientation towards career success predisposes them to decide not to have children.

### Work and family timetables

Only a minority of women (12/34) reported early deliberations concerning their future job. Only one *certain* woman left school with an identifiable career plan which she then followed through. By contrast, *all* of the six *accepting* women were included amongst the career planners. This seems to make the *accepting* group distinctive. The pathways of *accepting* women are exemplified by Moira Gloucester and Lillian Waters. Both women established their career paths in their late twenties and early thirties. Lillian remained single, while Moira was in a long-term relationship. Moira and Lillian reflected on the simultaneous demands of work and partnership at this time:

> . . . where I was at the time, work wise, career wise and all that, it would have been a phenomenal struggle [to have children], it really would have been a lot of upheaval, and probably a lot of heartache as well, so yes, in lots of ways I think gosh it would be nice, even if I just had one child, to have one child and be a mum now. But that's with hindsight, that's if I was now 30 and my situation now if you like, where I am a lot more established and everything's going on a lot more nicely than it was at the time.
>
> Moira Gloucester

> . . . in my 20s, work was the most important thing I guess until I got to my early 30s. All the people around me, all my colleagues, friends had got married and started having families, and I got to a stage in my early 30s where I thought, 'hang on, have I missed out on something here, is there something that I should have been doing that I haven't?' and they all seem to be happy, I'm on my own and so then I started to have this shift in 'well maybe work isn't that important'.
>
> Lillian Waters

So labour force attitudes and attitudes towards future partnering and parenthood were found to be intertwined. At the time of interview, both women were in partnerships with older men who already had children. Both had changed their working arrangements recently – Lillian through retirement and Moira by reducing her hours. Lillian's account of her retirement decision reveals how the centrality of her job diminished further when she eventually married in her forties. For her it was a new form of freedom:

> I think because I kind of moved on more into the job being a secondary thing, and now I was married and I had an ambition to be a housewife, sort of looking back on the early parts of marriages that my friends had

had where they were able to leave work and leave the responsibility and the worries of work behind and have a home life? that to me was a form of freedom. Freedom is very important to me? it wasn't necessary for me to work because Ivan was earning enough to be able to support us both. I had these vague ideas of going back to work if after six months I was ever bored out of my brains with being at home and it wasn't exactly what I'd imagined it to be, erm, but I never did get bored with it [laughing].

A new partnership could transform work/home balances. Moira Gloucester and Lillian Waters had formed successful partnerships relatively late in life and gave work more of a back seat. Resolving finally not to have children can perhaps be seen as giving permission to retreat from the workforce as much as to become more involved, a point which is not often made in the literature on interactions between employment and fertility.

Women who were *certain* in their choice of childlessness were not keen to identify themselves as career women. Kay Farr explained why she had some regrets about not focusing more on work earlier:

I just don't know what I want to do career wise, which I think is a waste, because I think we're part of the first generation that's really had a choice as to what we do and to choose not to have children and have a career or whatever. I feel I've wasted that.

This is a useful reminder that the sense of choice is not the same thing as acting upon it.

The recognition that work *could* afford opportunities for self-actualization was perhaps the marker for these women, even if their experience had not always matched up. Other *certain* women talked of 'still looking' for the thing that they really wanted to do. They valued work chiefly as a means of supporting themselves in their life outside. For the respondent group as a whole, it was through reference to their retirement plans that they provided some of the most interesting occupational data.

### Early retirement

Altogether one-third of respondents – ten women and five men – mentioned it as a future wish or plan, or had already taken retirement. The popularity of early retirement among respondents again contradicts the 'either/or' picture of work and having children. Only one respondent (a man) suggested that retirement might lead to their pursuing professional interests in a different way. For most, the idea of leaving work was in itself attractive. Almost half of those who were in the *certain* category of voluntary childlessness looked forward to early retirement, suggesting again that a definite choice of childlessness does not indicate that work is the priority in life.

One of the main attractions of early retirement was the opportunity to sell up and move house (often to a rural setting). Early retirement gave the people without children a context in which to leave work legitimately – in the same way that parental leave may function for parents at an earlier stage in life.

A widespread aversion to risk and poverty meant that financial planning and provision for retirement plans are paramount. The desire for financial security and independence was further reflected in respondents' perceptions of parenthood. Having children was often thought of as representing an unacceptable cost, while positive childless identities were connected with freedom and individual responsibility for the future.

## Childless identities and perceptions of parenthood

In the final part of the interview, respondents were asked about their views of the term 'childless'. The ways in which people responded reflected their position on the continuum in interesting ways, as the examples below illustrate. Only five individuals agreed that they might describe themselves as 'childless'. For a sizeable minority of respondents, 'childless' meant involuntarily childless, and was therefore not an appropriate term for themselves.

The *certain* respondents distinguished themselves most clearly from involuntarily childless people. They had made a positive choice not to have children and often did not see it as a relevant part of their identity. Rosemary Kensit (*certain*) said that 'childless' meant:

> Somebody poor who hasn't been able to produce, you know, somebody who's actually missing out on life somewhere and dreadful . . . feel so sorry for them, you know, that type of image . . . I don't relate to that at all.

If someone called her childless, she would react strongly:

> I would think they were idiots, they were missing an awful lot of what I am, that being childless isn't really even half a percent of what I am, they were describing what I'm not rather than what I am.

In the *ambivalent* grouping, the difference between voluntary and involuntary childlessness was recognized, but respondents did not situate themselves clearly:

> Well, in a purely medical sense, it's entirely accurate but it implies . . . either an inability to or a decision not to [have children] and neither in my case, I mean it's just I don't happen to have any children . . . at the moment, but I still think of it as something that might happen one day.
>
> Stephanie Cannon

Men were no more likely to embrace the term 'childless' with enthusiasm than their partners, and their responses were similar according to their position on the continuum. Where they ventured alternative visions of themselves, respondents emphasized their personal qualities, their freedom and their individuality. To be seen as a person apart from their reproductive choices was the widespread ideal.

## Parenthood as responsibility, commitment and sacrifice

Parental responsibility was variously described as *huge* and *imperative* and its permanence stressed through phrases like 'they never ever stop being responsible for them'. Childlessness represented freedom to be independent adults who pursued their own interests. As Isobel West said:

> I quite like this independence, and you know just being free and easy and not the constraints of like having to provide breakfast, lunch and dinner, and not being able to go out to the theatre.

Similarly, Simon Mann said:

> The advantages are that you have a freer schedule and the time that
> you have, that is time away from your career, is then the time that you
> can spend enjoying each other's company . . . maybe time that you can
> go and pursue some other hobby if you want to go off fishing . . . or
> whatever the case may be . . . you are not leaving someone else holding
> the responsibility and therefore putting the burden on them, so I mean
> both as a couple and individually there are advantages.

These assessments respectively from a single women and a married
man highlight not only the freedom which remaining childless
affords, but also the association of parenthood with marriages
where the duties of care and the freedom to pursue outside interests
are unevenly distributed between mothers and fathers – not having
children means fewer compromises.

Parental responsibility was also found to be linked to commitment. This was sometimes seen as the condition upon which a
decision to have children should be made:

> I think it's absolutely lovely if that's what you want and you're totally
> committed to it, . . . there isn't room for . . . giving anything less than
> 100% to parenthood.

The impression of *total commitment* was touched on further by
references to children being around *24 hours a day* and the view that
children *take over your life completely*.

Parental sacrifice was frequently identified by respondents, who
recognized that their own parents 'did without' for them and also saw
that their friends and relatives 'give up' social lives, spending money
on themselves, and (in the case of women) jobs to have children.

Faith Mann described friends as *coming pretty close to divorce* as they
coped with sleepless nights and the new balance of husband at work
and wife at home. The financial demands of parenthood were also
a strain:

> . . . some of them [friends] have stayed in careers they hate. One of my
> friends in particular, who's just had a child, her husbands earns half her
> salary, she has to go back to work, she doesn't want to but she has to
> pay the mortgage.

Even relatively well-off parents may find it hard to balance earning and caring. Research increasingly identifies the gulf between two-earner families with time pressures in parenthood, and no-earner families with few economic resources for children (e.g. Ferri and Smith, 1997). Although money was not put forward as the *reason* for choosing childlessness, the advantage of sustained earnings meant that childless women living alone, and those in partnerships, compared their financial position – and especially their housing situation – favourably with parents' circumstances.

While they could clearly identify the negative aspects of parent-hood, respondents were not generally 'anti-family'. Approximately one-third of respondents reported actively supporting relatives. Two unmarried women in their forties lived with and cared for their elderly mothers, while others had nursed ill parents, or been their primary support for considerable periods.

Respondents had also supported children. The major examples of this had occurred where siblings were single parents or were experiencing difficulties in their relationships. These instances involved both financial and emotional support. Without compara-tive information concerning family support for all adults, or a matched group of parents, it is impossible to be conclusive about the levels of care and support provided by our childless respondents. However, they did frequently show willingness to involve themselves in their families, and several respondents identified supporting their parents and nieces and nephews as a priority for the future. These observations lead into further discussion of the links between values and fertility choices, in both demographic and qualitative literature.

## Values and childlessness

The importance of seeing the choice of childlessness as a process cautions against viewing voluntary childlessness as a one-off moment that defines subsequent experience. This suggests that we should be cautious about seeing the voluntarily childless as 'parti-cular types of people' with coherent values – broadly characterized as individualist and 'anti-family' – apart from the parenting majority. This caution is lent further weight by the evidence in population data. Lynda Clarke's recent analysis indicates that childlessness (albeit in *all* of its forms) is becoming more prevalent amongst women with middle-range and lower academic qualifications, rather than being isolated in the best-educated groupings. Indeed, a distinctive group of young women with little education is increasingly differentiated through early motherhood from those who postpone, reject or cannot achieve parenthood.

Before placing the findings of the qualitative study in the context of previous in-depth research findings, it is important to review briefly some of the developments in demographic research linking values and fertility behaviour.

## Demography and social values: some integrative work

Easterlin (1980) argued that deciding to have children must be seen within the context of the other goods, services and quality of life which a couple could potentially enjoy. A strand of Easterlin's work that has influenced modern demographers is the concept of taste or preference. He argued that the sense of status and competition for social position would influence families differentially, and that competition would be affected by potential parents' childhood circumstances. Prosperous families tend to be the product of smaller birth cohorts: less competition for resources means fewer constraints on family size. Children growing up in prosperous circumstances will form a large birth cohort, and therefore their own chances of a secure family lifestyle is diminished through competition, with their own fertility rates consequently constrained. Therefore 'taste' for children must fit into a wider context of secure living and the acquisition of material goods. A 'decision' about whether or not to have children must be influenced in some measure by the value ascribed to children and parenthood. Perhaps even more importantly, one must have some concept of the perceived costs (social, psychological as well as economic) that parenting activities are seen to carry.

Van de Kaa's (1987) description of a shift away from religiosity and towards secular individualism has been of central interest to many demographers. The recognition of the importance of changing attitudes in influencing social behaviour has led them to analyse attitudinal survey material concerning 'family values' in the context of changing fertility rates. Simons (1986, 1995) has examined changing values and changing fertility rates, and also changing attitudes to preferred family size, through the European Values Surveys of 1981 and 1990. Simons has explored ways in which changing social values can be related to fertility behaviour through theorizing that 'the factors which determine the importance to lifestyle of producing children are those which arise from the religious character of the relationship between the individual and society' (Simons, 1986).

The term 'religious' does not refer here to conventional adherence to doctrines, but rather as arising out of the individual's stake in society and the level of belief in a notion of collectivity. To chart changes in values, Simons developed a matrix in which aggregated responses to survey questions concerning reproductive behaviour and family life can be plotted. One axis of the matrix represents degrees of individualism versus collectivity, indicating the 'hold' of social norms and conventions on the individual; the other axis represents degrees of absolutism versus relativism. Absolutists believe in a set of universal values (often associated with religious doctrines) governing family behaviour, while relativists make judgements based on particular individual circumstances.

Simons (1995) concentrated on two contrasting groups of countries in the European Values Survey: those which experienced a decline in fertility during the 1980s and those where fertility increased. Responses to a range of questions reflecting the individualism/collectivism and absolutism/relativism continua were plotted for each country using data from the 1981 and 1990 survey rounds, so as to identify any value shift over the decade. Questions used to represent the individualism/collectivism continuum made extensive reference to marriage: its significance as an institution and the importance of fidelity, for example. Changes in the position of aggregated scores relevant to this axis were more highly associated with fertility change than those along the absolutist/relativist axis. Simons sees attitudes has having begun a 'swing back' towards more traditional expectations of relationships and family life, but this has not yet been supported by trends in the 1990s.

Coleman (1998) agrees that values and the culture of parenthood in a country at a specific time are important potential explanatory factors in fertility rates. The correlation between period total fertility rates and levels of religious practice is quite good, as is the correlation of fertility rates with changing attachment to the notion of parental duty. However, he points out that the correlation between values and family intentions and preferred family size is weaker, and, furthermore, some countries have sets of values and behaviours which cannot be neatly set into any one of the individualist/collectivist and absolutist/relativist categories. For example, Sweden has both a high overall fertility rate, suggestive of strong family (collectivist) values, and the highest rate of births outside marriage in Europe, a statistic which conforms with individualist values. There is still a need, therefore, to improve our understanding of how and why values concerning family life change over time, and how behaviour can be better predicted from observed values.

In the qualitative study we found plenty to challenge the view of childlessness emerging as a consequence of alternative values. Conventional views about parenthood were expressed by those who had chosen childlessness. For women living alone, single parenthood was not considered a viable option. Most people emphasized the individual responsibility that choosing parenthood entails. Their picture of childlessness versus parenthood is one of independence contrasted with constraint; material security with financial risk. Parenthood was clearly identified with disruption and change, which people considered ill-suited to their organized and predictable lifestyle. Rather than radically reframing the social face of womanhood and motherhood, the voluntary childless people in this study emerged as thoughtful and responsible about what parenting might mean. They find it variously undesirable, difficult or impossible to incorporate it into their lives. Far from being a generation who can 'have it all', respondents saw themselves as making considerable effort to maintain a reasonable quality of life without children.

Parenthood requires decisions to be made about the division of labour within a relationship. This study indicates that a wish for joint parenting strategies is frequently an issue for voluntarily childless women: if they feel their partner will not readily share the domestic responsibilities of parenthood, it is an additional disincentive affecting any decision to have children. Men in the study also highlighted the benefits of egalitarian partnerships and viewed parenthood as incompatible with these values.

Our conclusions regarding the motivations towards childlessness and the wider attitudes accompanying such a choice echo findings in earlier research. In her review of the literature concerning voluntary childlessness, Veevers (1983:80) asserts that, 'assessment of the costs and benefits of parenthood seems more closely related to sex role attitudes and anxieties than to any single background characteristic. A major component of antinatalist views is the suspicion that parenthood is a potent force for inducting conventional sex roles in marriage.'

Morell (1994) found that there was a strong perception of the negative conditions in which mothering takes place, and the way it 'conflicted with desires for economic and emotional autonomy and self-expansive activity' (Morell, 1994). Women over 50 felt that there had been no possibility for them of 'having it all', and that there was a choice between work and children. The younger respondents saw the work/parenthood dilemma somewhat differently, and felt that the possibility of combining work and children would not permit them to be 'the *kind* of student or scholar or artist or architect they wanted to be, nor the *kind* of mother they felt their children needed' (Morell, 1994). The women aimed high and were cynical about being able to pursue both career ambitions and parenthood. Morell therefore argues that 'choice' about childlessness is a misleading conceptualization which colludes with pronatalism. She asserts that, 'the word choice fabricates the individual subject as an autonomous entity with rights to privacy and personal happiness. Such a notion emphasizes personal decisions and distracts attention away from social relations of power. The insistent focus is on the internal as opposed to the institutional and sociopolitical' (Morell, 1994). Thus it is vital to account for the fact that parenting does not have equal status with labour market activity, and that women are largely left to deal with children while men pursue their careers. That 'having it all' is so unfeasible may lie at the heart of the process of remaining childless for many women. Campbell (1985) does not see childless couples as particularly radical in their outlook – they are childless through commitment to one another, and through recognition of the scale of sacrifice involved in parenthood. Marshall (1993) agrees, seeing childless couples as nonconformists operating *within* an ideology of parenthood, rather than radical opponents of childbearing and family life. 'They [the couples] decide not to have children because they in fact accept fully the prevailing ideas about what parenthood represents,' (Marshall 1993).

These perspectives on the process of childlessness and its connection with values bring us back to Veevers' (1983) critical question, 'On the issue of childbearing, are the persons involved getting what they want?' (Veevers 1983), a question which cannot be ignored from a social policy perspective. With the research literature often suggesting that voluntary childlessness is a product of the constraints of parenthood in contemporary society, it is vital to explore what policy analysts have to say about the significance of fertility rates and childlessness, and to examine the evidence concerning the effectiveness of family policy in influencing these trends.

## Policy implications and conclusions

There is a consensus in the literature addressing the relationship between fertility levels and public policy, that effective policy is unusually difficult to design (e.g. Bane and Jargowsky, 1988; Macintosh, 1987; McDonald, 1997). Most active policy measures in this area are related to supporting parents and children in diverse and often diffuse ways – via the tax and benefits system and through provision of public services – and so are implicit. Infertility services represent the other end of the spectrum, where explicit regulations govern the circumstances of assisted reproduction. At what point might voluntary childlessness warrant policy interventions?

## Concern for future population levels

As we have pointed out, the inadequacies of current survey data are a considerable obstacle to assessing the need for future policy regarding voluntary childlessness. Large-scale surveys could be more sensitive to the issue of choice as a *process*, with questions tapping into stages of certainty, rather than simply asking whether people (crucially men as well as women) expect to have children. With better data, we would be more readily able to ascertain precisely the magnitude of any increase in the proportion of people choosing childlessness. As we outlined earlier, the proportion of British women aged 16 to 22 who currently state that they do not wish to have children (10%) still remains well below the proportion of those women projected to remain childless (20%). The difference between these two figures is accounted for in part by involuntary childlessness, but also by the groups represented on our continuum who may commit themselves to childlessness later in life. The emphasis laid on having both a stable partnership and a reasonable level of economic security in order to consider having children suggests that there may be levers in the 'climate of possibility'. These suggest three main areas to monitor with respect to fertility choices. First, there is the issue of compatibility between domestic and working life. For people in the key years of decision-making concerning parenthood, the difficulties of integrating secure employment and any desire for children are important issues. These have private dimensions in terms of men and women negotiating reasonable balances between work and child care, and public dimensions in that policy could respond to desire for greater equity in parenthood through more flexible employment. In Britain, there is no tax relief for working mothers using employer-provided child care and the provision of State-subsidized child care is less than in other European countries. Child benefit levels have also fallen below the cost of living, and policies to reverse this decline and enhance child care options would help parents bear the costs of family life more easily. Younger people support more flexible and gender-neutral experiences of parenthood. For example, in the 1992 British Social Attitudes Survey, two-thirds of 18–34 year olds disagreed that a husband's job is to earn money and a wife's to look after the home and family, compared with one-third of 45–54 year olds and one in eight people aged 60 or over (Kiernan, 1992).

Second, it emerged clearly in our study that housing conditions can influence the priority that people place on parenthood. Demographers have charted the relationship between housing tenure and fertility trends, and Murphy (1989) has noted the persistent relationship between local authority housing tenure and high fertility rates. In contrast, owner-occupiers, with their high initial mortgage costs, may delay childbirth, and may find they have little surplus income at key points in the childbearing life cycle.

Finally, there is an argument for policy intervention in terms of information and health education about fertility levels (Beets, 1995; Bouwens *et al.*, 1996). A continuing trend of delaying parenthood means that women (and men) need to be well-informed about the declining chances of conception in their thirties, just as they are regularly reminded of the costs and implications of teenage pregnancies and unplanned childbearing.

All these areas are concerned with creating more awareness of the trends in population and their implications for individuals and society. They contribute to an atmosphere of informed choice, rather than constraints being experienced by default. The evidence presented here suggests that now is not the time for direct intervention in Britain – fertility rates may be low, but in fact the U.K. has one of the higher fertility rates in the European Community. Moreover, the relationship between policy support for additional children and national fertility behaviour is by no means clear, as experience in other countries demonstrates.

Pronatalist measures have been notoriously unsuccessful in influencing long-term fertility rates. In the extreme case of Romania, where abortion was outlawed, fertility rates rose dramatically in the short term, but fell to their previous levels within a few years. In Sweden in the early 1990s, generous parental leave policies were associated with an immediate rise in the birth rate, but in the long-term fertility rates have dropped to below the levels of the late 1980s, so that policy changes appear to affect the timing of births rather than overall fertility levels. France and the former

West Germany have both provided considerable financial incentives for parenthood (e.g. favourable tax rates for couples with children; increased child allowance for third children; generous maternity leave and benefit; state-subsidized education and childcare services) and yet their birth rates have dropped – the rates in France are comparable to those in Britain while those in Germany are lower.

On the other side of the coin, in developing countries where there are concerns about overpopulation, the policies which have brought about the most effective reductions in fertility rates are those related to improving the status of women. These have involved encouraging a change in values concerning women's roles in society, and suggest that the interplay between social culture and fertility behaviour is key in impacting on birth rates in the long term.

The ageing population of Western countries, characterized by below replacement-level fertility and decreased mortality, shifts the balance of social investment away from young families and towards older people. Voluntarily childless people may actually find funding old age easier than do parents, because of their unbroken careers and relatively constant expenses. Weighed against this advantage is the fact that they cannot count on any care being provided by children. This social cost of childlessness raises wider issues to do with care and responsibility towards others, outside of traditional family structures.

There is nothing to suggest that directives to bear children for the sake of one's old age would be practicable or desirable. Our study found that the voluntary childless were highly resistant to the notion that care in old age justifies childbearing, and there is little to suggest that the parenting population sees their children in this light. Indeed, such directives would fall on deaf ears if the demographers' argument that trends are indicative of a shift towards individualism holds any water.

The main policy issues, therefore, seem to come back to the parents' ability to support their children adequately, economically and socially. The chances of this happening are higher where parents are sufficiently established to have regular earnings, decent accommodation and time to devote to educating and supporting their children. These conditions are less available to young parents, who are more likely – especially in Britain – to be poor. Teenage parenthood is also associated with a range of social disadvantages and with greater risk of instability in partnerships. These factors mean that the main policy concern is likely – rightly – to be that of reducing teenage pregnancy and enhancing opportunities for teenagers to educate and support themselves. However, if parenthood itself is not valued, the youngest parents will remain a disadvantaged and stigmatized group, while nonparents will look on with caution at the quality of life of British fathers and mothers.

The trend towards later parenthood makes this an issue in all Western countries. Adults who value equality in relationships, a stable and adequate domestic environment, a reasonable job and economic security may find it increasingly hard to make the decision to become parents. Indeed, choosing not to have children can be seen as one logical response to the pressures of adult life at the turn of this century. Cliquet (1997) has drawn attention to the high expectations in societies of young people, who are supposed to acquire education, occupational success, a secure home and having children in a tight time span. With the added pressure of a finite period of fertility in women, it is not surprising that increasing childlessness is one outcome.

In a Dutch study of delayed parenthood, Bouwens and colleagues (1996) see reliable contraception and the incompatibility of work and childcare as influential in making decisions about childbearing 'a matter of planning and doubt' (Bouwens *et al.*, 1996). The Netherlands have among the lowest rates of teenage pregnancy in Europe accompanied by high rates of assisted conception. They therefore see the balance and nature of individual and social costs in childbearing as transformed through later motherhood. The costs of assisted conception are likely to increase for both individuals and society as more people seek to bear children later, and more technology is available. The individual choice not to have children may also be viewed as more unusual as the possibility of childbearing extends to new groups. Thus the boundaries between people who consider themselves potential parents, involuntarily childless and voluntarily childless are subject to wider changes.

The evidence concerning damaging effects of low fertility is so far inconclusive: concern over the impact of ageing populations is balanced by the global perspective which points to the over-population of the developing world and the wastefulness of industrialized countries. This is a popular counterpoint to concerns over the continuing fall in our fertility rates. In all of this discussion, it is important to remember that declines in overall fertility rates reflect the trends towards smaller families as well as trends in numbers remaining childless.

Many people think twice before subjecting themselves to the economic and emotional insecurities of parenthood, and those who choose not to have children have a sense of how difficult it is to achieve a secure, sustainable existence, even without the demands of children. If society places a low value on parenthood as an activity and identity, and nonparents do not see social support for having children as readily forthcoming, then the individual decision not to have a child may become more frequent.

# References

Armitage, B., Babb, P. (1996) Population review: (4) Trends in fertility. *Population Trends* **84**:9–10. Summer 1996.

Bane, M. J., Jargowsky, P. A. (1988) 'The links between government policy and family structure: what matters and what doesn't'. In: Cherlin, A. J. (ed.) *The changing American family and public policy* (pp. 219–61). Washington: The Urban Institute Press.

Baum, F. E. (1983) Orientations towards voluntary childlessness. *Journal of Biosocial Science* **15**:153–64.

Beets, G. (1995) 'Does the increasing age at first birth lead to increases in involuntary childlessness?' Paper presented at the European Population Conference, Milan Italy. (Available from the author: Netherlands Interdisciplinary Demographic Institute, PO Box 11650, 2502 AR, The Hague, Netherlands.)

Bongaarts, J., Potter, R. G. (1983) *Fertility, biology and behaviour: an analysis of proximate determinants.* New York: Academic Press.

Bouwens, A., Beets, G. C. N., Schippers, J. J. (1996) Societal causes and effects of delayed parenthood. Utrecht: University of Utrecht Economic Institute. (Report written on behalf of the Commission of the European Union.)

Burghes, L., Clarke, L., Cronin, N. (1997) *Fathers and fatherhood in Britain.* London: Family Policy Studies Centre.

Campbell, E. (1985) *The childless marriage: an exploratory study of couples who do not want children.* London: Tavistock.

Campbell, E. (1983) Becoming voluntarily childless: an exploratory study in a Scottish city. *Social Biology* **30**:307–17.

Clarke, L., Cooksey, E. C., Verropoulou, G., Van Willigen, M. (1996) The experience of parenthood: fathers and mothers compared in Britain and the United States. Paper presented to the British Society for Population Studies Conference, University of St Andrew's, Scotland.

Clarke, L., Cooksey, E., Verropoulou, G. (1998) Fathers and absent fathers: socio-demographic similarities in Britain and the United States?' *Demography* **35**:217–28.

Cliquet, R. L. (1997) 'Below replacement level fertility and gender politics.' Paper presented at the European Sociobiology Society, Alfred U.S.A. Brussels: CBGS (Centrum voor Bevolkings en Gezinsstudie) Document 1997–2.

Coleman, D. (1993) Britain in Europe: international and regional comparisons of fertility levels and trends. In Ni Bhrolchain, M. (ed.) New perspectives on fertility in Britain. London: Office of Population Censuses and Surveys (OPCS).

Coleman, D. A. (1995) Male fertility trends in industrial countries: theories in search of some evidence. Paper presented at the Seminar on Fertility and the Male Life Cycle in the era of Fertility Decline, Zacatecas, Mexico. (Available from the author, Dept. of Applied Social Studies and Social Research, Oxford University, Barnett House, Wellington Square, Oxford, OX1 2ER, U.K.)

Coleman, D. (1996) (ed.) *Europe's population in the 1990s.* Oxford: Oxford University Press.

Coleman, D. (1998) Reproduction and survival in an unknown world: what drives today's industrial populations, and to what future? The Hofstee Lecture 1998, The Trippenhuis, Amsterdam, 7 May 1998.

Condy, A. (1991) Orientations towards motherhood and childlessness and social pressures to conform. Unpublished thesis for the Degree of the European University Institute, Dept of Social and Political Science, Florence. (Copy held at Family Policy Studies Centre).

Cooper, J., Shaw, C. (1993) Fertility assumptions for the 1991-based national population projections. *Population Trends* **71**:43–9.

de Wit, M., Rajulton, F. (1992) Education and timing of parenthood among Canadian women: a cohort analysis. *Social Biology* **39**:3–4.

Easterlin, R. A. (1980) *Birth and fortune.* London: Grant-McIntyre

European Commission (1994) *The demographic situation in the European Union.* *Luxembourg.* Office of Official Publications for the European Communities.

Ferri, E., Smith, K. (1997) *Parenting in the 1990s*. London: Joseph Rowntree Foundation and Family Policy Studies Centre.

Hajnal, J. (1965) European marriage patterns in perspective. In: Glass, D. V., Eversley, D. E. C. (eds.) *Population in history*. London: Arnold.

Jacobson, C. K., Heaton, T. B. (1991) Voluntary childlessness among American men and women in the late 1980s. *Social Biology* **1–2**:79–93.

Joshi, H. E., Davies, H. B., Land, H. (1996) *The tale of Mrs Typical*. London: Family Policy Studies Centre.

Kiernan, K. (1989) Who remains childless? *Journal of Biosocial Science* **21**:387–98.

Kiernan, K. (1992) Men and women at work and at home. In: Jowell, R., Brook, L., Prior, G., Taylor, B. (eds.) *British social attitudes: the 9th report*. Aldershot: Dartmouth.

Knudsen, L. B. (1996) Fertility trends in Denmark in the 1980s. Statistik. Copehagen: Danmarks.

McAllister, F., Clarke, L. (1998) *Choosing childlessness. Family and parenthood: policy and practice series*. London: Family Policy Studies Centre and Joseph Rowntree Foundation.

McDonald, P. (1997) Gender equity, social institutions and the future of fertility. Working Papers in Demography 69. Canberra: Australian National University.

Macintosh, C. A. (1987) Recent pronatalist policies in western Europe. In: Davis, K., Bernstram, M. S., Ricardo-Campbell, R. (eds.) *Below replacement fertility in industrial societies*. Cambridge: Cambridge University Press.

Marshall, H. (1993) *Not having children*. Melbourne: Oxford University Press.

Middleton, S., Ashworth, K., Braithwaite, I. (1998) Small fortunes: spending on children, childhood poverty and parental sacrifice. York: Joseph Rowntree Foundation.

Morell, C. M. (1994) *Unwomanly conduct: the challenges of intentional childlessness*. London: Routledge.

Morgan, S. P., Chen, R. (1992) Predicting childlessness for recent cohorts of American women. *International Journal of Forecasting* **8**:477–93

Murphy, M. J. (1989) Housing the people: from shortage to surplus?. In: Joshi, H. (ed.) *The changing population of Britain*. Oxford: Basil Blackwell.

Nason, E. M., Poloma, M. M. (1976) Voluntarily childless couples. *Sage Research Papers in Social Science* **5**:90-040.

Noack, T., Ostby, L. (1983) Childless or childfree? About infecundity and intentional childlessness (only summary available in English). Statistik Sentralbyra. Oslo: Konigsviger.

Office for National Statistics (ONS) (1998*a*) *Birth statistics 1996*. London: HMSO.

Office for National Statistics (ONS) (1998*b*) *Birth statistics 1997*. Series FM1 no. 26. London: HMSO.

Prioux, F. (1993) L'infecondite en Europe. In: Blum, A., Rallu, J.-L. (eds.) *European populations, Volume 2: Demographic dynamics.* London: John Libbey, pp. 231–51.

Pol, L. G. (1983) Childlessness: a panel study of expressed intentions and reported fertility. *Social Biology* **30**:318–27

Rimmer, L. (1981) Families in focus: marriage divorce and family patterns. London: Study Commission on the Family.

Rindfuss, R. R., Morgan, S. P., Swicegood, G. (1988) *First births in America: changes in the timing of parenthood.* Berkeley: University of California Press.

Rovi, S. L. D. (1994) Taking no for an answer – using negative reproductive intentions to study the childless childfree. *Population Research and Policy Review* **13**:343–65.

Ruddock, V., Wood, R., Quinn, M. (1998) Birth statistics: recent trends in England and Wales. *Population Trends* **94**:14. Winter 1998.

Schneewind, K. A. (1997) Marriage, yes, children, no – a lifestyle with a future? *System Familie* **10**:160–5.

Shaw, C. (1989) Recent trends in family size and family building. *Population Trends* **58**:19–22.

Simons, J. (1995) 'Fertility and values in 15 Western countries during the 1980s.' In: de Moor, R. (ed.) *Values in Western societies.* Tilburg: Tilburg University Press.

Simons, J. (1986) Culture, economy and reproduction in contemporary Europe. In: Coleman, D., Schofield, R. (eds.) *The state of population theory.* Oxford: Blackwell.

Templeton, A. A. (1992) 'The epidemiology of infertility.' In: Templeton, A. A., Drife, J. O. (eds.) *Infertility.* Berlin: Springer-Verlag, pp. 23–31.

Thomson, K. (1995) 'Working mothers: choice or circumstances?' In: Jowell, R., Curtice, J., Park, A., Brook, L., Ahrendt, D. (eds.) *British social attitudes, 12th Report.* Aldershot: Dartmouth.

Van de Kaa (1987) Europe's second demographic transition. *Population Bulletin* **42**.

Veevers, J. E. (1983) 'Voluntary childlessness: a critical review of the research.' In: Macklin, E. D., Rubin, R. H. (eds.) *Contemporary families and alternative lifestyles: a handbook of research and theory* (pp. 75–96). Beverley Hills: Sage.

Veevers, J. E. (1980) *Childless by choice.* Toronto: Butterworth.

Veevers, J. E. (1973) Voluntarily childless wives: an exploratory study. *Sociology and Social Research* **57**.

Werner, B. (1996) Family building intentions of different generations of women: results from the General Household Survey 1979–83. In: *Population trends 84.* London: Office of Population Censuses and Surveys.

Wrigley, E. A., Schofield, R S (1983) English population history from family reconstructions. Summary results 1600–1799. *Population Studies* **37**:157–84.

## 7

# Sexual orientation and fertility

C. J. PATTERSON AND L. V. FRIEL

## Abstract

There has been much controversy lately about the role of sexual orientation in parenthood. Despite this, reliable information about lesbian, gay and bisexual parents and their children is limited both in nature and scope, and many intriguing issues have as yet been little studied. For example, until recently, basic issues such as possible associations between sexual orientation and fertility have gone almost entirely without systematic investigation. Are lesbian, gay and bisexual adults less likely than heterosexual adults to become parents? Although common sense might suggest that they are, the results of recent systematic research suggest that accurate answers to such a question are more complex than often realized. In this chapter, we offer a review and critique of previous attempts to estimate the size of lesbian/gay parent populations, describe recent efforts to make such estimates based on data from representative samples of American adults, and comment upon the likely biases inherent in different estimation processes. When all available data are considered together, the resulting estimates of fertility among lesbian and gay adults are lower than expected by some but higher than anticipated by others, and they highlight the complexities of assessing both sexual orientation and parental status among lesbian and gay adults.

# Introduction

There has been much controversy recently in the United States and Western Europe surrounding lesbian and gay parents and their children. In a number of European countries, debates about same-sex marriages have included questions about the extent to which same-sex couples, if granted the right to marry, should also be allowed to become foster or adoptive parents (Henson, 1993). In the United States, when courts have heard cases that focus on same-sex marriage, issues related to childbearing have often been seen as central. Such debates are described in a number of sources (e.g. Baird and Rosenbaum, 1997; Sullivan, 1997).

These controversies have given rise to a number of questions (Patterson and Redding, 1996). For legal and policy reasons, the most insistent among these questions are those focusing on the mental health of lesbian mothers, gay fathers and their children. Issues surrounding the development of children with lesbian and gay parents dominate formal judicial proceedings and informal courts of public opinion. Judges have often inquired about the development of the sexual identity of children of same-sex couples (e.g. will the children grow up to identify as gay or lesbian?), about other aspects of their personal growth (e.g. will children of lesbian and gay parents have more behaviour problems than other children?), and about their social development (e.g. will these children be teased and stigmatized by their peers?). Because many people do not knowingly count among their friends, relatives, and acquaintances either lesbian/gay parents or their children, there is a substantial amount of ignorance and curiosity focusing on the ways in which children of lesbian or gay parents compare with those with heterosexual parents. It is clear from recent research (King and Black, 1999) that college students expect children of lesbian mothers to have more behaviour problems than other children, and this bias may be shared by judges and policy makers.

In the last 30 years, an increasing amount of research has been published about the development of children with lesbian, gay and heterosexual parents. There is now a fairly substantial body of evidence with which to address questions about the normative development of children with lesbian or gay parents (Patterson, 1992, 1995, 1998). In the main, the results of this research reveal that, far from suffering various problems as envisioned by some, children of lesbian and gay parents appear to develop much as do the children of otherwise comparable heterosexual parents. For instance, children of lesbian mothers have been found in several studies to be no more – and no less – likely to display behaviour problems such as depression and anxiety, on the one hand, or disruptive and aggressive behavior, on the other (Patterson, 1998). Indeed, a recent longitudinal study reported that the offspring of lesbian mothers are no more likely to report sexual or romantic attraction to same-sex others, or to describe themselves as non-heterosexual, than are children of heterosexual mothers (Tasker and Golombok, 1997). In general, empirical research has failed to confirm the fears about the well-being and adjustment of children growing up with lesbian or gay parents (Patterson, 1992, 1995, 1998).

However, the controversy remains, despite the increasingly clear research evidence. Both stereotypes and actual information about lesbian mothers, gay fathers, and their children continue to figure prominently in custody disputes, adoption and foster care actions, and related public policy debates both in the United States and elsewhere (Patterson and Redding, 1996). In the United States, for instance, a recent Mississippi State Supreme Court decision denied custody of a 15-year-old boy to a gay father, ordering instead that the boy live with his mother, even though she lives with a man who has a history of violence and substance abuse and who has beaten her in the presence of her son (ACLU, 1999). Dissenting from the majority, Justice Charles Macrae described the majority as having been 'blinded by the fact that [the child's] father is gay' (ACLU, 1999).

In the context of such controversies, fundamental questions have sometimes been overlooked. Perhaps the most basic one is about the extent to which lesbians and gay men can be correctly assumed to be parents at all, and, if so, in what numbers. Are there significant associations between sexual orientation and fertility? Are lesbian and gay adults less likely than heterosexual adults to become parents? How many lesbian and gay adults are parents, and how many children are growing up in their households? When considering these questions, another related question arises as well. Who should be counted as lesbian or gay, for purposes of such tabulations? And who should be counted as a parent? These are questions about a contested terrain, and they do not have a single easy answer. The basic task of enumerating the population of lesbian and gay parents is made more complex by the need to give answers to questions of this kind.

In this chapter, we aim to review the available information about associations between sexual orientation and fertility. First, we review the range of estimates of the numbers of lesbian/gay parents in the population of the United States, and describe the information upon which these estimates seem to be based. We then describe the earliest large-scale attempt to estimate the numbers of lesbian and gay parents, based on the landmark study of Bell and Weinberg (1978), and offer some commentary on its strengths and limitations. We then review more recent attempts to study such questions that have been reported recently by Badgett (1998). Finally, we present new calculations, based on information from the National Health and Social Life Survey (Laumann *et al.*, 1994), for which data were collected in the United States in the early 1990s. Finally, we offer some conclusions and ideas about potential directions for future research in this area.

## Early estimates of the numbers of lesbian mothers, gay fathers and their children

There are a number of widely acknowledged difficulties in estimating the numbers of lesbian mothers, gay fathers and their children. For instance, because of fears related to possible prejudice and discrimination, many individuals are afraid to act upon their same-sex sexual and romantic attractions; furthermore, if they act upon such attractions, they may do so in secret without identifying themselves as lesbian or gay (Herek, 1995; Herek and Berrill, 1992). Even if individuals act upon same-sex attractions and identify themselves as lesbian or gay, they may be unwilling to reveal this aspect of their identity to an interviewer, again for fear of adverse consequences. As the prevalence of hate crimes against lesbian and gay people demonstrates, such fears are not entirely unfounded (Herek, 1995; Herek and Berrill, 1992). Efforts made by many lesbian and gay adults to hide their sexual identities can be extensive, and these are important obstacles to the accurate enumeration of sexual orientation in the adult populations in both the United States and in Europe (Michaels, 1996).

In addition to notorious difficulties involved in counting lesbian and gay *adults,* there are other difficulties associated with enumeration of lesbian and gay *parents.* Particularly in light of the history of discrimination against lesbian and gay parents in many parts of the United States, some parents take great pains to hide nonheterosexual identities. These parents fear that, if their true identities were to be known, they might lose custody of, or visitation with, their children. In many cases, parents' efforts to conceal their lesbian or gay identities have extended even to hiding these aspects of their lives and identities from their own children (Patterson, 1992). Without question, the perceived need to hide nonheterosexual identities provides an important obstacle to the accurate enumeration of lesbian and gay parents.

Even in light of acknowledged obstacles, however, some estimates of the numbers of lesbian and gay parents and their children have been offered, but not surprisingly they show considerable variability. For instance, widely repeated estimates have put the numbers of lesbian mothers in the United States at anywhere from one to five million, and the numbers of gay fathers anywhere from one to three million. These same estimates tend to put the numbers of children of lesbian and gay parents at between six and fourteen million (see, for example, Editors of the Harvard Law Review, 1990). Although these estimates have been widely repeated, no empirical studies are cited in connection with them. Hence, it is difficult to be certain about the origin of these figures or to evaluate their reliability.

One way in which these kinds of estimates might be generated is to rely on what is known or believed about the then-available research findings. Some appear to have been based upon a figure taken (incorrectly, as it happens) from Kinsey *et al* (1948), suggesting that approximately 10% of the adult male population of the United States could be considered nonheterosexual. Drawing from large-scale studies of lesbian and gay adults, some of which asked about parental status, one can calculate the percentage of lesbian or gay adults who describe themselves as parents, and extrapolate these numbers to the population at large. Since the samples of men and women who participated in Kinsey's landmark studies were not representative of the population of the United States, and since the 10% figure appears to have been based on a misreading of Kinsey's data, estimates based on this will, of necessity, be inaccurate (for further discussion of this point, see Laumann *et al.*, 1994; Michaels, 1996). Furthermore, Kinsey's research was conducted many years ago, long before the current controversies surrounding lesbian and gay parenthood had emerged into public discourse. Since estimates can only be as good as the data upon which they are based, and since the Kinsey data are seriously flawed for the purpose at hand, estimates based upon his findings are not likely to be accurate.

Another early large-scale study upon which estimates of the numbers of lesbian mothers and gay fathers could be based was that of Bell and Weinberg (1978). In the 1970s, these investigators interviewed a convenience sample of over 4000 adults in the San Francisco Bay Area who identified as lesbian, gay or homosexual, and compared their responses on a number of items to those of a group of heterosexual respondents who had been selected to match the lesbian/gay/homosexual respondents on age, education and gender. The lesbian/gay/homosexual participants were recruited from homophile organizations, gay bars, personal contacts, and so forth, and one cannot determine the degree to which the resulting group of respondents is representative of the population from which it is drawn.

In the course of lengthy interviews, Bell and Weinberg (1978) asked each participant if they had ever been married, and, if so, if they had ever 'had children'. Participants were free to interpret this question as they chose. The average age of participants was about 35, but there was considerable variability around this average, with at least 25% of the lesbian/gay/homosexual sample under 25 years of age. Because of the relatively young overall age of the sample, a sizeable proportion of even the heterosexual sample had not yet had children. Even so, because all participants were asked the same question, the study does provide a comparison between the responses of heterosexual and nonheterosexual participants.

Lesbian and gay adults in Bell and Weinberg's study were considerably less likely to report having had children than were same-aged heterosexual participants. Indeed, 21% of lesbian women, but 51% of the heterosexual women reported having children. Among men, 10% of gay or homosexual men, but 47% of heterosexual men reported having children. Thus, more than twice as many heterosexual women, and more than four times as many heterosexual men than lesbian/gay/homosexual women and men reported having children. Sexual orientation was a significant predictor of having had children for both men and women, with the effect being stronger for men than for women.

As interesting and important as this finding remains, even more than 20 years later, there are some limitations to which its interpretation should be subject. First, as noted above, the Bell and Weinberg (1978) study is not based on a representative sample. All of the participants lived in a single geographical area (namely, the San Francisco Bay Area), and the degree to which the findings apply to those in other areas of the country or abroad is not known. Only Caucasian and African–American participants were recruited for the study, so there was no information about those from other ethnic groups. The participants were relatively young at the time of their interviews, so their ultimate levels of fertility (e.g. at age 50) cannot be determined. The Bell and Weinberg (1978) data were collected over 20 years ago, and their relevance to today is not known. Finally, the definition of fertility ('having children') was vague, and different interpretations of the term 'having children' may have been used by different participants. For these reasons, the Bell and Weinberg (1978) findings, though valuable, cannot be seen as definitive.

Overall, it is impossible to determine whether or to what extent figures drawn from Bell and Weinberg's (1978) study are reliable.

Indeed, it is even difficult to know whether they present greater risks of overestimating or underestimating the fertility of lesbian/gay/homosexual adults. Because only participants who had been married were asked whether they had children, the study may have underestimated actual fertility by omitting those who had children outside of marriage. On the other hand, if participants interpreted the question about having children as including adoptive and foster children, then the resulting figures may be overestimates. To develop better estimates, we need to examine population-based, representative samples of respondents, with questions about the matters of principal interest framed in more precise terms.

## Recent estimates of the numbers of lesbian mothers, gay fathers and their children

Badgett (1998) recently attempted to estimate the numbers of lesbian mothers, gay fathers and their children based on population-based, representative samples. Drawing from two databases of relatively recent vintage, Badgett evaluated the likelihood that participants in two surveys identified themselves both as lesbian/gay/homosexual and as having children. The first sample was drawn from the Yankelovich Monitor, which drew a probability sample of all adults in the United States. In face-to-face interviews, participants were asked to select from among a large group of labels all those that described them. The labels were printed on a card, and included personal characteristics such as 'idealistic' and 'competitive', as well as 'gay, lesbian, or homosexual'. Participants responded by calling out the code associated with each descriptor; thus, it was possible to identify as being gay or lesbian without having to pronounce the terms aloud in front of an interviewer. Interestingly, 5.7% of the participants in this research described themselves as lesbian, gay or homosexual. The participants were also asked both, 'are you a parent?', and 'are there children under the age of 18 in your household?'

The second sample was from a Voter Exit Poll, and involved a random sample of voters in the United States. In this study, participants completed a written survey, and selected from among a group of labels the ones that fitted them best. One of the choices was 'gay/lesbian/homosexual', and 3% of participants selected this description. Since the participants were all American voters, they had a profile that is characteristic of this group. They were all at least 18 years old, and most had more years of education and higher incomes than average for the population. These individuals were also asked whether or not there were 'children under the age of 18 in your household'.

For present purposes, the specific questions asked in these two surveys had both strengths and limitations. The question 'are you a parent?' was defined as having at least one biological child, and thus excluded adoptive or foster parents, as well as any other route to nonbiological parenthood. Thus, regardless of sexual orientation, this question may exclude many adults who became parents in nontraditional ways. Similarly, the question about children under the age of 18 in the household can be expected to yield under-estimates of parenthood, since those with children away at school or grown children living on their own would not be counted as parents. On the other hand, this definition could include adoptive, foster, and other nonbiological parents. Each approach to assessment, then, has its strengths and weaknesses.

The results of Badgett's (1998) calculations were presented separately for men and for women. Using data from the Yankelo-vich poll, Badgett reported that 32% of lesbian women, and 36% of heterosexual women reported having children in their households. Using the Voter Exit Poll data, Badgett found that 31% of lesbian women, and 37% of heterosexual women reported having children in their households. Using data from the Yankelovich poll about whether or not women were parents, Badgett found that 67% of lesbian women and 72% of heterosexual women described themselves as parents. None of the comparisons based on sexual orientation was statistically significant. Although all of the comparisons suggested, as expected, that heterosexual women were somewhat more likely than lesbian women to be parents, the differences between lesbian and heterosexual women were small and not statistically significant. Unlike Bell and Weinberg (1978) then,

Badgett (1998) reported that lesbian women were as likely to be mothers and as likely to have children living in their households as were heterosexual women.

For men, Badgett's (1998) findings were more in concert with those of Bell and Weinberg (1978). Using data from the Yankelovich poll, Badgett reported that 15% of gay men, and 28% of heterosexual men reported having children in their households. Using data from the Voter Exit Poll, Badgett found that 23% of gay men and 33% of heterosexual men reported having children in their households. Finally, based on the Yankelovich data, Badgett reported that 27% of gay men, but 60% of heterosexual men described themselves as parents. All of the comparisons based on sexual orientation were statistically significant; as expected, heterosexual men were more likely than gay men to be parents and to have children living in their households.

Based on Badgett's (1998) results, one might be inclined to conclude that fertility is significantly related to sexual orientation for men, but not for women. In the data analysed by Badgett (1998), lesbian women were as likely as heterosexual women to describe themselves as parents and as having children living in their households, but the same was not true among men. Gay men were significantly less likely than heterosexual men to be parents or to have children living in their households. These conclusions, if sustained in other studies, would certainly be important from a number of different perspectives.

How valid are the conclusions based on these data? Badgett (1998) was the first to provide estimates of fertility among lesbian women and gay men based on data from representative or near-representative samples of American adults, and in this way, her work improved markedly upon earlier studies. On the other hand, some limitations of Badgett's approach can also be noted. For instance, although her research is based upon nationally representative or near-representative samples, there were relatively small numbers of lesbian and gay respondents in each of the two samples she used, and estimates based upon them must therefore be more tentative than they would be if samples were larger. Second, the datasets with which Badgett worked defined sexual orientation in only a single way – as *identity*. To be identified as lesbian or gay in this research was to apply the label to oneself, and no way to assess the degree to which such labels did or did not match up with actual sexual behaviour or sexual desire was available. The importance of this issue cannot be determined on the basis of data available in either the Yankelovich or the Voter Exit Polls, but it is suggested by the fact that another recent survey reported that a third of adults reporting a same-sex sexual partner within the last year did not identify as lesbian, gay or bisexual (Michaels, 1996). Overall, more complex assessments of sexual orientation would certainly be desirable.

Earlier efforts to assess possible associations between sexual orientation and fertility, then, have not yielded particularly clear conclusions. The results of Bell and Weinberg's (1978) pioneering study suggested that both lesbians and gay men are less likely than their heterosexual counterparts to have had children. More recent work by Badgett (1998), however, suggests that while gay men are less likely than heterosexual men to be parents or to have children currently living in their households, lesbian women are not markedly different from heterosexual women in these areas. The methodologies used in both studies had both strengths and weaknesses, however, and the questions remain open.

To address the issues raised by earlier research, we drew upon the resources of the National Health and Social Life Survey (Laumann *et al.*, 1994), which involved a large nationally representative sample of American adults. Because this study had, among other things, assessed sexual orientation as well as parental status, it provided an excellent opportunity to address issues surrounding the possible associations between sexual orientation and fertility.

## Estimates based on the National Health and Social Life Survey

The National Health and Social Life Survey (NHSLS: Laumann *et al.*, 1994), a comprehensive survey of sexual behaviour conducted in the early 1990s, provided the data for the current project. The

Table 7.1. *Percentage of women and men who reported same-sex identity,*
*behaviour, or desire in the National Health and Social Life Survey (NHSLS)\**

| Those categorized as lesbian/gay on the basis of: | Women % (*n*) | Men % (*n*) |
|---|---|---|
| Identity | 1.4 (24) | 2.8 (39) |
| Behaviour | 4.1 (72) | 4.9 (69) |
| Desire | 7.5 (131) | 7.7 (108) |
| Identity, behaviour or desire | 8.6 (150) | 10.1 (143) |
| Entire sample (*n* = 3159) | 55.4 (1749) | 44.6 (1410) |

\* Frequencies and percentages are taken from Laumann *et al.* (1994).

NHSLS involved face-to-face interviews with over 3000 English-speaking American adults, ranging from 18 to 59 years of age, and living in households. Thus, the study did not sample older adults, those living in institutional settings, or those who do not speak English. The focus of the study was on the social organization of sexuality, and it included questions about sexual orientation as well as about parental status.

Most important for the present purposes, the NHSLS (Laumann *et al.*, 1994) included questions that permit more complex definitions of sexual orientation than have generally been available from other sources. In particular, respondents were asked not only about sexual identity (i.e. heterosexual, lesbian/gay, or bisexual), but also about their same-sex sexual behaviour, and about their desire for same-sex sexual opportunities. The proportions of respondents giving nonheterosexual replies varied considerably across questions (see Table 7.1). Thus, the results suggest that identification of lesbian women and gay men may be somewhat more difficult than often believed. On the basis of information available in the NHSLS, four possible approaches to identification of lesbian women and gay men can be identified.

The most common way of identifying gay men and lesbians in research of this kind is based on *identity*. Taking this approach, one attempts to separate those who identify themselves as gay or lesbian from those who identify themselves as heterosexual. In the NHSLS, respondents were asked, in the context of face-to-face interviews, 'do you identify yourself as lesbian, gay or bisexual?' Results showed that 1.4% of women and 2.8% of men indicated to the interviewer that they identified themselves in this way (see Table 7.1). This approach, which requires that lesbian and gay respondents identify openly and in person to a stranger, is the most stringent of all the assessment techniques for identifying nonheterosexual respondents.

Another approach to identifying gay men and lesbians is based on *behaviour*. From this perspective, one attempts to separate those who have engaged in same-sex sexual behaviour from those who have not done so. In the NHSLS, respondents were asked, 'have you had any same-sex sexual partners since the age of 18?' This question was part of a 'Self-Administered Questionnaire' (i.e. written questionnaires to which participants responded in writing, and then sealed into privacy envelopes before handing them back to the interviewer). Results showed that 4.1% of women and 4.9% of men reported same-sex sexual partners during their adult years (see Table 7.1). Relying upon same-sex sexual behaviour reported in this way results in a larger group of 'lesbian, gay and bisexual' respondents than does the measure of identity described above.

A third avenue to the identification of gay men and lesbians is based on *desire*. Taking this approach, one attempts to separate those who see same-sex sexual contacts as attractive and desirable from those who do not. In the NHSLS, respondents were asked, 'does the idea of same-sex sexual behavior attract you, or seem appealing?' Participants responded by reporting a number from a handcard presented by the experimenter (on which 1 = 'very appealing' and 4 = 'not at all appealing'). Results showed that 7.5% of women and 7.7% of men described same-sex sexual behaviour as appealing or attractive (see Table 7.1). These numbers are clearly greater than either those for behaviour or identity. More adults see same-sex sexual behaviour as attractive than have actually engaged in the behaviour or identified themselves as lesbian or gay, and hence the criterion of *desire* identifies more individuals as lesbian or gay compared to the other two, taken singly.

A fourth approach to the identification of gay men and lesbians is based on a combination of all three of the earlier criteria. Taking this approach, one separates those who were identified on the basis of identity, behaviour, *or* desire from those who were not identified by any of these criteria. Results showed that, in the NHSLS, 8.6% of women and 10.1% of men would be identified as gay or lesbian on the basis of at least *one* of the three criteria (i.e. identity, behaviour, or desire – see Table 7.1). Clearly, this is the least stringent method of identifying lesbian and gay adults, and it results in the largest estimates.

Our concern here is not to recommend one method for identification of lesbian and gay respondents over another, but to point instead to the different results that one obtains if one uses different methods, and to ask what implications these may have for estimating fertility rates as a function of sexual orientation. Clearly, larger samples of lesbians will be obtained if women are identified on the basis of desire for same-sex contacts than if only those who claim a lesbian identity are selected. The NHSLS data (Laumann *et al.*, 1994) reveal that those claiming a lesbian identity are also very likely to express desires for same-sex sexual behaviour. The group of those expressing desire, but reporting no same-sex sexual experience and no lesbian identity, are likely to have lived in different ways than those who have made their relationships with women central to their daily lives. What implications do these facts have for assessments of fertility?

The NHSLS (Laumann *et al.*, 1994) also included questions about fertility. Most important for the present purposes, respondents were asked, 'how many children have you ever had, counting only live births?' From replies to this question, respondents were categorized as 'having biological children' or 'not having biological children'. Thus, data gathered in this study are relevant to biological parenthood, and do not include foster or adoptive children.

Using data from assessments of sexual orientation and of parenthood, we examined the associations of the two, both for men and for women. For women, results showed 30% of those who were classified as lesbian on the basis of identity, 49% of those who were classified as lesbian on the basis of behaviour, 58% of those who

Table 7.2. *Percentages of nonheterosexual women and men who reported having had at least one biological child in the NHSLS as a function of categorization criteria\**

| Those categorized as lesbian/gay on the basis of: | Women % (*n*) | Men % (*n*) |
|---|---|---|
| Identity | 30 (7) | 14 (5) |
| Behaviour | 49 (35) | 32 (22) |
| Desire | 58 (76) | 29 (31) |
| Identity, behaviour or desire | 58 (76) | 38 (54) |

\* Frequencies and percentages were calculated from information supplied by Laumann *et al.* (1994).

were classified as lesbian on the basis of desire, and 58% of those who were classified as lesbian on the basis of at least one of the previous three criteria also identified themselves as having at least one biological child (see Table 7.2). For comparison, 73% of heterosexually identified women in this sample described them-selves as having had at least one biological child. As expected, the fertility estimates varied dramatically as a function of the criteria employed. Also as expected, however, fertility among lesbian women – however identified – was lower than among heterosexual women.

For men, results showed that only 14% of those classified as gay on the basis of identity, 32% of those classified as gay on the basis of behaviour, 29% of those classified as gay on the basis of desire, and 38% of those classified as gay on the basis of at least one of the previous three criteria also described themselves as having at least one biological child (see Table 7.2). For comparison, 59% of heterosexual men in this sample identified themselves as having had at least one biological child. Again, as expected, fertility estimates varied widely as a function of the criteria for identification of gay men. Also as expected, however, fertility among gay men – however identified – was markedly lower than among heterosexual men.

In all, then, data from the NHSLS suggest lower fertility among lesbian and gay than among heterosexual adults. In general, lesbian and gay adults – no matter how identified – were less likely to report having children who were biologically related to them. As expected, however, the *degree* of association between sexual orientation and fertility depended strongly upon specific defining criteria for sexual orientation. The smallest numbers of lesbian and gay adults (and thus also parents) were identified with the *identity* criterion, whereas larger numbers were identified with criteria related to *behaviour* and *desire*. Regardless of the criterion used, however, sizeable numbers of people were identified.

To assess the extent to which associations between sexual orientation and fertility might be due to extraneous factors, we examined a number of demographic variables that are related to fertility in heterosexual populations. Specifically, we studied age, race, education, and income – all variables for which information was available in the NHSLS. Confirming Badgett's (1998) findings, results showed that lesbian and gay individuals did not have higher incomes than heterosexual individuals. Similarly, although larger proportions of lesbian and gay than heterosexual adults described themselves as white, this difference was not statistically significant. Men who identified as gay were, on average, four years younger than men who identified as heterosexual, and this difference may have contributed to their reduced fertility, but there were no such differences among lesbian versus heterosexual women.

The single most striking difference between lesbian/gay and heterosexual adults in the NHSLS sample was related to education. No matter how they were identified, lesbian and gay respondents reported significantly higher educational attainment than did heterosexual respondents. This difference is particularly interesting because many nonrepresentative samples of lesbian and gay adults have revealed higher than average educational levels among participants. It has not, in general, been clear whether this finding results from characteristics of the population in general (i.e. lesbian/gay adults are generally better educated than heterosexual adults) or from biases in sampling procedures (i.e. better educated lesbian/gay adults were recruited more often to participate in research and/or were more willing to volunteer). Because the data for the NHSLS were drawn from a nationally representative

sample of American adults, and because lesbian/gay and heterosexual respondents were recruited for the study using the same
procedures, the higher educational levels reported by lesbian and
gay respondents here are not likely to be the result of sampling
biases. This finding suggests that it may be worth considering the
possibility of association between educational levels and the willingness to adopt lesbian or gay identities, as well as to report same-
sex sexual behaviour or desire. If there are indeed general associations between education and sexual identities, this fact would be
worth further exploration, in an attempt to clarify the demography
of lesbian and gay populations.

In the present context, differences in educational attainment
between lesbian, gay and heterosexual respondents raise the possibility that differences in fertility might be due at least in part to
education rather than to sexual orientation. In the United States
today, fertility rates are lower among women with higher levels of
education (United States Bureau of the Census, 1999). Because
lesbian women and gay men report higher levels of educational
attainment, their fertility would be expected to be lower than
average on this basis alone. To assess this possibility, we calculated
relative risk scores, taking into account age and education, as well
as income and race. The results of these relative risk analyses were
essentially identical to those described above; differences in educational attainment did not explain differential fertility as a function
of sexual orientation.

Overall, though associations between sexual orientation and
fertility were quite robust in the NHSLS sample, the data were also
subject to a number of limitations that affect the strength of
conclusions that may be drawn from them. First, the sample of
nonheterosexual adults (identified on the basis of identity) was
again rather small ($n = 56$). For this reason, generalizations made on
the basis of these data should be treated with caution, pending
replication in other samples.

Second, the criteria used to identify nonheterosexual individuals
in the NHSLS had some intrinsic limitations that probably resulted
in them being very conservative. To be classified as lesbian or gay
on the basis of identity, for example, participants had to describe

themselves in this way in the context of face-to-face interviews with a researcher with whom respondents had no prior relationship. That many lesbian or gay individuals may have been afraid or embarrassed or ashamed to give honest answers in this kind of setting is suggested by the very low rates of classification by identity (only 1.4% of women identified themselves as lesbian, and only 2.8% of men identified themselves as gay). In other population-based samples, when self-identification required the respondent only to call out a coded identifier, self-classification was markedly more common, exceeding 5% of the entire sample (Badgett, 1998). Thus, it seems likely that *identity* criteria employed in the NHSLS identified only that subset of lesbian and gay adults who were most open about their sexual identities, and most willing to share them with an interviewer.

A third limitation of data based upon the NHSLS is that they are based exclusively upon reports of biological parenthood. Although this certainly has some advantages (e.g. precision), it fails to identify those who are parents of children to whom they are not biologically related. Among those excluded in this way would be foster and adoptive parents, and nonbiological parents in lesbian and gay communities. Because nontraditional forms of parenthood are probably more common among lesbian and gay than among heterosexual adults, it is likely that this bias results in greater underestimation of the numbers of lesbian/gay as compared to heterosexual parents.

A fourth issue, related to the previous one, concerns the average age of the adults studied in the NHSLS. The average ages of respondents in this sample were in the early to mid thirties. Since the obstacles encountered by lesbian and gay adults who wish to become parents are likely to delay their attainment of this goal, lesbian and gay individuals who become first-time parents are likely to do so when they are older, on average, than heterosexual adults. To the degree that this is the case, the comparatively young average age of the NHSLS respondents introduces a bias that is likely to reduce estimates of lesbian and gay parent numbers, as compared with those of heterosexual parents.

Taken together, these several limitations combine to yield a dataset that, although strong in many respects, is likely to under-estimate lesbian and gay fertility in particular, and also the numbers of lesbian and gay parents in a more general sense. Laumann and his colleagues underscored this point when they characterized their estimates of the numbers of nonheterosexual individuals as consti-tuting 'lower bound estimates' of the true numbers (Laumann *et al.*, 1994). Estimates developed from the NHSLS data should therefore be viewed as conservative.

## Conclusions

Overall, then, despite acknowledged difficulties in making estimates in this area, we conclude that there are almost certainly associations between sexual orientation and fertility. In the United States, NHSLS data show that lesbian and gay adults are less likely than heterosexual adults to have biological children. Because these data contain many biases, the true associations between sexual orienta-tion and fertility in the United States today may be somewhat less than the current findings suggest. At the same time, however, it is also clear that large numbers of lesbian and gay adults do have biological offspring. Biological parenthood may not be as common among lesbian and gay as among heterosexual adults, but neither is it unknown.

It is valuable to compare the present results, based on data from the NHSLS, to those based on data from the Voter Exit Poll and the Yankelovich Monitor (Badgett, 1998). The NHSLS data are relevant to biological parenthood, and suggest that lesbian women are less likely than heterosexual women to have children who are biologically related to them. The Voter Exit Poll and the Yankelo-vich data concern 'parenthood' (without requiring a biological linkage) and 'having children in the household', and these datasets show no associations with sexual orientation. Thus, it appears that, although lesbian women are as likely as heterosexual women to regard themselves as parents and to have children living in their households, they are less likely to have biological children. In other words, lesbian women seem to be more likely than heterosexual women to have become parents in nontraditional ways (e.g. adoption), but equally likely to be parents. Among gay men, the difficulties involved in becoming parents are more pronounced, and no form of parenthood is as common as among heterosexual men.

Taking all the available information together, then, how many lesbian and gay parents are there, and how many children do they have? In the United States today, United States Bureau of the Census data show that there are 105 million women and 97 million men aged 18–59 years. Using the most conservative numbers available (i.e. those from the NHSLS, based on 1.4% of women and 2.8% of men who identify as lesbian or gay, and the 30% of lesbians and 14% of gay men who describe themselves as biological parents), then the numbers of lesbian and gay parents are estimated at just under one million. If it is assumed that each parent, on average, has two children, then that would put the number of children with lesbian or gay parents in the United States today at just under two million. Because of the strong likelihood that lesbians and gay men may have failed to self-identify in the NHSLS, however, and because there must also be lesbian and gay parents who are older than 59 years (who would not have been sampled in the NHSLS), these estimates are likely to be smaller than the true numbers.

Consider, in contrast, estimates based on Badgett's (1998) calculations, from the Yankelovich data. In these data, 5.7% of respondents identified as 'lesbian, gay or homosexual'. Using the United States Bureau of the Census population figures given above, the Yankelovich data would lead to estimates of about four million lesbian mothers and one million gay fathers, for a total of more than five million lesbian and gay parents. If, on average, each parent has two children, that would put the numbers of children with lesbian or gay parents at ten million.

Clearly, estimates based on more liberal criteria suggest that there are even larger numbers of families in which children have lesbian or gay parents. For instance, if lesbian and gay individuals are identified in the NHSLS data based on the presence of *any of the three* criteria (identity, behaviour or desire), then 6.9% of women are identified as lesbian and 7.7% of men are identified as gay. Larger

proportions of individuals identified in these ways describe themselves as parents in the NHSLS data (i.e. 58% of women and 38%
of men). Using these figures, the number of lesbian and gay parents
in the United States today might be estimated at just over seven
million. If each parent can be assumed to have, on average, two
children, this would put the numbers of children with lesbian or
gay parents at approximately 14 million.

In short, even when estimates of the numbers of lesbian and
gay parents and their children are based on representative or
near-representative samples of American adults, they may nevertheless vary widely. Most important among the reasons for such
variations would appear to be the operational definitions of sexual
orientation employed, the specific methods used in assessing
lesbian and gay identities, and the breadth of the definitions of
parenthood that were adopted in each study. Different approaches
to each of these issues may be appropriate for different purposes,
and no single approach is likely to provide a complete solution.
Even in view of the variability, however, it would be reasonable to
conclude that there are almost certainly millions of gay or lesbian
parents in the United States today. Exactly how many millions of
lesbian and gay parents, and exactly how many millions of their
children live in the United States today are questions that do not
have simple answers.

Our conclusions about the prevalence of parenthood among
lesbian and gay adults are similar in many respects to those
described by Laumann and his colleagues with regard to the
prevalence of homosexuality itself:

> Put simply, we contend that there is no simple answer to questions
> about the prevalence of homosexuality. Rather, homosexuality is a
> complex, multi-dimensional phenomenon whose salient features are
> related to one another in highly contingent and diverse ways.
>
> (Laumann *et al.*, 1994:320).

Just as there is no single answer about the prevalence of homosexuality, we suggest that there is no single answer to questions about
the prevalence of lesbian/gay parenthood. Estimates of the
numbers of lesbian and gay parents vary widely as a function of

research methods, criteria for identifications of homosexuality, and breadth of definitions of parenthood.

When taking all of the available data into account, however, there is considerable evidence of an association between sexual orientation and fertility. The data suggest that both lesbian and gay adults are less likely than heterosexual adults to have had biologically related children. Even when assessment tools consider a broader definition of parenthood (i.e. one that includes both biologically related and unrelated children), the same linkage between sexual orientation and parental status seems to emerge for men: gay men are less likely than heterosexual men to be parents. Interestingly, the situation for women appears to be different. Although lesbians are less likely than heterosexual women to report biological parenthood, they are as likely as heterosexual women to describe themselves as parents or to report children living in their households, presumably because lesbian women often become parents in nontraditional ways. When all available data are taken together, the resulting estimates of fertility among lesbian and gay adults are lower than expected by some but higher than expected by others, and they highlight the complexities of assessing parental status among lesbian and gay adults.

# References

ACLU (1999) Mississippi Supreme Court denies child custody to gay father in favor of violent stepdad. Press release dated February 8, 1999. Available via the Internet at http://www.aclu.org/news/1999/n020899b.html.

Badgett, M. V. L. (1998) The economic well-being of lesbian, gay, and bisexual adults' families. In: Patterson, C. J., D'Augelli, A. R. (eds.) *Lesbian, gay and bisexual identities in families: psychological perspectives*. New York: Oxford University Press.

Baird, R. M., Rosenbaum, S. E. (eds.) (1997) *Same-sex marriage: the moral and legal debate*. Amherst, N.Y.: Prometheus Books.

Bell, A. P., Weinberg, M. S. (1978) *Homosexualities: a study of diversity among men and women*. New York: Simon and Schuster.

Editors of the Harvard Law Review (1990) *Sexual orientation and the law*. Cambridge, MA: Harvard University Press.

Henson, D. (1993) A comparative analysis of same-sex partnership protections. *International Journal of Law and the Family* **7**:282–313

Herek, G. M. (1995) Psychological heterosexism in the United States. In: D'Augelli, A. R., Patterson, C. J. (eds.) *Lesbian, gay and bisexual identities over the lifespan: psychological perspectives*. New York: Oxford University Press.

Herek, G. M., Berrill, K. (eds.) (1992) *Hate crimes: confronting violence against lesbians and gay men*. Newbury Park, CA: Sage Publications.

King, B. R., Black, K. N. (1999) College students' perceptual stigmatization of the children of lesbian mothers. *American Journal of Orthopsychiatry* **69**:220–7

Kinsey, A. C., Pomeroy, W. B., Martin, C. E. (1948) *Sexual behavior in the human male*. Philadelphia PA: W. B. Saunders.

Laumann, E. O., Gagnon, J. H., Michael, R. T., Michaels, S. (1994) *The social organization of sexuality: sexual practices in the United States*. Chicago: University of Chicago Press.

Michaels, S. (1996) The prevalence of homosexuality in the United States. In: Cabaj, R. P., Stein, T. S. (eds.) *Textbook of homosexuality and mental health*. Washington, D. C.: American Psychiatric Press, Inc.

Patterson, C. J. (1992) Children of lesbian and gay parents. *Child Development* **63**:1025–42

Patterson, C. J. (1995) Lesbian mothers, gay fathers, and their children. In: D'Augelli, A. R., Patterson, C. J. (eds.) *Lesbian, gay and bisexual identities over the lifespan: psychological perspectives* (pp. 262–90). New York: Oxford University Press.

Patterson, C. J. (1998) Family lives of lesbians and gay men. In: Bellack A., Hersen, M. (eds.) *Comprehensive clinical psychology, Volume 9: Applications in diverse populations*, Singh N. N. (volume ed.) (pp. 253–73). Oxford, UK: Elsevier.

Patterson, C. J., Redding, R. (1996) Lesbian and gay families with children: public policy implications of social science research. *Journal of Social Issues* **52**:29–50.

Sullivan, A. (ed.) (1997) *Same-sex marriage: pro and con – a reader*. New York: Vintage Books.

Tasker, F., Golombok, S. (1997) *Growing up in a lesbian family: effects on child development*. New York: Guilford Press.

United States Bureau of the Census (1999) Resident population of the United States by sex, race, and Hispanic origin: April 1, 1990 to July 1, 1999. Available via Internet at http://www.census.gov/population/estimates/nation/intfile3-1.txt.

# Index